G000075139

The Return

The Return

Traveling with Mother Mary

As Narrated by John the Apostle

WILLIAM FRANCIS STURNER

© 2022 William Francis Sturner

Other Dimensions Publishing

All Rights Reserved

ISBN: 978-1-66781-098-0

Other Books by William Francis Sturner

BIOGRAPHICAL
Love Loops: *A Divorced Father's Personal Journey (1983)*

CREATIVITY
AhA: *Creating Each Day with Insight and Daring (2000)*

LEADERSHIP AND ORGANIZATIONAL CHANGE
Action Planning *(1974)*
Impact: *Transforming Your Organization (1993)*
Superb Leadership: *The 12 Essential Skills (1997)*

MYTHIC SPIRIT TALES
The Three-Legged Deer: *Exploring the Miracles of Nature (2010)*
Kindred Spirits: *Celebrating Angels, Mystics and Miracles (2011)*

THE PSYCHOLOGY OF RISK AND CHANGE
Calculated Risk: *Strategies for Managing Change (1990)*
Risking Change: *Ending and Beginnings (1987)*

SPIRITUAL COMMENTARY
Mystic in the Marketplace: *A Spiritual Journey (1994)*
The Creative Impulse: *Celebrating Adam and Eve, Jung and EveryOne (1998)*
Trust Your Immortal Soul: *A Guide to Spiritual Living (2012 & 2016)*
Yeshua: *The Continuing Presence of the Master Soul (2017)*

Other Dimensions Publishing

The Open Heart Sanctuary III
Nokomis, FL

wfsturner@mac.com

Presenting
Mystic-Spirit Tales and
Spiritual Commentary
For the Childlike,
the Curious,
the Loving
and
the Spiritually Inclined

Dedicated

To Linda Ward

Dear Friend,
And Mentor,
Ever the
Spirited, Joyful
And Blessed
Soul:
Brimming Over
With Talent,
Resilience,
Love
And
Compassion

Cast of Characters

Mother Mary

Mother of Yeshua

Manifest under various spiritual guises throughout history

Now perpetually manifest in the physical realm as the feminine
aspect of the Master Soul

Referred to as Mother Mary or Mary

Yeshua

Incarnate Son of Mother Mary

Manifest under various spiritual guises throughout history

Now perpetually manifest in the physical realm as the masculine
aspect of the Master Soul

Frequently referred to as 'the Lord' or 'Lord Yeshua'

Prime Source

Aka: God, God the Father, Our Lord, The Lord, and God Almighty

Creator and Sustainer of both the spiritual domain and
physical cosmos

Creator of the process of Incarnation - by which many of Its
component parts, i.e., immoral Souls incarnate as embodiments in
the physical domain.

Archangel Gabriel

Archangel Raphael

Archangel Michael

Joseph
    Husband of Mother Mary
    Earthly father of Yeshua

John the Apostle
    Disciple of Yeshua
    Narrator of this story

Mary Magdalene
    Disciple of Yeshua
    Referred to as Magdalene or Mary Magdalene

Essenes
    Jewish Spiritual Sect, Qumran, Judea

John the Baptist
    Herald of Yeshua

Ana and Joachim
    Parents of Mother Mary

Elizabeth and Zechariah
    Aunt and Uncle of Mother Mary
    Parents of John the Baptist

Members of the Community
    Those who interact with Mother Mary and Apostle John as they
        return to Jerusalem
    Neighbors of Mary and Joseph in Jerusalem

Contents

Chapter I

Yeshua Opens the Conference

Celebrating Mother Mary

"LOVING SOULS, ALL," SAID A BEAMING YESHUA.[1] "WE THANK you for accepting our invitation to join in this celebration of Mother Mary - beloved Soul, wife of Joseph of Nazareth and the Mother of My most recent and now perpetual incarnation."

"Prime Source – Our Loving Lord Almighty - has authorized Me to act as honorary chairperson of this conference. Our Lord is - of course - known to the traditionalists as 'God', and to the many who consider themselves modern or progressive, as 'Prime Source.'"

"I have long learned to revere the person who is today the special focus of our sharing. I speak, of course, of My and Our - beloved 'Mother Mary' - the miraculous spirit who has incarnated on Earth numerous times

---

1 *'Yeshua'* is the anglicized Hebrew name for *'Jesus'*, used here because the common biblical name of 'Jesus' has become so loaded with often erroneous theological interpretations that it seemed best to use the neutral and original Greek term *Iesous* - as transposed into its English-Hebrew equivalent of *Yeshua*.

as a special representative of Prime Source, and then became the bearer of My most recent Incarnation."

"After years of devotion on Earth, She was called home by Prime Source, honored with the Assumption - Body and Soul - into Heaven - and designated as a Master Soul in perpetuity - to serve the incarnate Souls of the Earth and even those scattered throughout the cosmos."

"Her return to the heavenly domain did not last very long, however, for Mother Mary yearned to return to Her work here on Earth. So She reincarnated once again. In a relatively recent and very triumphant return, She reentered the physical domain at the same spot from whence She had departed, namely our Sanctuary in Glastonbury, Britannia."

Earlier, during the events on the Temple Mount, I entrusted Her to our own John the Apostle ('Woman here is your son. To [John]: Here is your Mother. And from that hour [he] took Her into his home.' John:19: 25-27). So I knew She was in good hands when they decided to return to Palestine, retracing the path we had taken years ago when we left the troubles of Palestine to establish a Sanctuary in Britannia. Thus did Mother Mary and John proceed back East - traversing Europa, again sailing the length of the Mediterranean and arriving back in Palestine many months later - where Mother Mary, as you know, continues to serve humanity until this very day."

"Need I say: there are testimonies galore to be told about this wondrous woman – and I know many of you are anxious to tell your story of Her contributions. Not surprisingly, Mother Mary also wishes to add some personal testimony regarding the various facets of Her life."

"So, we have a vast amount of territory to cover, and I will try as best I can to monitor the portrayals with an eye to continuity. Thus we will recall the most salient aspects of Her recent travels – beginning with the one described in John's earlier book. [2] There are so many facets to Mother's life

---

2   See *Yeshua: The Continuing Presence of the Master Soul* by William Francis Sturner as Narrated by John of Jerusalem. (Osprey, Florida: Cre-

of service that we hope to keep our celebration of each set of specifics as focused and brief as possible."

"Did you say 'brief' and 'focused'?" asked Father Joseph as everyone laughed.

"I think the operative term is ...'as possible'," Yeshua responded – smiling broadly. "And that applies to ev-ery-one, including Me, I now realize - after being so pointedly reminded of the need for focus and brevity," He said wagging His index at his father. "That is the only ground rule I want to offer at the moment - and that will be difficult enough – obviously for all of us," He said - continuing to grin ear to ear.

"But let's face it: everything is related, so comments on any one aspect of Mother Mary's life may stimulate recollections of a number of related issues. Perhaps the best way to proceed is to follow a natural or sequential timeline - 'beginning' with Mother's most renowned reincarnation into this physical realm - this time as the daughter of Ana and Joachim."

Birth of Mother Mary

"Okay," said Ana, walking slowly *to the microphone.* "This seems like a good spot for Joachim and I." Ana, of course, was the Mother Mary's biological Mother - the Soul that volunteered to conceive, carry and – in turn - deliver the incarnated embodiment of Mother Mary into the physical arena during the biblical period known as the New Testament.

"As you probably know by now," said Ana wrapping Herself in the colorful afghan She had recently crocheted. "Joachim and I had almost given up on my getting pregnant."

"We had both grown older and we were beginning to reconcile our-selves to the fact that despite our desire to produce a child. Unfortunately, that desire had not been realized and we were ready to concede the issue."

---

ateSpace and Other Dimensions, 2017), especially Part I: Recollections (Jerusalem).

"Then, suddenly, in our darkest hour, as you now know," said Anna giggling, "God helped us to move things along – and as it turned out, very rapidly and completely!"

"Our Lord blessed us with a pregnancy - and so I carried our precious Mary to birth. To behold a child of any size or either sex would have been joy and a miracle. But then to give birth to the being who turned out to epitomize what was sacred in life: oh my goodness. It was and continues to be a bit overwhelming. We were awestruck, first by Her inception, then Her birth, then Her development as a sacred being, and then – of course – by Her ultimate contribution when She in turn gave birth to the incarnated form of our Beloved Yeshua."

"This is how it all unfolded. First, my wondrous husband, Joachim - a man you know who gave generously to all in need - had his offering to the Temple rejected by Ruben, the resident priest. Why? He told Joachim that 'it was not proper for him to bring an offering to the Temple because he and his wife had not produced any children.' Can you imagine the humiliation!"

"So my dear husband went to the desert for weeks, fasted, prayed."

"It was at the end of his fasting that each of us was visited individually by an angel of the Lord. Can you believe it: we were each – individually and separately - told I would conceive and bear a child."

"I was at home, alone - when an angel delivered the message of my pregnancy. And a few days later, when Joachim was finally on his way home – having been delayed by the need to complete an earlier building project – oh, it was then that he too was visited by an angel and told quite emphatically that I was pregnant! Can you imagine our shock - and our delight! When the child arrived, we named Her Mary."

Life in the Temple

"Now my dear husband, Joachim - Mary's father - of course, you know him – he will finish our part of the story," said Ana. Using her cane, she then pulled an empty chair closer so she could at last sit down beside her husband as he addressed the crowd.

"Thank you, Ana. Well done, my luv," said Joachim – nodding repeatedly and smiling broadly at his wife.

"So we wondered: how could we best respond to God's word, to the angelic announcements that Ana was pregnant despite the fact that She had been barren for so many years. And I had been away for several months. When I confronted her with my fears that she had taken another man in my absence, she assured me she had done no such thing – and emphasized that both angels made it clear that the child was a gift of God. People still talked and wondered, as did I – but less so every day. So we carried on - assured by the words of the angels that Ana's pregnancy was indeed intended by God."

"And thereafter, Ana, bless Her heart, regularly sang a song to the Lord God." Bending over, he chatted briefly with his wife. "Don't worry. I heard it so often that it is ingrained in my heart. Besides, if I forget something, you will remind me."

Turning to the assembled friends and relatives, Joseph said, "It went something like this" – then responding to the tug on his sleeve, he quickly corrected himself. "Actually - it went exactly like this."

> I sing a holy song to you, our Lord God,
> For You have visited us
> And removed us
> From the reproach of our enemies.
> The Lord God has given us His righteous fruit,
> Unique and abundant before Him. [3]

"Of course, we then dedicated the life of our beloved Mary to the Lord.

When She was three we took Her to the Temple where the priest of the Lord received Her, gave Her a kiss, blessed Her and said:

'The Lord will make your name great for all generations.

---

3   'Protogospel of James', Translation by Bart D. Ehrman, *Lost Scriptures* (New York: Oxford University Press, 2003), p 66.

Through you will the Lord reveal his redemption
To the sons of Israel at the end of time.'" [4]

"So we had some additional decisions to make," said Ana, rising once again to stand next to Her husband. "Under the circumstances, as Mary grew, we thought it only right and proper to bring Her to live in the Temple so She might be guided directly by the Lord. Once we got there, however, we were concerned that She might not want to stay at the Temple but rather insist on returning home with us. But lo and behold, we knew all was well when She literally danced for joy and became the delight of all who witnessed the scene."

"We visited, of course," said Joachim, "we to Her and She to us – and such arrangements did not change for years, that is until the priests informed us She had turned twelve and had become pubescent. We – that is, Ana and I - asked the high Priest, Zachariah, to go into the holy of holies, pray for Her and ask God for guidance."

"An angel did appear to the priest, and asked him to gather the widows of the town together. Each widow was directed to carry a staff – because, the high Priest noted, Mary would marry the widow who receives a miraculous sign."

"The widows convened, their staffs were collected and the priest took them all into the inner sanctum and prayed over them. Upon his return he redistributed the staffs to each widow. Nothing miraculous occurred, that is until Joseph, last of the widows, had his staff returned to him. Immediately a dove flew out of it and landed on his head."

"Stunned, Joseph was overcome, emphasized that he was old, that he came to the gathering only because – as a widow - he was summoned by the high Priest. He even emphasized that he already had a family by his deceased wife, and feared – if now designated as Mary's husband – that he would be ridiculed for taking such a young virgin into his house."

---

4   *Ibid.*

"The priest reminded him of the fate suffered by those who refused God's offering. And so, Joseph went to Mary, spoke kindly to Her and vowed that he would indeed marry Her and then take Her from the Temple to his home in Nazareth."[5]

Looking over to Ana, Joachim asked: "Did I get it right?"

"Yes, yes, yes - and thank you for clearly recalling all the details – some of which I had forgotten already," she said laughing. "As a summary it was perfect."

Magdalene then stepped forth to fill in the rest of the story.

"I personally do not become part of this sacred saga until much later – of course - when I become a disciple of our Lord Yeshua," said Magdalene. "But I have always been interested in our Lady's life and have tried to recover what facts I could regarding Her remarkable unfolding. It is not totally clear how it all happened. Perhaps our Lady will add Her recollections as well - if the issue is not too delicate. Either way, here is what I have been able to figure out."

"So it was that, you, Mother Mary left the Temple after so many years, married and went to live with Joseph in Nazareth."

Joseph's Boys

"Now the record gets a bit confusing. For example, when Joseph and Mary later responded to the order from Augustus that all persons register, one source also has Joseph referring to the need to register 'his sons.'" [6]

"Either Joseph had as many as four sons by an earlier marriage. Or – according to Mark 6:3 - all four were the natural offspring of Mary and Joseph – that is, each arriving years after the miraculous pregnancy and

---

5   Jaroslav Pelikan et al. *Mary: Images*, cited earlier, 15-16.

6   Cited by Ehrman, *Lost Scriptures, op.cit.*, "The Proto-gospel of James", 17:1, page 69. One can only speculate on the age of the four sons - although James is usually mentioned first in the various biblical texts and so presumably was the eldest.

birth of Yeshua. But Matthew 1:25, for example, tells us "[Joseph] had no marital relations with Her until [after] She had borne (Her firstborn son)". To complicate things, Matthew 13:55 refers to "all His [Yeshua's] sisters" - raising the possibility that Joseph also had daughters by an earlier marriage."

"Allow me to note immediately," said Mother Mary. "What you say is true. Joseph had fathered both boys and girls during his earlier marriage. His wife had died several years earlier and he did a wonderful job of continuing to raise his family. I, of course, was delighted to learn of his devotion to his children, and that I would thus become a member of a family already filled with such youthful energies."

"As it turned out, the four boys - James, Joses, Simon and Jude – came to live with us, but the two girls – having married many years earlier - had since followed their husbands and established separate households."

The Annunciation

"Inheriting and thus being immediately faced with the responsibility of raising such a large family – and all boys," Magdalene continued, "a new reality that involved Her making a a commitment of unconditional love - even though it must have tested Her immediate parenting skills. And there She was about to face Her true destiny – as Archangel Gabriel suddenly appears on the scene."

"Most of the depictions of the Annunciation – as rendered by the world's famous artists down through the ages have portrayed you - Mother Mary - as being surprised by the sudden appearance of Archangel Gabriel. You are portrayed as startled, and seemingly over-whelmed both by His initial greeting and the fullness of His announcement. As we understand it, Gabriel said the following: 'Hail Mary, full of grace, blessed is the fruit of thy womb Jesus (Yeshua).'" (Luke 1:28)

Mother simply nodded: "Exactly."

"Now artist after artist – throughout the ages," Magdalene suggested, "have depicted the physical setting of the Annunciation as one that most would call shimmering, sacred, otherworldly. More precisely, the paintings suggest the Annunciation occurred in a unified space that was divided into two sections."

Fra Filippo Lippi, *The Annunciation* (1440-1453), National Gallery, London. Almost every artist of the Middle Ages and the Renaissance has painted or sculpted their interpretation of this miraculous event. Among the most famous are: Simone Martini (1333), Fra Angelico (1426), Botticelli (1485), Donatello (1436), Giovanni de Paulo (d. 1488) and el Greco (1577).

"The left side of the room invariably depicts Gabriel as kneeling, leaning toward you, with or offering you a flower. He is the first among the Archangels and messenger of The Lord. So His presence - and subsequent affirmations - surely symbolize the union of God's heavenly presence with your earthly receptivity. In so doing, God - or Prime Source - was apparently combining Its sacred intention with your human capacity to conceive the incarnation of Its divine child."

Everyone seemed to grasp at Magdalene's directness. Mother Mary simply listened and continued to nod in agreement. Several moments ticked by before Magdalene took a deep breadth and resumed Her narrative.

"So, to continue: the right panel of most paintings of this monumental event invariably show you – Mother Mary - as stunned yet receptive - sitting or kneeling in what appears to be a bed chamber. The mood of the room seems to transcend ordinary time and material space. It is indeed seems like a very sacred moment. Most subsequent paintings of the scene either display the figure or symbol of God the Father as being higher in the room or up among the rafters. The Lord - later symbolized as a white dove by the artist Tanner - releases a stream of golden light that reaches down diagonally and points directly at Your womb."

"Please forgive me, Mother Mary," said Magdalene. "I hope I have not misunderstood or presumed too much. But the specifics I summarize have seemed crucial to nearly every artist who attempts to convey the story of the Annunciation. Please correct me or fill in any essential blanks as I - with your blessing - catch my breath and sit down."

At the Core

"First: You are doing just fine," said Mother Mary. "Besides, I greatly enjoy hearing how others have viewed My life. And," She said - while looking over to Yeshua. "I am sure to have My turn. I have nothing to say but 'thank you'. Perhaps I will add some details - but later on. You are doing just fine and everything you have said is completely accurate."

"Dear Mother, be assured: You shall have as much time as You want," said Yeshua. Everyone smiled and nodded - and many even shouted their approval.

Henry Ossawa Tanner (American): *The Annunciation* (1888),
Philadelphia Museum of Art.

"Meanwhile, Anna, Joachim, Magdalene, Mother: please proceed,"
said Yeshua. "Who wishes to finish this portion of the story?"

The foursome looked at each other. Finally, Joachim said, "I am finished for now."

"As am I," Ana added.

"That makes three of us," laughed Magdalene.

"Mother, the floor - apparently and fittingly – is all yours."

She rose slowly, walked to the dais and after adjusting Her shawl, she began to speak.

"Thank you, all. Well, first a few particulars. Almost all of history's great artists are likely to depict Gabriel adorned with ornate wings - whether folded or hovering. Actually He had none - but the wings I guess try to convey His heavenly demeanor. And He apparently will be depicted as kneeling - which He did. And the prayerful extension of His arms hands emphasized the fact that which may have been an obstacle that just seconds before had disappeared."

"His gaze - and His hands - thus easily unified the celestial and human spheres - the arena of inspiration thus nurturing Yeshua's latest incarnation. There was Prime Source's intent on the one hand and Me as the recipient of His grace on the other. The energy was flowing - symbolized by Gabriel, uniting both heaven and earth, The Lord and I."

"Among the artists that best capture My sense of the awe - and the sacred tremor I was experiencing - is an American artist by the name of Henry Tanner. In fact, Tanner is the only one I know of who is inspired enough to accurately depict the appearance of Gabriel not in human form – but literally as Gabriel appeared to Me – namely as a full length sphere of shimmering white light surrounded by an elongated and glistening areola of gold. It was absolutely dazzling.".

"And Tanner captures it exactly as I experienced it. I was seated on a bed wearing a long, sweeping robe. My hands were folded. My head apparently was tilted forward and upward, at an approximate 45-degree angle. Tanner depicts Me as I remember it: stunned, overcome with emotion, humbled to the core."

"How soon was My destiny fulfilled?" Mother Mary whispered, Her head bowed. Looking up, She exclaimed: "In a moment, in a flash - I felt internally transformed. I remember how light and airy I felt – spellbound and as if floating on a cloud."

"For a long while thereafter... I remember feeling as if in a trance. There was a sense of profound silence – and I was overwhelmed with feelings of intense love and thanksgiving."

"Tanner's depiction of the room also captures the details: the dazzling white-yellow radiance of Gabriel, the earth-tone of My flowing robe – striped with long lines of black – every corner of the room filled with shades of dark red, bright maroon and a piercing glow of gold."

Mother Mary paused...took a series of deep breaths...then lapsed into a deep silence.

Finally, She sighed, raised Her face - seemingly still starring into space. Slowly She straightened Her back and smiled.

"It was - and still feels – other-worldly, a blessing beyond belief, a true and overwhelming experience of the divine."

"Fini," is all She finally said, then adding, "at least for now."

The total gathering was silent: all that could be heard was gentle sobbing, and occasional whispers of 'oh my', 'thanks be to God', 'three cheers for The Lord - and Gabriel', and 'thank you Mother Mary, thank you'.

Joseph and I

Following a short lunch, the conference resumed. The attention was firmly focused on hearing more from Mother Mary – and She obliged.

"Obviously, few if any, know My story as well as I do," She said laughing. "So I had best volunteer to tell what else I remember – in fact, remember so well and so vividly." Everyone nodded, clapped and cheered.

"It is very difficult to speak of My Son apart from the fact that I realize again how wonderful it is to be His Mother. As any parent knows, it is the Mother – especially in the early weeks, months and years who is primarily responsible for the child."

"It is the Mother who not only conceives but carries, nurtures, delivers, feeds and cuddles the child. But please know that my husband, Joseph - and Yeshua's mortal father - was wonderful, supportive to a fault, from the day of Yeshua's conception to all the times thereafter. He was always checking on me, always present for both of us, always attentive to Yeshua – always the deliverer of care, nourishment and abundant love."

"But initially there were issues that had to be resolved. For example, Joseph did wonder – initially and occasionally thereafter – after I told him about about Gabriel's appearance and that I was pregnant with Yeshua. At first, even I was mystified and had difficulty absorbing the full impact of Gabriel's announcement. I was not only stunned by the news that I was blessed with a child - but that my pregnancy was ordained through the direct inspiration of the Lord."

"I explained the entire incident to Joseph, again and again – always citing Gabriel's exact words. I also remember using our conversations to revisit the reality of Yeshua's incarnation and relive the specifics of Gabriel's appearance and God the Father's inspiration."

"Nothing like that ever happened - to Me - before or since. I remember my astonishment. In fact, I am still astonished!"

"I told Joseph of my initial and ongoing response: 'how can this be, since I have not yet been with you, my husband.'"

"I also repeatedly shared with Joseph the fullness of Gabriel's response: *The Holy Spirit will come upon you, and the power of the Most High will overshadow You. Therefore the child to be born will be called holy, the Son of God*,' is exactly what He said."

"We went over the experience in every detail, again and again. With a great deal of prayer and petitions for guidance, I - and Joseph - realized ever more fully that it was not only believable but absolutely true."

"I meditated upon Gabriel's words – over and over again, not only to placate Joseph's initial fears that I had been intimate with another man – but also to convince Myself that The Lord had chosen Me – of all woman – to conceive and deliver His divine Son."

"Oh my: those were indeed blessed, heady and remarkable days. My head and heart are still spinning."

There was a long silence, Mary repeatedly taking out Her handkerchief to weep, sigh, then wipe the tears from Her eyes.

"Sorry," She said. "Allow me now to get back to My main point. Both of us, Joseph and I - shared a great deal in the birthing and upbringing of Yeshua. We worried, we prayed, and slowly we learned to celebrate the impact of the Lord's announcement together. We also shared jointly in the raising of the four boys Joseph fathered before the death of his first wife.

Joined together we were a family and Joseph - in all his devotion, protection and goodness - was the head of it."

"As to the actual birth of Yeshua, we had journeyed from Nazareth to Bethlehem in order to complete the registration required by Caesar - since Joseph and I had been descended from the house and family of David. We were on the road to return home when My time arrived. Unfortunately we were unable to find an inn or shelter so Joseph, God love him, improvised, finding a stable with dry grass and a solid roof. As it turned out, the animals were a wonderful extra, their joyful sounds adding to nature's way of honoring the sacred moment of creation."

Again, She stopped and muttered to Herself, said only that "I will share more on all that - later on."

"So not only did Joseph and I became a couple but then loving and caring parents as well. We had no other children together and frankly had no longing or need to bring another child into the world: Yeshua – the Son of God - surely was the only gift and blessing we needed or deserved. And we knew Yeshua was both our - and The Lord's child, but now we, His earthly caretakers, were responsible for loving Him with delight and devotion."

Pregnancy

"Regarding My pregnancy, it has been a while, of course, and there is so much to share - so I ask that you please be patient with Me. Some impressions are indelible...chief among them the ease with which Yeshua literally allowed Me to carry Him in My womb lo those many years ago."

"As you can imagine, He would – like any other child - kick and seemingly stretch His entire body. He was also especially active when responding to My comments and questions. Yes, we would interact frequently and even had an internal dialogue about the world's moral issues as well as our individual and combined development and future. Much was foretold - even during those months of pregnancy - all of which both frightened, uplifted and humbled me."

"I would also often ask Him if He was feeling well, or if He needed anything. Of course, I would tell him how much I loved Him, and relate the latest comings and going in our village and surrounding area. He did not respond to everything I said or shared. But when He did, He communicated His messages or responses through His responsive kicks, stirrings, 'verbal' uttering and what can only be described as His communicating with me through a kind of inner sense or intuition, making me aware of His needs and wishes instinctually through direct awareness and knowing. I assure you His reactions and requests - and even assertions - came through with great clarity."

"Outer and internal signs of My pregnancy soon indicated it was time to share the news with My mother and father, Ana and Joachim. I told them the story of Gabriel's visit and My pregnancy, and waited for their response. I was not surprised but I was relieved to see that they listened attentively to everything I said – even coming immediately - to sit by My side, thanking Me for the what they called the 'glorious' news, and offering their immediate support."

"I still remember My mother's reaction. 'Ah – my daughter,' she said, stroking My face. 'We have sensed - even *known* from your birth - that You are blessed. Remember: we have known you for a long time - and watched you grow in God's favor all these years.'"

"We are reminded as well," said she, "of the divine intervention that also enabled your father and I to become pregnant with You. And now You are to have a child of Your own – and blessed by God's direct intervention! Astounding. Miraculous.'"

"As to My father, Joachim: he keep nodding, tearfully adding - in a hushed tone - that he was so very proud of Me."

"Oh, My dear parents," I remember saying. "First - it is so very good to see you and share the good news. And I am ever so aware that it was you who led the way in miracles. The fact that you had Me in your wisdom years was indeed cause for celebration – and your blessings have been passed on to Joseph and Myself - and soon will be to Yeshua as well!"

"I admitted to them – and now to you, My extended family and friends – that after the angel of God visited Me, called Me 'blessed' and told Me I was pregnant with God's child, I could still scarcely believe it; the enormity and sheer wonder of it all was almost too much to absorb. For weeks I prayed and kept mostly to Myself – not knowing what to say or do."

"But then Joseph and I talked and prayed at length together - and were supported by a very assuring dream he had three nights in a row: he was visited, comforted and assured by an angel that all was proceeding according to God's will. Surely it was the same Archangel Gabriel that appeared to me."

Mary bowed Her head – and softly walked back to Her chair on the podium. En route, She stopped suddenly – as if awakening from another realm - and reached over to grasp the hands of Her mother, then Her father as well. In a voice quaking with tears, She spoke directly to them: "Thank you both – again. With your support I felt stronger and more affirmed each day. It does appear that we have all been wondrously blessed. For reasons I still cannot fully understand or justify – I realize more fully every day that the Lord was consistently honoring Me and thus trusting Me to bring forth a divine child into our everyday world."

"And now look at Him." She said pointing to Yeshua. "He is as incredible as ever – now even, years later – being the Master of a ceremony that honors His own Mother. I am - indeed - doubly, triply – truly blessed."

Yeshua – tears in His eyes - came instantly to the side of His Mother, putting His arm around Her, kissing and kneeling before Her as He whispered something that no one else could hear.

"Thank you, My loving son," Mother Mary could be heard saying again and again. Finally She looked up and then stood facing the crowd: "Please, everyone: know that I am fine, as strong as ever. Yes – I am finished for now. Perhaps I will have more to share with - but later on. Now - it is time for me to give thanks - and to rest."

He Arrives

Time passed, juices and orange slices were served along with sweet cakes. After a while, Yeshua tapped on the podium, asked everyone to be seated, and again turned to the panel of potential presenters.

"Anyone ready or anxious to comment?"

"Well," said Mother Mary, "I am fully revived and would like to continue."

"Why am I not surprised?" said Yeshua laughing. "Dear Mother: again - the floor is Yours."

"Thank you all for Your patience," said Mother Mary. "Your indulgence is greatly appreciated. I will not be long – I promise - but it is best I complete what I have started. Thus a few more details."

"So, you may remember, a major annoyance emerged during My late pregnancy. Caesar Augustus – God love him - ordered a census to be taken of all Roman territories. Since Joseph and I were from the house of David, it was our obligation to travel to and register in Bethlehem, the ancient city of David."

"We took the donkey but the roads were still difficult - covered as they were with people - coming and going to the lands of their ancestors - all in order to satisfy the Roman demands regarding a census."

"As you already know, we prepared to return to Nazareth immediately - that is until I realized My time had come and we had to stop and find a place to rest and deliver our baby. By then we were in a town called Bethlehem, looked for an inn but could not find a room in the immediate area. Not knowing anyone, we encamped on a farm, in a barn - with the permission of the owner, of course - and soon thereafter delivered Blessed Yeshua - there in the manger - surrounded by hay and cows and horses."

"All this you know already - but I do love talking about it! But now: here's a few details I never shared before. Given the setting, I think Yeshua learned to moo and nay before He learned to speak! Really, the setting was so unique, delightful and loving - 'totally down to earth' if I may say so – so representative of Yeshua's instinctual love of everything He then and still deeply loves and appreciates. The setting – there in and on the earth - surely symbolized and expressed the core of His incarnation and subsequent mission."

"You probably know the outlines of the story of His birthing. But - again: here are some significant details. He was a big, robust baby, crying out - and even giggling although only an hour old - kicking His blankets and waving His arms with what we interpreted as joyful exuberance."

"What else could it be," said Mother Mary, punctuating the air with raised arms and shoulders. "Surely that was it: what else could it be – the One whom God had selected to guide and heal individuals and nations, the One who had agreed to incarnate on Earth as the Master Soul – who gloried in being greeted by the combination of cows, camels and horses – as well as seemingly hundreds of angels – and all the folks from the nearby farms - and then being honored by guests from other lands who were drawn to celebrate His coming. Amazing. All of it: simply amazing."

"Through it all, He was the happiest of babies. One heavenly choir after another arrived along with who knows how many shepherds, and - as noted - several kingly figures from the surrounding lands - whose camels were loaded with such precious gifts as gold coins, rare frankincense perfume and the medicinal incense known as myrrh."

"Oh my: how glorious it all was. Me – a Mother! Can you imagine! And Joseph, God love him, the devoted father. And Prime Source – Yeshua's heavenly Father. Ooh, oh, ohhhh: such a magnificent baby, already beaming – already the fount of joy, a blessed being – intended to inspire, to love... and to guide us all."

Mother Mary took a deep breadth, sighed deeply, smiled broadly, then resumed Her comments.

"A major obstacle then arose - when Herod, fearing the birth of a special child who might jeopardize his reign and power, took drastic action. Would such a new born become a powerful ruler, perhaps the rumored 'King of the Jews'? Not so fast, Herod apparently concluded: just in case, why not kill all the baby boys born to Jewish parents throughout the kingdom who are less than two years old. If he didn't know the whereabouts of 'the one' child who allegedly could threaten his regime - the child whom some in the Jewish community had long hoped would be the messiah who would free them from the Roman yoke - then that child would surely be among the recent and still very young infants of Jewish parents."

"Fortunately, Joseph received warning of Herod's decree – from an angel, no less - during a dream. Surely it was Gabriel guiding us again: He advised us not to return home to Nazareth - but to go to Egypt. We knew enough to trust His advice - so we took the long journey to Egypt (that's another story filled with its own difficulties and miracles). We ended up staying in Egypt for over two years, that is until word arrived that Herod had died and the threat of losing our son had passed. We returned to Palestine and thus Nazareth soon thereafter."

Yeshua's Childhood

"To learn a new skill - all baby Yeshua needed was to see it demonstrated. By the time He was two years old, He could cook, even bake a pie; at four, He built a small barn and a cart; at seven He learned how to fashion an iron tool; and by the time He was ten He could deliver a newborn calf, mend a roof, and teach a lesson to the other children at school on almost any subject: carpentry, how to tend to and heal a wound, and even recall and comment on sacred writings and poetry."

"The sublime moment, the experience Joseph and I actually needed to witness - the one that provided us with a most important sign of and key to Yeshua's true and highest calling - came was when we went to Jerusalem to celebrate the feast of Passover. By then, Yeshua was almost twelve years old. When the festivities ended, Joseph and I left for home with a number of neighbors and traveled quite a way before we realized Yeshua was not among us."

"Quickly we returned to the city, searched everywhere for Him, and finally found Him in the Temple, sitting among the teachers, listening, asking questions, making learned comments of His own."

"Of course we confronted Him mildly – or so we thought given our anxiety. But also pointedly: "We have been seeking you. Why have you treated us so?"

"His answer was equally direct: 'How is it that you were anxious and sought Me? Did you not realize I would be about My Father's business?'" [7]

"Ah, the transition was made: He had made the reason for His incarnation demonstrably clear and concrete. So it was that we were alerted

---

7   Luke 2: 41-50.

– this time with thunderous clarity – of His need to fully affirm His divine nature. As His biological parents we needed to - how shall I put it: *release* Him – yet fully *support* Him – so He might fully embrace and enter whole-heartedly into His sacred mission."

"So it was that we learned – slowly but surely – to fully accept His spiritual reality, which henceforth was His every-day reality. He was not only extraordinarily 'gifted' but also 'special'. Moreover, He had been and was blessed from on high. He was the latest incarnation of the Lord Itself and was now and thenceforth a full expression and manifestation of a Master Soul!"

"So we did whatever we could to support His process of becoming and being who He truly was. We prayed for Him - of course - and did what we could to enable Him, to help Him determine what He needed to do next – always encouraging Him to do what He must - given the enormity and sacred nature of who He really was."

"For example: an incident - which occurred much later but is illus-trative. We were at wedding in Cana, and were informed there was no more wine. We instinctively realized the potential of the moment. Yeshua looked over at Me, in essence declaring, that His "hour had not yet come." But I – being a Mother - sensed otherwise - so told the servants to 'do whatever He tells you.'"

"Yeshua smiled, signed, nodded and responded immediately. He asked the servants to fill six jars with water and then take them to the stew-ard. The steward tasted the contents of the jars and was startled. 'Every man serves the good wine first,' is what he said, 'and when everyone have drunk freely, then you serve the poor wine. But you have kept the good wine until now.'" [8]

"Thereafter," said Mother Mary, "Transformation - literal, trans-for-mation - became the overriding theme of His life – and ours as well."

There was a long silence. A pensive mood pervaded the group.

---

8   John 2: 1-12.

Finally, Mother Mary shook Her head, clapped Her hands gently, and took a moment to breathe deeply. Finally, She said: "I have said enough – at least for now. If you don't mind, I will now sit down and welcome the comments and testimony of others."

Shouts of "hear, hear," echoed throughout the gathering. Mother Mary turned, waved to the assembled guests, and took Her seat next to Yeshua. She took His hand, leaned over and cried quietly into His arms – occasionally looking up, patting His face - and then smiling through Her sobs. Finally She looked up, saying merely: "Sorry – but sometimes it is difficult being a Mother."

Moments passed – no one stirred. Finally Father Joseph moved to the dais.

"Perhaps this is a good time to stretch, walk about, get something to eat. I know there is water, wine, bread and olive oil. And I am sure I saw cheese, grapes, dates and even some honey. Enjoy. We'll reconvene in a little while – for we still have several important events and issues to cover."

We Thank You

Yeshua tapped on the wooden table.

"May we please resume. Of course, of course - bring the food with you to your seats."

"The next theme is the foundation for everything My Mother reviewed, and is crucial for understanding what was likely to unfold in Her life and Our entire 'Sacred Family.'"

"We use the descriptive term 'sacred' because it invokes the themes of love and sanctity that energizes both our individual lives, our immediate biological and spiritual family and the life force permeating everyone who is physically and spiritually part of this gathering."

"We wish especially to thank all those who journeyed with us to Britannia, everyone we met en route, and all the local villagers who helped us create our Sanctuary in Glastonbury [9] and then - more recently - return to resettle here in Palestine.

"Special thanks also goes to those who supported Us when Prime Source called Mother to heaven for Her Assumption; all those Souls who supported Her decision to return to Earth; and everyone She and our beloved John met during their recent journey back to this beloved land."

"Our sense of 'family' also includes all of those who originally befriended and supported Mother Mary, Father Joseph and Me during the difficult yet glorious time of My incarnation in Bethlehem, our subsequent journey to and from Egypt, and then during our long stay in our beloved Nazareth - the town in which I became a youth and now an adult."

"Through it all, I also want to pay special tribute to the two persons who have played such crucial roles in every aspect of Mother's cumulative comings and goings – from here, to Britain, to heaven and now back again in Jerusalem. I bow in humble appreciation to our spiritual companions, Mary Magdalene and John the Apostle."

Setting the Record Straight

"Before turning to the record of Mother Mary's recent return to Jerusalem - as narrated by John the Apostle, the companion who gallantly agreed to assist Her - I would like to offer some testimony of My own. It concerns issues of primary importance to understanding the historical backdrop to their journey, and to understanding the preeminent place Mother Mary continues to play in the sanctification of the world."

"First, as you see, both of Us are alive and well. Our present faculties are in tact - or so it seems," Yeshua said laughing, looking over at Mother Mary and receiving only Her affirming nod.

"This reality is particularly important to Me - since as you know - I was long rumored to have been crucified and then resurrected. Unlike Mother Mary, I never left, was never assumed and thus had no need to

---

9   See *Yeshua: The Continuing Presence of the Master Soul,* as above.

return. I have been here all along - awaiting My mother's triumphant return to this hallowed of incarnate life. I raise these issues again now because they are crucial to understanding both the past and the future of Mother Mary's role as My Mother and My sacred partner. The Lord designated Me a Master Soul at the time of My inception as the child of Mother Mary. She also assumed that role at the time of Her Assumption back into Heaven following Her work at the Sanctuary in Glastonbury."

"As a backdrop to all this, allow Me to refer to the stories of My alleged passion and crucifixion on or about the year 33 ACE (After the Common Era). Unfortunately, such stories have gained a foothold in the proclamations and practices of a long list of groups and churches. The result is a cross here, a cross there, a cross seemingly everywhere – the symbol of My alleged death and Mother Mary's deep sorrow have since been propagated as the essence of 'christian' religious belief and practice."

"There is nothing wrong or inaccurate in depicting *what actually happened* with a simple equilateral cross - one with its equal arms or extensions indicating the four directions or the world-axis, the resulting symbol of the plus + sign affirming Life and the interplay between the complementary forces of heaven and the earth - it's midpoint or center symbolizing Prime Source as Life's point of creation and manifestation."

"If a religious body persists in using a cross of any kind to emphasize the contribution of My life in particular, then let it be a simple + cross on which is displayed a flower or bunch of them - perhaps a long-stemmed lily, bouquet of roses or a collage of colorful wildflowers - something that is alive with perennial energy and that celebrates the eternal presence of God in the world of everyday living."

"Yet look at the discrepancy: I allegedly underwent a fierce and total humiliation that included whips, a crown of thorns, the carrying of a heavy cross, a sword piercing My side and then ultimately being nailed to a vertically aligned cross upon which I surrendered My life through suffocation. Woe is me: is not that a horrible and sad-sad story? A divine figure – vilified as a religious leader who feared for His own life and that of His followers - condemned by Jewish Temple leaders and crucified by order of the Roman command - thus justifying the adoration of the elongated cross as the symbol of My alleged death and Mother Mary's alleged eternal sorrow. Amazing. How gargantuan can a distortion be."

"In truth My alleged death was a charade, a staged mirage literally orchestrated by Prime Source and I. We used the ready availability of lasers – a spiritual methodology used for eons by Spirit - although it will not be fully honored on Earth until scientific awareness affirms it in the twentieth century."

"In our case, lasers were used to induce others into thinking they had witnessed a set of events that portrayed My alleged passion and crucifixion while We – Mother Mary, our extended Holy Family and I - watched the illusion safely from a nearby hill. That is a fact and that is the ultimate reality. If the scene is to be symbolized then all that is needed is a simple yet ageless + sign or depiction of a lovely flower - both wonderful symbols of eternal life and Our everlasting triumph."

Isaiah's Prophecy

"But the staged mirage did enable Us to set the record straight regarding the misinterpreted prophecy of Isaiah - the one that predicted the humiliation of a 'sufering servant', When placed in a trance by Spirit's use of lasers, many allowed themselves to experience what they wanted. Actually Isaiah's words were referring to Israel itself. [10]

---

10   Isaiah's reference to a 'suffering servant' appeared as part of the four songs in the Hebrew Book of Isaiah known as the Servant poems or the 'Songs of the Suffering Servant'. See Isaiah 42:1-4; 49:1-6; 50:4-7; 52:13-53:12; and 53:7,11-12.

Such passages have generated a wide variety of interpretations over the years, each expressing the tradition they represented. The following quote from 'Old Testament Messianic Prophecies' in Wikipedia is instructive:

"Isaiah 53 is probably the most famous example claimed by Christians to be a messianic prophecy fulfilled by Jesus. Jesus is said to fulfill this prophecy through His death on the cross. The verse from Isaiah 53:5 has traditionally

Unfortunately, once falsely ascribed by a mixture of Temple officials, Sadducees, Pharisees,[11] the errant view was adopted by the hierarchy

---

been understood by many Christians to speak of Jesus as the Messiah."
Yet the interpretive note to the fourth servant song contained in *The New Oxford Annotated Bible: An Ecumenical Study Bible* (New York: Oxford University Press, 1991), p. 939, interprets the term 'servant' to refer to Israel. Rabbi Joseph Hertz [also] argues that the passage refers to an event that had already passed - given the frequent difficulties and dispersals suffered by the Jewish people throughout their history including their deportation to Babylon in ca. 597 BCE. Modern Jewish scholars, like Rabbi Tovia Singer as well as Rashi (1040–1105) and the Christian writer, Origen (184/185 – 253/254 CE), also viewed the phrase, 'suffering servant', as a reference to the whole Jewish people.

Bernhard Duhm in his 1892 commentary on Isaiah interpreted the relevant passages in Isaiah in the same way, concluding that the reference to the 'servant of YhWh' is actually Judea/Israel - called by God to lead the nations but itself horribly abused in the process.

For more information, see Wikipedia under the various headings of 'Isaiah', the 'Songs of the Suffering Servant' and the names of those who shared their various analyses and comments.

11   The *priestly Sadducees,* representing the aristocratic, wealthy and traditional elite withi the hierarchy, worked with the Romans on issues of civil governance and dominated the decisions of the Sanhedrin regarding all aspects of Jewish living. They were a strongly conservative group, openly opposed to any of the 'modernizations' proposed by the Pharisees, as well as any reconciliation with the newly emerging Christian groups.

Their rivals, *the Pharisees,* came mostly from the so-called lower economic and social classes. Yet they too were opposed to reconciliation with the new Christian groups. Being less doctrinaire and conservative, however, they openly differed with the Sadducees on many doctrinal issues. The Pharisees, for example, believed in resurrection and the afterlife. They also believed in of the emerging Christian groups. It was a good story and although Isaiah's words referred to Israel and the Jewish people - and not Me - the more gruesome account appealed to many, enabling both the contemporaneous and subsequent generations to rally around a very sad yet galvanizing heroic figure."

"The gnostic author of the Apocalypse of Peter [12] - however - rightly depicted Me as smiling if not "laughing" as the laser-induced mirage of the alleged passion unfolded. Actually My facial expression was more like a grimace than a smile - as Mother Mary, John and Magdalene and I witnessed the laser-show and its projected 'mirage' from the safe distance of a nearby hill."

"Admittedly, there was good reason to allow others to conclude We had disappeared from the scene; it slowly but surely stopped all the turmoil that had gathered around My mission and My repeated advocacy for a new law of love and compassion - both of which greatly disturbed the Jewish and Roman hierarchies."

"In particular, it stopped the Temple leaders from dogging our every footstep - for they feared We were disturbing the people's allegiance on their interpretation of the Torah and certain ethnic traditions. Our leaving Jerusalem and then Palestine also helped to neutralize Roman fears that I, as the alleged Messiah and future king of the Jews, would, if successful, lead

---

the wisdom of their ancestors - thus leading to the adoption of an Oral Law, a set of understandings and observances passed on to each new generation and which in turn became open to interpretation and modification.

The Sadducees, however, rejected such 'additional traditions' because they were considered 'extra' extensions - not originally or overtly included in the laws of Moses or the written Torah. The Sadducees also considered these first five books of the Hebrew Bible, often referred to as the 'Jewish Testament', to be the only source of divine wisdom.

12 See *The Nag Hammadi Library*, James M. Robinson (General Editor), (San Francisco: harper & Row, 1978), p. 377.

an overthrow of their rule in Palestine. So our departure for Britannia not only put the tensions of Jerusalem behind Us but it so doing greatly expanded the geographic reach of Our Mission."

"Unfortunately our departure also enabled other groups to propagate their false claims of My demise; redefine our original and highly 'spiritual' message into a series of prescribed do's and don'ts; later propagate threats of an alleged 'hell' instead of heeding our continual invitation for everyone to display love and compassion for all - including themselves; justified the need for a new 'Christian' church that glorified a hierarchical structure; and made the new corps of bishops and priests the designated and prime intermediaries to Prime Source. Meanwhile. the ordinary citizenry was slowly reduced to the role of being subservient to a strict system over which they had little say. This power grab by the self-ordained bishops was and still is a preposterous case of ego-inflation."

"Despite all the bickering over doctrine, role and jurisdiction, many of the subsequent clerics, monks and everyday parishioners adopted a more personalized approach to the new sets of rules. Many became ever more mystic, interpreting the emerging gospels metaphorically rather than literally. Such dissenters thus paid lip service to the many legalities and complex theologies that soon emerged while bearing the brunt of subsequent inquisitions exactly because they tried to live - not by the Jewish, Roman or allegedly new-Christian edicts - but by the norms of love and compassion Mother Mary and I have always espoused."

"Our beloved disciple, John the Apostle, has since corrected the record of My alleged passion and crucifixion. He personally witnessed the reality of everything that transpired that day - having followed Me into Jerusalem dressed as a Roman officer on what has become known as 'Palm Sunday', thereafter joining Mother Mary, Mary Magdalene and I on the nearby hill as we all watched the laser-induced illusion unfold."[13]

---

13   See *Yeshua: The Continuing Presence of the Master Soul,* as noted earlier. See in particular, Part One: Recollections: Jerusalem, pages 1-7.

"Then these false claims of My supposed death and Mother Mary's eternal sorrow led to a series of claims and innuendo - propagated throughout the centuries by various church leaders and councils blaming the Jewish people for our alleged tragedies. As noted, whatever difficulties We allegedly experienced the day, although propagated by members of the Temple in Jerusalem, were carried out by authorities of the ruling Roman Army. The effects of this false blaming of the Jewish people have been disastrous ever since." [14]

---

14   Note, for example, the very early injustices suffered by the Jews under Assyria and Babylonia, then Ancient Greece and Rome. Then the false blaming of the Jews en masse by various members of the Catholic and Christian hierarchies and laities, brought about a series of sustained persecutions of the Jewish people throughout history. Most recently such lies and resulting persecutions reached an extreme in Nazi Germany. Gross discrimination and atrocities, of course, continue into the modern era - in both muted and overt forms - as both advocated and tolerated by political and cultural groups in various areas of modern society.

Despite it all, Judaism and its many leaders and communities have throughout history continued to make enormous contributions to society in general - and in particular to religion, mysticism, science, music, art and the social sciences. Fortunately, a UN resolution following World War II established the State of Israel as home for Jews with the intent that it serve both its Jewish and Arab citizens as an independent, democratic and multi-faceted nation. Unfortunately that vision has been sullied of late by a series of very conservative religious and political alliances within Israel itself.

For a warm and delightful depiction of the age-old and still very current Jewish devotion to tradition, family, love and joy see the play or film entitled, *The Fiddler on the Roof.*

Overriding Purpose

"For Me to undergo a gruesome passion and death, and Mother Mary to suffer a life of sustained sadness - would hardly serve Prime Source's intention to expand and deepen divine presence throughout the universe. It has always been Our intention as Master Souls to extend and glorify the process of incarnation – not just of all the Souls who have gathered here today – but for all the Souls who have ever incarnated and especially those preparing to do so in the future."

"Souls are the cells or particles of Prime Source's identity and divinity. By empowering them to incarnate in the physical domain, Prime Source has enabled all of us to deepen and extend Our awareness and experience as We become ever more loving and compassionate. As each of Us deepens and extends our service to others, thus do We support the power of Prime Source to spiritualize the entirety of Our ever-expanding universe."

A Silly and Harmful Interpretation

"While we are clarifying things and setting the record straight, allow me to correct another serious error," Yeshua continued. "And it started with some egregious misinterpretations propagated by some of the early Christianity writers and clerics. Unfortunately such views were solidified soon thereafter - all under the formal auspices of the newly emergent Roman Catholic Church, and then accepted by Emperor Constantine at the Council of Nicaea in 325."

"Once the Church consolidated its power, it adopted the gross distortion that alleged My supposed degradation and crucifixion was payment for the alleged disobedience of Adam and Eve in the mythic Garden of Eden. The whole idea was silly and utterly counter-productive. But - I admit - We greatly underestimated the emerging hierarchy's need to then invent rationales for happenings they badly misinterpreted. Compounding the allegation of My alleged demise, for example, they reached the conclusion that the human Soul was forever corrupted when Adam and Eve (who actually were the respective manifestations of My Soul and that of Mother

Mary) committed the 'original sin' when We metaphorically ate the forbidden fruit of 'the tree of the knowledge of good and evil.'"

One of its leading theologians, Augustine of Hippo, even reached the conclusion that there was a perpetual need for all Souls to suffer remorse, penitence, fear and self-loathing. Why? - the original human Soul itself had been corrupted shortly after Its infusion into Its initial embodiments. Only through My incarnation and death was humankind to be redeemed, the price paid for the original disobedience by Eve and I. What those church officials could not fathom, however, is that Eve and I together were actually manifestations of the Master Soul.'"

Realities

"As to Our alleged expulsion from the Garden of Eden, reality was once again turned on its head. By leaving the mythic Garden, We - the twin aspects of the Master Soul - inaugurated the process of incarnation: We - and all Souls who consequently chose to follow us and embody themselves in the material realm - were able to take a good portion of our heavenly empowerments with Us as We then entered the land of everyday physicality. In following Our Lord's mandate, We were - by intention and practice - thus empowered to spiritualize the material realm." [15]

"To put the story of Mother Mary in full historical context, then, please realize that the creation story outlined in the Hebrew Bible was merely one in a string of cultural tales symbolizing the beginning of life on Earth. Our early incarnations as Adam and Eve were merely the Middle Eastern way of describing the emergence of the physical realm. Once manifest, we were destined to attain full development as the twin or masculine and feminine aspects of the Master Soul - manifesting ourselves in a myriad number of appearances throughout history in every area and culture of the Earth."

---

15   See William Sturner, *The Creative Impulse: Celebrating Adam and Eve, Jung and Everyone* (Melbourne Beach, FL: Helicon Publishing, 1998).

"Thus Mother Mary and I have incarnated umpteen times - together and separately throughout the eons of time – appearing as spiritual leaders in many different cultures and geographic areas of the Earth and the cosmos. Here on Earth My personal appearances have been categorized as the 'Godman' - manifest during biblical times in the personages of Seth, Enoch, Moses, David, Joseph, Joshua and Melchizedek, Zend and Asaph (better known as the Essenian 'Teacher of Rigteousness') – all of whom served as progressive stages in My full development as Yeshua, the Master Soul and masculine aspect of Prime Source."[16]

"During My development as a Master Soul I have also appeared in many diverse cultures as such spiritual adepts as the Egyptian Osiris, the Olympian Dionysus, the Persian Mithras, proponents of mystery religions such as Hermes and Asclepius,, the Sumarian Dumuzi and Mesopotamian Marduk, the likes of the oriental Confucius, mystics like Lao-Tzu, the Vedic deity Indra, the unfolding of Brahman-Krishna-and-Kali, the Persian Zend, the appearances of the Buddha in India and Japan, and later the Grecian triad of Socrates, Plato and Pythagorus."[17]

"As the masculine aspect of the universal Divinity, my post-biblical appearances have also included the Aztec Quetzalcoatl, various kings of the post-classical period of the Mayans, and avatars and medicine men of Hopi, Navaho and Shoshone Native American tribes. I go where Prime Source deems I am needed - all part of Its commitment to infuse the

---

16   See Glenn Sanderfur, *Edgar Cayce's Past Lives of Jesus* (Virginia Beach, VA: Association for Research and Enlightenment, A.R.E. Press, 1988); and the works of Timothy Freke and Peter Gandy, especially *The Jesus Mysteries* (New York: The Three Rivers Press, 1999). For more on these themes, see Chapter VIII, above, especially the section entitled, 'The Eternal Presence'.

17   See Joseph Campbell, *Occidential Mythology* (New York: Penguin, 1964), and *The Masks of the God: Oriental Mythology* (New York: Viking, 1962), as well as David Adams Leeming, *The World of Myth* (New York: Oxford University Press, 1990).

spiritual perspective into every culture and tradition of the universe. As Edgar Cayce later wrote: 'There never has a time when there wasn't a Christ' - or put in historical context, 'a Christ-in-Training' - that is until I was blessed as the Master Soul by Our Lord at the time of My incarnation as Yeshua." [18]

"None of these appearances were complete in themselves. But each played a part in revealing and affirming an aspect of My unfolding Master Soul - slices, if you will, of the full 360 degree circle that finally unfolded with My perpetual incarnation as *the Christed one.*"

"This was equally true for the unfolding of Mother Mary. Her many earlier incarnations were all inputs to the completion of Her final and perpetual manifestation as the feminine aspect of the Master Soul. Her biblical appearances included Deborah, Esther, Hagar, Jezebel, Lililth, Miriam, Rebekah, Sarah, Tamar and of course Eve. [19] The many global guises that advanced Her full development included such diverse cultural embodiments as Kuan Yin, Nut, Kali, Sophia, Aphrodite, Spider Woman, Astarte, Corn Mother, Demeter and Persephone, Isis, Cybele, Rhea, Lilith, Circe, Athena and Artemis, Hecate and Maya, and the medicine women and shamans of various North and South American tribes.. All of these manifestations led gradually but increasingly to Her incarnation as Mother Mary, and then Her elevation to the status of Master Soul following Her Assumption into Heaven during the later stages of the biblical period." [20]

---

18   Sanderful, *op. cit.*, pp. 202-209.

19   M.L del Mastro, *Woman of the Bible* (Edison, NJ: Castle Books, 2004); and Patricia Monaghan, *Goddesses and Heroines* (New York: E.P. Dutton, 1981).

20   See Joseph Campbell, *Goddesses* (New York: New World Library, 2013); Marija Gimbutas, *The Living Goddesses* (Berkeley, CA: University of California Press, 2001); and David Leeming & Jake Page, *Myths of the Female Divine Goddess* (New York: Oxford University Press, 1964).

Evolutionary Progress

"In each case of earlier appearances, Yeshua and Mother Mary made real, progressive but admittedly only partial contributions to our eventual emergence as full Master Souls, and thus gradual adoption of God's norms of unconditional love and compassion. Until then - and thus throughout our many appearances in the ancient world - We were only able to infuse those increments of spirituality that were tolerated by cultures that continued to rely primarily on power, violence and egotism."

"Prime Source, however, persisted - as did We, Its twin Master Souls. And so it was Our role - through out many ancient appearances - to slowly but increasingly advance the message of love and compassion in the many regional and ethnic groupings We served. We were assisted throughout, of course, by the Archangels, and sets of Angels, Ascended Masters, prophets, adepts and incarnate Souls such as you. As civilization advanced, each set of progressive incarnations - yours as well as Ours - has worked in tandem with the related advances made in human consciousness and thus societal norms. We are ever more confident that the principles and behaviors of *Universal Spirituality* will be increasingly adopted throughout the world. This is especially true given our now perpetual roles as resident Master Souls, coupled with a human consciousness that is increasingly aware of its spiritual roots and thus is ever more willing and able to shower the world with love and compassion."

Continuous Unfolding

"Be assured: Mother Mary and I - as the twin personifications of Prime Source Itself, Souls - having evolved into fullness through many iterations - are here to serve on the Earth - and the entire universe, in perpetuity. So it is with special thanks to the Lord God Itself, that Mother Mary and I are here with you today."

"In particular, the Lord God has ordained the unique role that Mother has and will continue to play forever in the grand unfolding and sanctification of our universe. It is She who has been tasked to align the workings of our world with the spiritual essence of Heaven. She is and always has been the lynchpin, the central and cohesive source that continues to nurture the birth and developmental process of the many Souls - such as you - who have been called on and blessed to serve as incarnates."

"Enough! Now to the main attraction and the testimony of John the Apostle - the wondrous being who so diligently and faithfully recorded the events of Mother Mary's series of returns. The first was Her return to Heaven for Her Assumption. Then came Her return from Heaven back to Her beloved Sanctuary in Glastonbury, Britannia. And then, Her decision to return to Jerusalem - the Holy City where it all started - there to celebrate Her reunion with Magdalene, John and I."

"Ah - what wondrous times. And what a fascinating story!"

Chapter II

There – And Back Again

The Glow

AS PREDICTED IN A DREAM, I DID INDEED SEE A DISTINCT GLOW on that third night of the new moon – beside the wooded area – just outside my room at the Sanctuary. The light came from the east – several degrees to the right of a line of trees.

It was a golden-and-whitish light that shone on the low horizon. A flock of starlings – squawking noisy as usual - had just flown overhead and were now landing next to that exact stop.

There was no missing the intended point of rendezvous - symbolic of the conjunction of heaven and earth. Mother Mary was in the process of re-entering the physical realm, renewing Her decision to both extend and deepen Her personal commitment to humanity and all living persons and things everywhere.

Having given birth to our Lord Yeshua by divine intervention, and having been only 'recently' reabsorbed - total mind, body and Soul - into the realm of divinity through the Assumption, Mother Mary was about to return, the instrument of Yeshua's perpetual incarnation and now Her own. She would follow in Her Son's footsteps, rededicating Her life to the people and fortunes of the Earth and any other material and spiritual realms to which She was called.

Suddenly, there She was – standing quietly amidst a stand of tall trees – the shine of Her golden aura amplified against a background of orange fruits, green leaves and tawny-brown tree trunks.

"Mother," I called... as I ran to Her.

"Oh, John. How I have missed your hugs!"

The birds suddenly stopped squawking and several of the tallest trees seemed to bend their boughs, enclosing us ever so gently in their protective arms.

Moments - seemingly years - passed.

Then a voice from the kitchen.

"Last call for breakfast!"

Honoring Her Return

"I can now - just barely recall what the heavenly realm was like," said Mother Mary. "I know I have just returned from 'living on the other side', but for how long I do not now remember. I experienced it fully – that I know, sense, feel. Yet apparently it was like all the other comings-and-goings we have all experienced - making our way from heaven to Earth and back again whenever our embodiments completed their service and our full Souls again readied themselves for a new incarnation. Apparently – like everyone else - I have already forgotten the specifics of my latest transition although I sense you think it was a very special one."

"Most important, now that I am back in the physical realm, I must be sure to guard against both overextending My embodiment's ego and forgetting - or minimizing – the terms of My latest or updated contract. The initial phases of reincarnation can also blur - if not distort and eliminate - recall of our latest mission and assignments. Empowered as I – and all of us are: none of us – no matter how fine our recall - has the power to instantly sidestep any of the challenges we also agreed to."

I smiled, thinking: how grand She is: the Mother of the divine Yeshua, just returned from Her Assumption by our Creator, and here She is already facing the reality of the work that lies ahead.

"Ah - to greet you again in person, dear Mother, is an incredible joy and blessing," said I, searching for words. "The entire process - or I should say - your record of accomplishments and contributions - is already staggering. It all seems incomprehensible...yet there is it: remarkable – in substance and proportion... and all so true."

United in Place and Purpose

"Yes, here we stand, thanks be to God," Mother Mary replied, "all of us immortal Souls and incarnates on the Earth, continuing to honor Prime Source's request that we nurture and protect one another and everyone we meet. And John – you and I are soon to fulfill our promise to Yeshua that we travel and live under the same roof - which, as you know may not consist of anything but tree branches and straw."

We both laughed. "I am – in short – overwhelmed to see you, Mother Mary, and am blessed by Your presence. And, of course, I am deeply, deeply honored to serve once again as Your vassal and traveling companion."

Mary took my hands in Hers, reached up to stroke my face, then with Her head on my shoulder, embraced me with the dearest of hugs. "My dear boy," said Her. "It is I who is greatly honored: here I am, an aging Mother, thankful for the strong arm of a youthful embodiment who is fast becoming a presence unto himself. May I also remind you, my dear man, that you already are the author of a revolutionary book about My Son, a wondrous account of how He honored the spiritual intentions of our Lord and ignored all the sectarian interpretations of His sacred mission."

"I have read and reread your account of how we joined Yeshua in dismissing the silly tales of His supposed crucifixion, then journeyed with Him west across Palestine and then the Mediterranean, finally to land in Britannia and establish our first Sanctuary in Glastonbury."

Then with a twinkle in Her eye, and a nudge of Her elbow, Mother Mary added: "I sense our continuing travels together will also encourage the emergence of still one more book."

"Yes, I replied. "With God's help, the new book will honor You. I will merely be the one who takes note of all Your creations: beginning now with Your triumphant return to this incarnated state, and as we proceed, to describe for prosterity all the miracles You invoke. No commentary will be complete, however, if I do not also note the special way in which you walk and talk, how you work with and heal others, and how you demonstrate your love of life with everyone and everything you encounter."

I celebrated the moment by crying, as did She. Two incarnates, one royal and now perpetual, the other awe struck by the nature of his companion and his commission to assist and protect Her. I still recall the words of Yeshua: "When [I] saw My Mother and you - the disciple whom I loved - standing beside Her, I said to My Mother, 'Mother, here is your son.' And to you John, 'here is your Mother.' And from that hour you, took Her into your home." [21]

Mother Mary and I also knew - instinctively - that it was our individual and combined missions to demonstrate how wondrous it was to be loving, joyful, fully engaged and appreciative of the awesome gift of living. We also realized instinctually that our individual and combined tasks included giving aid, comfort and healing to everyone we met. That seems more true each day - especially as we subsequently prepared to leave the Sanctuary, get back on the road, head west-southwest to London, ever intent on traversing Europa once again and eventually completing the circuit by returning to our beloved Palestine - perhaps even daring to reenter Jerusalem once again.

Morning Rituals

It was a morning ritual – the first of two - perhaps three - such 'honorings' that Mother Mary enacted every morning.

Initially, there was Her greeting the day. She admittedly smiled each morning as the physical world slowly came back into view.

"Good morning My Lord," She would say – and instinctively add: "Thank you for the blessings of this new day." She would slowly rise to a sitting position as She stroked back the hair that had fallen across Her face.

---

21   John 19: 26-27 – with the appropriate modifications in personal pronouns.

Easily finding Her slippers on the side of the bedding, She rose, placed a shawl around Her shoulders and walked out to whatever stream or pond we had instinctively camped near the evening before. Mother Mary would reach down and grasp a handful of water, sip some of it then splash some along Her face and neck.

She would then crouch down, twirl a finger into the mud and draw two intersecting figure eights, one on the horizontal and then another drawn on the vertical - thereby creating the outline of a flower with four petals.

Ah, yes," She would remind Herself: "the four loops, a symbol of life, the love and unity of an all-inclusive flower."

The highest petal was assigned to God the Father, while its opposite at the lower end represented the incarnational process. On the horizontal plane, the petal to the left stood for one's soulful intentions while the petal or loop to the right stood for the ways in which one wanted to manifest those intentions that day. The point at the center where all four petals met was the domain of one's immortal Soul and its power to infuse its divine heritage into its earthly responsibilities.

"I give thanks for the infinite nature of our universe," Mother Mary would say as She swished and then washed Her fingers in the pond, saying: "May each moment of our mortal existence on Earth honor and reflect divine inspiration."

Mother Mary would return to our tent, lean-too, barn or whatever had served as our encampment for the night, and then call out to me to insure I was awake. It was then that She would gather the grains and fruits we usually had for breakfast – a simple meal yet filled with universal symbols.

After filling Her bowl with grain, She would place a slice of fruit at its symbolic center. Then She would place a slice of the fruit at each of the quadrants. Voila: the outlines of a mandala: the four major directions - centered, balanced and consciously invoked. Mother Mary would bow in tribute to the spiritual significance of the mandala - followed by a moment of deep reflection. She would then invariably bow deeply, thanking the

Lord for enabling Her to participate in the continuous unfolding of the universe.

Exuberance

And so it was that Mother Mary was back, grounded, here on Earth, now within sight and touch, renewing Her dedication to use the details of Her most recent embodiment as offerings to God and opportunities to again express love and thanksgiving in the tangible ways of the Earth.

She would invariably wash Her dishes one by one in the large basin, and in the course of the day find time to mend Her garments (and mine), and at end of day carry a basket of clothing to the water, and wash them using rocks and a mixture of animal fat and salts. As time allowed, She also applied Her skills at weaving – something She picked up from various artisans who lived both near Glastonbury and the many towns we visited as we subsequently traveled along the western shores of Britannia.

She also loved to walk – deep into the woods where She would inevitably find nuts to add to our meager dinners, and flowers for Her hair and the harness of our donkey. She even picked and wove stands of tall grasses to augment our improvised shelters as we traveled. And the waves of the sea were the source of much delight. Invariably She would spot a path down to the ocean – crying aloud as She slipped out of Her skirts and triumphantly rode the waves.

Discretely separated as we were for modesty sake, we were nonetheless within distance to hear each other's cries of joy. "Ahhhh," "wondrous", "delightful" came the yelps that glanced along the ocean surface. We mindlessly lost tract of time as we finally tumbled onto the shore, waved to each other, dressed and then walked the beach as far as it would take us. "Oh to feel the healing power of God's great ocean," is what Mother Mary would often say once we stopped to sit and absorb the sights and sounds of the sea.

Her aura was greatly enhanced by the sun and magnified by the misty spray. She was, indeed, a godly figure – twice blessed and exalted beyond measure – an anointed one who allowed Herself to be transfixed by the gifts of nature.

"We need not wish to profit from these waters," She would say, "for the waters do it all naturally: healing, energizing, caressing us with their sheer bounty and exuberance. How fortunate it is to be alive on planet Earth."

At such moments, a look of reverie would often come across Her face – and suddenly She seemed far away. Silent, seemingly subsumed by an awareness unknown to me - then suddenly returning with a few deep breaths, seemingly waking from a deep sleep - extending Her arms and open hands as in offering a gift, finally clasping them in prayer as She nodded several times - before bowing deeply.

"The sights and sounds of outer space – which I sighted once again during My Assumption into the heavenly realms - are indeed dazzling, allowing Me to pay homage to the creative genius of our Lord once again," She once cried over the roar of the sea. "Being immersed in the soaring reaches of the cosmos, listening to its majestic music and yes, witnessing both its exquisite color and delicate touch - was indeed breathtaking. But this, these waters, here and now: oh my – it is as if I was steeped in the very jubilance of love."

Remembering

"I do not remember all the details of My recent journey to the heavenly side," said Mother Mary. "Yet I clearly remember our Lord's gracious offer to honor Me with the Assumption – and His patience when I resisted continuous absorption, My asking rather that He grant My wish to return to Earth - there to continue serving My incarnate family and friends."

"Either way – both transits - agreeing to return to heaven and then deciding to incarnate once again to this physical realm – were difficult decisions: giving up My immediate contact with all of you here in the incarnate world, and then again leaving My beloved friends in heaven. Thank goodness for the power to meditate and contemplate – which I continue to invoke wherever I am. Such empowerments enable Me to open fully to the majesty of the Lord – and thus communicate directly with everyone on either side."

"I remember cleaning My room at the Sanctuary, making My bed, knowing I would hurt those who would grieve My going – especially the incarnations of My Son and My husband. Gradually, I sensed the onset of thunder, the gathering strikes of lightning and various overlays of soaring music. Inspired by the increasing strains of a mighty choir, I felt Myself letting go of My embodiment, accepting, yielding - being slowly transported by and enclosed within Our Father's embrace. I experienced a gentle jolt, then realized I was indeed back in the heavenly realm. I recall giving special thanks to our Lord – again, and again - for blessing Me with the capacity to bear Yeshua and launch Him on His ever-lasting manifestation in the physical realm."

"Oh, my," She kept saying, "Oh my, oh my, ohh my. I could hardly catch My breath. Here – there - then back here again - knowing that Prime Source, as part of My Assumption, had - in the process - also designated Me as a Master Soul. What an absolutely majestic world-wind."

Deciding to Return

"I requested this return to Earth because I could not possibly remain in the rarefied atmosphere of Heaven forever – not when so many Souls on Earth and throughout the physical domains of the cosmos were struggling to recall, affirm and live according to the goals they set for themselves when they chose to incarnate."

"I knew I had to return to where I was most needed. Fortunately, Prime Source agreed. But unfortunately, shortly after My return, Yeshua decided to leave Glastonbury and extend His mission in other lands and realms. Fortunately His travels thereafter always included 'fly-bys' and even intermittent 'landings' and personal interactions with us as we eventually made our way back to Palestine."

"Yeshua knew – of course - that it was not His mission alone to further spiritualize the material realm. Once assumed into Heaven and thereupon anointed by Prime Source to be the feminine aspect of the Master Soul - I realized it was also My responsibility to care for every Soul who incarnated: the villagers who continued to help Us support the Sanctuary, those We were to meet as we returned to Palestine, and all the future incarnates with whom We would share the glories of this planet."

"As Yeshua departed for parts immediately unknown - you John, and I, began to consider bringing our version of our missions to other places – including the possibility of literally circling all the way back to Palestine, something that was always on My mind, I now confess, even though you persistently urged that we take one day at a time. Mary Magdalene decided not to travel with us at that time but we were certain we would meet up with Her again in the not too distant future."

"Father Joseph, Joseph of Arimathea and Nicodemus, however, chose to stay on in Glastonbury, continue to guide developments there before – they too inevitably chose to assume other assignments in other areas."

Companions

"You, John, were then known as 'John of Jerusalem – but quickly became known as well as 'John the Apostle', author of the fourth Gospel as well three Epistles. Your contributions came as no surprise to Me given your desire to write - evident in your recording everything we did in that little book of yours. And how could either of us forget my Son choosing you to become My guide, benefactor and traveling companion. With His blessings and encouragement, and that of my dear husband, Joseph, you and I decided to continue our spiritual journey together. And so it was that we departed Glastonbury one lovely spring morning, headed west, thinking about Palestine but open to discover where we would best serve next."

"It was a bittersweet decision. We had grown so accustomed to our work in Glastonbury, made so many friends – gradually training others to continue and perfect what we had started so many years before."

"You may remember, John, that a few months earlier - while I was still in Heaven - I visited you in your dreams, reminding you of Yeshua's words that we care for each other when and as I returned to Earth. So it was not long after I returned to the Sanctuary that we announced to the group that we too had been called to embrace the next phase of *our* earthly mission. All we knew or confessed to - at that moment - was that we would travel east toward Plymouth, perhaps go as far as London, then maybe sail to the lands in the north of Europa - and who knows - maybe even wander closer and closer to completing a full return to Palestine."

Instant Reconnect

Mother Mary was walking along the shore of the North Sea one day – as we continued our journey east - when suddenly She stopped and reported that She felt a familiar shudder. Then She heard singing – and in looking over the horizon saw a faint sign and then a clear outline of light. Soon it materialized into the semblance - then the physical presence - of Her Son, Yeshua.

"I did not mean to frighten you," said Yeshua. "I hope I did not. I realize I have no excuse for not visiting you sooner but My work has carried Me to many different spots of this Earth and beyond. As you know, I create many different aliases and extensions – each helping Me to fit into various situations, remain anonymous yet spread some good will and healing as I respond to calls for assistance."

"Given your Assumption and now return to incarnate status," Yeshua continued, "you too are now capable of flowing into whatever manifestations or appearances help You achieve Your goals - a young girl, a beggar, a merchant, whatever. Through the Assumption, you too have in essence become a Master Soul and a divine being, meaning that you - an incarnation of Divinity - now possess the spiritual empowerment to become anyone or anything You wish - that is, adopt whatever disguises, appearances or extensions you choose that enable you to achieve Your intentions." [22]

"On My side, I have waited to complete some essential projects before feeling free and relaxed enough to visit You again - in the flesh, so to speak. I assure you this is no apparition or a mere quickie response to one of your

---

22   Note that the pronouns used to describe Mother Mary begin with a capital H or S following Her Assumption - when She was also designated as a Master Soul.

many call-outs. 'Tis really Me, your everlasting Son and partner in transformation - Yeshua."

"Oh, My boy," Mother Mary responded: "Who cares how You arranged to be here or which divine empowerments You activated to be present again in the flesh. I am delighted to see You - and hug You - and now walk arm and arm with You. I have missed You so."

"I realize You are busy with our heavenly Father's work, yet I must admit I have waited patiently for You to turn some of Your personal attention to Your earthly Mother as well. I too have a selection of wondrous stories to share with You since I rejoined the realm of the incarnated."

"Please tell me more," was all Yeshua said.

"Well," answered Mother Mary. "You may know this intuitively - already - but allow me to tell you in My own words."

"Prime Source indeed was most loving when It chose to have Me assumed back into heaven. But thereafter My life was consumed with too many ceremonies, too many heavenly choirs, too easy a life. I yearned to be back here serving My many incarnate friends, so I asked to come back as My incarnate self. Fortunately Our heavenly Father understood, as did your earthly Father as well. So here I am: hugging My son of both natures – and using both My spiritual and corporeal arms to do so. What could be better: is not this another kind of heaven, like the one We can and are in the process of creating here on Earth."

Missions Dovetail

"Your work, however, seems always to be shrouded in mystery," said Mother Mary as She continued to walk the ocean path, arm and arm with Her Son. "Perhaps because Your mission involves the largest and most complex issues and the deepest long-range problems of society. My focus, on the other hand, is more concerned with the immediate, the here and now, the everyday particulars of traveling with and entering into the lives of specific parents, children, farmers and tradesmen. These are the folks who currently inhabit the many villages and hamlets of this Earth and who eventually will also live and toil in its many cities."

"Well put my dear Mother," Yeshua replied with a full grin. "Our work does indeed dovetail - yet often overlaps. Witness the many times You too help to resolve the complex issues of a family and community while I am also attending to those who need anything from a little nudge, the bump of an inspirational word or a simple but direct intervention. We each do what we do - bing-badda-boom - our everyday kind of stuff although the recipients often perceive it as miraculous," He said laughing.

"You have Your special purviews – with occasional adventures in other and larger spheres. Although I am meant to attend to My more expansive emphases, I too am often asked to resolve issues at their most granular level. Whether so-called 'big' or 'small' - if it helps, we love being of assistance."

"I dare say," Yeshua continued, "having a loving impact – on anything from society to individual citizens - are arenas in which every incarnate also possesses substantial empowerments. In fact, it often seems that the most loving and the powerful impacts are initiated by the least celebrated incarnates - those who just happen to be involved in a situation that demands they exercise their capacity to call on divine energy and help if not heal another. Obviously, the most recent and most humble of incarnates can grow substantial 'wings' as needed and act with enormous insight and love – even at a moment's notice."

"Since my return to Earth," said Mother Mary, "I too have become aware that every loving word and action can, in its wake, create a series of repercussions. A word, a gesture, an act of caring - can impact not only on those immediately involved but also generate a 'domino effect' - each person in turn passing their 'blessing' on to others. Individual acts of love literally beget a stream of similar actions thus effecting tens of others. So it is with any action - especially the loving ones - for they are passed on and thus multiply down the line. What started as a singular and even spontaneous action of goodness can create a cascade of goodwill throughout an entire community."

"Is it not wonderful that an individual action can have such multiple and long-range effects - potentially resonating throughout a family, a region and even the cosmos. Hate and egotism have certainly yet to disappear from the intentions and careless actions of those incarnates who go astray. Yet expressions of love and compassion are especially capable of going viral, one act being repeatedly replicated and creating a veritable cascade of love."

"And so it seems," Yeshua concluded, "that our sharing today is part of that process. The smallest intervention on behalf of love and compassion – can and often does create a deep, long and most lasting impact. It loosens hardened dispositions, gives permission to the hesitant, motivates the stout-hearted, and inspires the instinctual goodness that is fundamental to all God-loving Souls. So brava and bravo to us all."

"I love, You, Yeshua," said Mother Mary.

"And it is no wonder that I so love, admire and adore You," answered Yeshua, as He leaned over to hug, kiss - and hold His beloved Mother.

Universal Empowerment

We walked for several minutes before Mother Mary stopped, turned to me with delight in Her face. The spontaneous meetings She has with Yeshua made Her intently aware of the fact that although Yeshua was not always at Her side physically, She knew He was actually at Her - and our - side every moment of everyday.

She went on to declare with utterly simplicity that "although He is My Son and fellow Master Soul, He is also everyone's guide and protector. He is God's anointed ambassador and His prodigious powers, of course, enable Him capable of doing just about any and everything. You know this very well, John - for you have lived and traveled with Him. The so-called itinerant we met on the road, yesterday: remember him? – a large staff, breaded, blue shirt and bright red scarf. He waved merrily to us. Then He blessed us as He rode by atop that big caravan."

"Of course, I remember him," I said. "I thought it could be an angel but it went by so quickly I was not sure – then thinking it was just some wondrous fellow in love with life and unabashedly willing to share his happiness with others. I remember in particular this fellow took great joy in his decorative clothing. So it felt so good to return his hearty greeting. We both even laughed at his antics and lavish outfit – but then bowed reverently at the sign of His blessing."

There was silence as Mother Mary tilted Her head at me. Suddenly it clicked. "Of course. So it was Yeshua after all," I exclaimed. "How wonderful. Who knows where He has gone since visiting with you earlier today, and what incredible thing He is now in the midst of initiating if not completing."

"Well, He told me He was headed for the Americas," said Mother Mary. "He wanted to learn from the Indians of what He called the 'great plains' area of a land beyond the ocean. He can - of course - be there in the blink of an eye – His divine eye, that is. Such instant travel is simple if you have access to Prime Source's eternal vision - and then focus your thoughts on achieving such instantaneous travel. Such powers, of course, also lie dormant in the hearts of every incarnate – as they too learn to trust and fully express their spiritual empowerments."

"Yes, it is all in everyone's capacity. With focused intention – and 'vroom,'" She added. "One's Soul can be can be off and away to wherever one wishes - an empowerment given to all incarnate Souls - and, mind you, is exercised by their Soul most frequently as its embodiment sleeps. The Soul is capable of arriving instantly wherever it wishes or is called. Sooner of later they will teach their otherwise grounded embodiments to use their minds to work the same wonders."

"In Yeshua's case there is always a need or opportunity. I see and understand Him thoroughly, of course, Soul to Soul, being twin aspects of the Master Soul and amplified by our Mother-Son bonding. The realization of this double connection - as unique as it is - is also, at times - overwhelming."

"One can only wonder how often He responds to any and everyone in need - and then uses whatever guises enable Him to blend in and contribute as needed. It is no wonder that we cannot forget it when He honors us with one of His sudden appearances and fly-bys: waving to us as He gallops by on a horse, appearing for but a moment at the edge a caravan, passing us briefly as a beggar at a market and even stopping to travel with us for a while as we continue our journey – always exuding His ceaseless capacity to be totally present. Amazing."

Chapter III

Everyday Adventures

Help En Route

WE HAD BEEN WALKING FOR THE BETTER PART OF TWO DAYS – due east, staying as close to the coast as we could, preferring the heavily beaten roadways to the trails that seemed to head in the same direction but then often veered off into cul-de-sacs. We also tried what we hoped were shortcuts only to track our way back through heavily wooded areas and reconnect with the main or established paths.

It was by good fortune that on the third day we came across a caravan of merchants who happened to be making their way to London. They were camping for the night on a small lake when we saw their fire and immediately headed in their direction.

"May we ride with you, good sir?" I asked a burly man barking out orders to the young men in his charge.

"Clear those trees there," he bellowed, "and bring the wagons round ready to leave promptly in the morning. And you there: get some more wood for the fire. We are meant to eat our supper before the sun goes down."

"A ride, is what you wish, eh?" is all he said at first. "You seem steady and in fine health. Are you willing to work for your passage?"

"Aye, I am. I also beg pardon for my Mother, a more middle-aged lady."

"Well, She is also welcome – as long as She helps to prepare the meal. Meanwhile, please give a hand to those weary souls watering and feeding the horses...and get a hurry to you...There is work to be done."

"So you will take us with you in the morning?" I stammered.

"Only if you heave to it as quickly as possible."

"To be sure: you are heading east, aren't you – toward London."

"And any of the markets and fairs big enough to pay a fair price for our fresh produce, housewares and mechanical parts."

"Tell you what," he continued. "I'll even throw in meals until we reach our destination – and a chance for you both to sleep with the grain – if you only hasten to help. I am short-handed and as much in need of your strength as you seem to be of bed and board."

The bargain struck, I walked with Mother Mary to the fire and the preparations for dinner, then quickly trotted off to join the others who were caring for the horses and redistributing the merchant's goods in the four caravans. Before long, we were indulging in a fine meal of grains, fruits and even roast lamb.

I sat with Mother Mary. We prayed, gave thanks, then agreed: surely someone is keeping an eye out for our welfare.

On to Bournemouth

Riding in a wagon pulled by horses was the perfect fit. We were prepared to walk the approximate 100 kilometers to Bournemouth – but our new friend with his several caravans just happened to come by. We know Yeshua can move individuals to help us, but entire caravans?

Thus did we traverse the distance from Glastonbury southeast to Bournemouth in less than four days. Fortunately the caravan was also scheduled to proceed farther east to the markets and the larger port of Portsmouth. From there we could take a boat to one of the major ports of Europa, and perhaps retrace the route from which we came: going southeast diagonally across Gaul to the Mediterranean, then hopefully sail eastward across the great sea and thus head in the general direction of Palestine. Lest our hopes exceeded reality, we also agreed that we were ready to settle anywhere en route that the good Lord indicated.

So despite our hopes and dreams, we continued to treat each leg of our journey as one more opportunity to carry the living message of The Lord to any who would listen. There was no sense hurrying to get anywhere in particular if we failed in our greater mission - that is, seizing on every opportunity to live with love and compassion with any person or situation we came across.

As it turned out, the ability of others to heed our message had little to do with what we said or the listening skills of those we met. Not surprisingly, our words were useful - but only as a means of solidifying the impact of what we actually did – particularly what Mother Mary did.

For example: during our trip to Portsmouth, a woman and her young child joined us in the caravan. The young child was suffering from a constant cough and chest congestion. The woman tried several times to quiet the child but to no avail.

Mother Mary shared that She too was a Mother, and sympathized with the woman's apparent anguish in not being able to cure or at least quiet Her child. So She asked if She could hold the child.

The mother, looking nearly exhausted, hesitated at first, asked Mother Mary if She was sure, then slowly allowed Mother Mary to cradle the child in Her arms.

The child reached out to Mary and her hands immediately clutched around Mary's fingers. She began to coo rather than cough, eventually sighing deeply – smiling, and dozing off.

The mother also felt asleep - as Mary stared at the child, stroked Her forehead and rocked Her ever so gently.

Otherwise there was silence.

Suddenly the child strained as if to sit up - so Mother Mary placed Her higher against Her shoulder. The child's hands moved to Mary's face and patted it gently. She then turned to look at her Mother – and reached out to her as well.

Stretching up and out – the child looked about the caravan, smiled broadly - then cuddled into Mother Mary's shoulder and fell back to sleep.

The coughing had stopped. So had the wheezing. All that could be heard was the rhythmic breathing of a small child and her Mother.

Threat and Triumph

And so it was that we safely reached the port of Bournemouth. The next morning we went down to the quay to check on the prospect of sailings to the Low Lands of Europa. There was a boat scheduled to make that trip but it was still en route back from Le Havre and then London. The harbormaster said the boat was also designated for repairs once it docked at Portsmouth, which meant departure could be delayed for at least another week or two – perhaps as long as a month.

The delay in making continued progress east was disappointing – at least at first – for it would further delay traversing the several lands that would lead us back to the shores of what we referred to as 'the Holy Land'.

"We are Jews, are we not," said I when we initially considered the general destination points of our travels. Palestine was our adopted home, the scene of so much of what had defined Yeshua, us and our work.

So we reasoned: if returning to Palestine was our approximate endpoint, then who really cared when, how and how quickly we got there. We would have preferred to board the right boat tomorrow but could easily use the extra time to complete a range of activities: visit the temples in the area, visit and comfort the residents of the nearby hospital, and volunteer to teach at the local school.

"Let's volunteer at least a half day - every day - for as long as we wait for the boat," said Mother Mary. "In the meantime you'll have the time you have needed to bring your record of our journey up to date."

We found a spot in the shade, and after fingering the beads She carried in Her pocket, Mother Mary also made it clear that She was ready and willing to review anything I wrote – with an eye, as She put it, "to help fill in some of the details".

The Need to Share

We found the local school, volunteered – I in the backroom carting wood, and Mother Mary teaching a set of ten-year olds how to sew and knit. At days end, we found ourselves lolling about our tiny cabin - waiting for word of the next boat to northern Gaul and/or the Low Lands.

Mother Mary drew pensive at first - and then was anxious to talk.

"It may make more sense if I talk it out," She said suddenly. "Things get a bit jumbled when I try to carry it all inside. I hope you have a receptive ear this evening, John – one that might help Me make some sense of a host of factors - you know, issues regarding Prime Source and Yeshua, and all this stuff about My being assumed - mind, body and Soul - into the heavenly realm."

"Wow," I remember saying. "Are you sure you want to tackle all that …tonight?"

"Well, I suggest we get started now, tonight…while I am in both an inquisitive and sharing frame of mind. If we only cover significant bits of the story tonight – that will be fine – as long you and I can return to any unfinished portions later on. I propose we cover whatever we can tonight, then resume, as needed, on another occasion."

"I can agree to that," I said with enthusiasm, "bit by bit, as we proceed, just as long as You don't overwhelm one or both of us in the process. I know You – and Your capacity to probe can easily overwhelm my capacity to listen - and dull my capacity to recall and record the essence of Your insights. You must admit that You have already lived the equivalent of multiple transformations in this one lifetime…more than most can even imagine. Then there is Your capacity to call on whatever comes through from Your many earlier incarnations. Some may see You – not me, of course - but others may see You only as a simple, middle-aged lady. I know better."

"The average citizens of these or any parts to which we have lived and traveled have no any idea what a powerhouse You are – born through the blessing of the Immaculate Conception, to a woman beyond Her normal life-bearing age, bequeathed to the synagogue for special blessings and study until you were 12, betrothed to the elder Joseph, visited by Archangel Gabriel and informed that you would give birth to the beloved Yeshua - the Son of Prime Source Itself, in of all places a manger - thereafter celebrated by barn animals and kings - who then by marriage inherited four additional sons, nurtured-taught-and-coached the young Yeshua in all the particulars of this and the divine realm, thereafter honoring His mission and suffering through the indignities heaped on Him by a small knot of ignorant clerics and soldiers. 'Oh my,' as you say. Allow me to catch my breath!"

"Remember: You then escaped with your divine and incarnated Son and the royal party, traveled to and helped Him found a Sanctuary in Glastonbury, served there for several years - before being consumed into heaven (which, as you must know, is - by ordinary standards - totally impossible and thus truly unbelievable!)."

"All of this – of course - served as a précis to your deciding to return here to the physical domain in order to rededicate Your life to teaching, healing and working with every person and situation You happen to meet. And all that brings us to now, this instant: where, my dearest of woman, You wish to re-evaluate some aspects of Your life. Where oh-where - do we possibly start? The whole thing dazzles my mere mortal mind."

We sat in silence for a long while. Finally I extended my hands – as did She. "We might begin with simple tears of joy and thanksgiving," is all She said.

She smiled, then laughed. I – as usual - could not help but follow Her infectious ways. I put my pen, then my pad aside – entering with Her into a realm I could only glimpse and follow - but hardly comprehend.

A Miraculous Baby

"He was a miraculous baby – unlike any in the village," Mother Mary finally said while laughing. "He was my first and only, of course, so I had no comparison to other births or how to raise a child – except to watch and learn from the children and parents we met en route as we traveled to and from Egypt."

"At the earliest stage, He would stare at things like a bowl of water and splash His hands in it and then giggle, time after time. When He learned to crawl on the earth He would revel in it, holding fistfuls aloft and letting the earth slowly spill from His hands. He would push the dirt into piles, then separate them into smaller mounds - which in turn He aligned along various geometric patterns. He would stare at His creations for a moment then look at Me and Joseph, throw His head back, laugh and with a resounding bellow, cry out with joy."

"Everything, everything delighted Him. It appeared as if He was on a great adventure - as if rediscovering the essence of whatever He saw or touched – all of which, He, of course - in His designed role as Master Soul - had helped to create in unison with The Lord Itself."

"By the time He was two He was able to speak in adult sentences, often repeating the new words He had learned that day. He loved to play with any and everything in sight: pieces of cloth, big and small rocks, the latches on a door. He also loved to examine His hands, wave them and then create a breeze by clapping."

"He seemed to learn intuitively, spontaneously - through intense interactions with whatever – referring frequently – even at such an early age – to what He called 'the essence'. By the time He was three, he would often mutter: 'Myy, oh myy, let us give thanks to Our Lord for blessing Us with such wondrous creations.'"

"Looking skyward and then at whatever He apparently deemed special or experienced *as sacred*, He would bow His head rapidly with a series of small nods, culminating in a long and full bow. Slowly He would then prostrate Himself upon the ground, forehead in the dust, palms upward, legs extended, feet arched slightly, His toes curled as if grasping the earth."

"Word of Yeshua's words and actions spread rapidly. 'Are you sure your eyes and ears did not deceive you?' one neighbor might ask another after they had spent time with Him. 'How can it be?' they would ask: 'He is only a child.'"

"I am sure He is inspired," said one elderly man. "He looks at you with such intense concentration – as if looking into your *Soul*. I swear Yeshua is a child-god.'"

"Others would even refer to Him 'a messenger from God'. His words and actions spoke for themselves. He was and always has been - special, very, very special.... incredible ...as you know: He was - from the very beginning - a divine gift of God."

Remarkable Development

"Yet over the years, many adults – and even children - seem puzzled, even fearful of Yeshua," Mother Mary said with a face that belied both sadness and pride.

"To many in the village He was - of course - considered to be very different from those of His age, a sort of odd fellow - yet one to be greatly respected, even feared - for He was no ordinary person."

"His internal development was soon matched by His physical development. At two, for example, He was still the size of an average toddler but by the time He reached four he was already taller than a man's waist. And once He opened His mouth, you knew now precocious, how advanced He was – expressing a depth of feelings and a remarkable range of knowledge regarding the earlier prophecies and the insights drawn from a wide range of spiritual traditions. His curiosity was insatiable and He loved everything He saw and touched and experienced."

He Who Hears

"One day, for example, we had some hay delivered for the animals, and as usual, Yeshua was quick to engage the farmer in conversation."

"What is your donkey's name," He asked. "And what is his lineage?"

"Well - I don't think he has a name - that is we never named it. It is a mere donkey, very stubborn – but in the end usually agrees to do most everything we demand of him."

"So you value his services?"

"Oh, very much so."

Then why not honor him with a name? It is sign of respect."

"Respect – for a dumb donkey?"

At that comment, donkey reared its back legs, battered the door of the barn, then shuffled its legs to align them with the body of the farmer.

"Best watch out," Yeshua warned, as the animal roared and scraped its hooves rapidly on the ground.

"It appears he was listening to our conversation," said Yeshua as the farmer retreated to the other side of the barn. "But that is impossible," said the farmer. "It is only a dumb donkey who does not deserve a name. What difference would it make anyway?"

The donkey – having maneuvered close to the farmer – turned around, then lunged its rear legs up and at the farmer, catching him in the buttocks and forcing him to clash against the barn door.

"You might want to rethink your assumptions," said Yeshua. "Lest you get hurt – now or whenever you dare to say such things again. I suggest you think of a name – and fast. You might even apologize – and with a some oats in hand, ask your loyal and hard-working donkey if it would like to carry that name you suggest as His own. You might also begin to address him as 'he' and him' - for he is indeed a male donkey."

"Talk to a donkey??"

"Yes - and you best be quick about it lest he continues to let his hoofs do all the talking."

The donkey looked back, snorted, his hinds legs repeatedly shuffling in the dirt.

"Yes - a real name for your donkey – not a throwaway, lest he reject it with another kick," suggested My very young Son.

"Hmmm," said young Yeshua. "How about 'Hoshama' - meaning 'he who hears'. Whenever you call him you would be able to commemorate the time he made you very much aware that he and all of God's creatures have the capacity to listen attentively to everything we say – along with a deep desire to be included, consulted and honored for the service and good well they provide."

"Okay - 'Hoshama' it is," said the farmer, shaking his head.

The donkey looked up and brayed - first softly and then loud enough to startle any one passing by.

Interacting with Other Children

"Yeshua would not play with other children so much as guide and counsel them," is how Mother Mary put it, "whether it involved planting seeds in the garden, stacking stones and bricks, cleaning a room or area or helping others who were ill or had a disability."

"And He also loved to laugh and express His love of life. Races were one of His favorites – and He would compete with boys much other than Himself. His legs were much shorter, of course, but He had the capacity to move them very rapidly, making Him – at the age of five and six - a fair competitor with boys who were ten or twelve. Once He entered His early teens He was practically unbeatable – even when the field consisted of 18 to 25 year olds. Once a race was over, He always thanked and congratulated everyone for their performance."

"He also loved teaching the others to play games that involved memory and thinking 'ahead'... like checkers and the ancient predecessor of what would someday be known as chess. Once He even organized a tournament involving several small towns. All the players from every team were His students – so He routed for all of them and reveled in the camaraderie He helped to create."

Inclusion

"He caused quite a storm one day when He approached the parents of girls and young women – urging them to encourage their daughters to join in any and all of the activities. Initially, the villagers were angered by such prompting for they feared their daughters would be corrupted by playing games – so less interacting so closely with boys."

"Then one day a young girl of perhaps seven appeared on the edge of the field when the boys were playing a game in which the goal of each team was to hit a ball into a net guarded by the opposition. Yeshua noticed Her immediately and beckoned to Her."

"This time it was the young boys who opposed Her inclusion. But Yeshua reasoned with them, chided them for fearing the skills of a female, and noted the advantages of having another very fast runner on their team. Yeshua did not know at the time whether the girl was a fast runner or skillful at kicking the ball down the field - so less kicking it into the net of the opponent. In retrospect, I now realize He may simply have intuited it - as He did with so many things."

"Then one of the boys by the name of Marc asked Her point blank: 'Are you good at running and kicking'?"

"Surely I am, or will be," said Ruth.

"So out she went - like the boys - yelling and screaming for the joy of involvement. When given the chance, she slowly teased the ball up field, passed to a teammate - and upon receiving it back, kicked it firmly into the net.

"The next game, Ruth brought Her sister and a friend."

"If they are as good as you," said the elected captain of the team, then we will find a way to get all of you into the game".

"Some of the other boys grumbled, until Marc reminded them that their team had always been humiliated - that is until Ruth and some of her friends joined."

"Some (referring to the girls) can run and hit while others are not as good. It is the same with the boys. Why not field the best of both and enjoy winning for a change?"

As interest in the game grew, Yeshua even helped to organize a tier of young adults. He loved it because he could now – despite His relative youth – both coach and play. Slowly both the boys and the girls learned to love and admire Him, His patience as a coach being matched by His sensational play on the field.

"It may sounds crazy to everyone but you, my Lady," said a spokesperson for the parents of the players, "but your Son has already proven to be 'beyond gifted.'"

"Then looking at Yeshua, he shook his head, and with a deep sigh said: "'And you, young man, have proven sensitive to – and seemingly the master of forces - the rest of us only fear or dream of'."

With Others, and When Alone

"In each of His activities, Yeshua was always delighted to help, to contribute, to learn. – whether that involved helping Me in the kitchen - cleaning dishes, stocking food or disbursing the grain, or assisting His father - and cutting the long boards into lengths that Joseph then finished and assembled into cabinets."

"Then there was all the work He did for the community - especially in times of sand storms, droughts, illnesses and disputes: finding lost animals, making bricks of dried clay, concocting remedies for the ill and always finding a way to quiet and then redirect flared tempers."

"He also spent a great deal of time guiding His kinsmen - especially the children and youth: talking with them, quieting their fears, answering their concerns, helping the boastful convert any negative energy into something positive, and helping the timid gain self-confidence - such that both became His partners in resolving problems."

Please Slow Down

"Mother Mary," said I - finally. "Please slow down. You speak so much faster that I can write. Please hold for just a minute or two..."

"Okay, I think I am ready...," I finally admitted. "Sooooooo, please feel free to proceed...but pl-easeee, at a slower pace."

Mother Mary took a deep breath, laughed. "I promise" She said – and then - in what was at least a slower cadence - She resumed.

"Besides all that, Yeshua still found the time and energy to be alone, out on the edge of every village He ever visited. When asked what He did during such times, He replied: 'It gives me time to think, to pray, meditate and even contemplate the wonders of the universe. I call out and converse with God My Father, chat with the angels, commune with learned Souls - and even walk with a few of the Archangels.'"

"And I noticed," Mother Mary added, "that at prayer, He would often prostrate Himself, lay flat on the floor or ground - and for some time, then slowly rise to His knees, extend His hands with palms up as He resumed a standing position. He would then rapidly shake His hands along His sides - as if shedding some thoughts or feelings. Eventually He would stretch His arms slowly over His head, finally assuming the form of a perfect Y - before uttering tearful cries of 'thank you, My Father in Heaven: thank you.'"

Everything, Everything

"He marveled at everything He could see, touch, hear or smell. His senses were for Him a constant source of admiration and inspiration."

"So this is what my Father has been up throughout the millennia," He would say occasionally, as He discovered one additional feature of the physical world after another. "Meandering in nature even helps Me recall many of the things I experienced, learned and developed in My many earlier incarnations. How wondrous it has all been."

"He was fascinated by almost everything that has evolved, marveling at how it all proved useful to the resident incarnates of the Earth. He had a special liking for the dazzling array of animals and birds, fishes and flora that have continued to emerge and even supersede themselves."

"He was excited, for example, to learn there were still large animals such as elephants, tigers and bears roaming the earth; and gigantic fish like whales, dolphins and sailfish swimming in our seas. What was the source of His information and understanding, He did not reveal. But given His divine heritage He apparently used His capacity to by-locate at will - enabling Him to go anywhere He wished, traversing time and place to experience any and everything first-hand."

"As if that was not enough, His Master Soul was able to travel - any time He wished - help others resolve their situations - any where in the world or the cosmos for that matter. All His embedded Soul needed to do was to fully engage that original and primary identity and temporarily disengage from His temporary incarnate or embodiment. This could happen at will during the day but was especially common at night while His embodiment rested."

"I, or course, was fully dazzled by this empowerment of His until I too acquired such powers later with My Assumption. Now I understand - however, that all incarnate Souls possess the same ability - although they may not be aware of it because it is their Souls that travel at night as their unconscious embodiments sleep."

"Oh I forgot to mention: on the everyday scale, He delighted so at the sight of puppies, kittens, frogs and butterflies. He would also make a special point of celebrating a given flower growing on a hillside, a crescent moon, a praying mantis, and especially a human couple taking turns carrying their newborn baby in their arms. And He marveled at the sight and sound of swallows, eagles, doves, dogs, kittens and even camels. 'What a glorious place,' he would exclaim, 'how truly wondrous and outrageously blessed is this place called Earth.'"

"He even memorized various bird calls and the utterances of animals – enabling Him – literally - to carry on conversations using a great variety of peeps and gawks and grunts and growls."

"As to the creepy-crawly things of the earth – including those insects that could also fly: all He had to do was lay on the ground and 'watch the show', delighting, as he put it – in the great variety of beings that busily moved into and over the ground, on the trees and amidst the blades of grass."

"The sight of grasshoppers flying and then tumbling over as they landed made Him laugh, and the sound of bees was reverie to His ears. He so admired the slow meandering routes of snails and worms, and was absolutely fascinated by the flutter of hummingbirds, the graceful multidirectional flutters of dragonflies and the total sudden, staunch then impatient hops of the blue jay."

It Was Like That...Everyday

"Every day was like the one before it," Mother Mary exclaimed. "He was literally in love with life and fascinated by every aspect of it. Animals, insects, birds, you name it. Each interaction with the world – especially anything living, even crawling - was a new experience, and He was dazzled by the variety and the unique features of everything He encountered."

"Horns, teeth, the teats of nursing cows and goats, the tentacles of various insects. He even brought home a snake one day, laid it on the table and began to question us about it."

"That is a snake, my dear," said I, "and it has no place in the home. Depending on the species, its bite can kill or paralyze a human being. So be extra careful."

"But its bite has not bothered me," He responded. "No wonder it has looked troubled and returned again and again to bite my hand. The poor guy seems exhausted."

"You may be insulated, my dear, but the rest of us are not. Please get that creature out of our house. In fact, carry him out to the farthest reaches of the village. His bite can be very harmful if not lethal. Out, out, please: this minute! He looked puzzled - but obeyed."

Curious, Curious, Curious

"He was curious about everything. He wondered why Prime Source made or at least allowed the creation of that which proved to be a menace to mankind. So He would ask us but neither Joseph or I had answers to many of the things He craved to understand."

"I will have to ask Prime Source at prayer this evening," He would say. "Perhaps if snakes stay close to their own nest, and the nest is close to someone's home, then its presence may ward off other - perhaps more dangerous creatures – creatures that can inflict more widespread harm on humans and other forms of life. There must be a reason for their existence. Yes, yes: I will ask Father."

"And what of the symbolism of the snake and its role in Egyptian myths and the Hebrew Book of Genesis? It sheds its skin, doesn't it? And of all creatures it moves so easily on – or slightly above – the ground. Perhaps, He reasoned, these facts alone explain why the advent the mythic symbol of the snake - such as portrayed in Genesis - signaled the advent of change and transformation."

"Surely it is a wondrous creature," He once told Father Joseph, pointing to the important role the snake has played in generating and expressing the spiritual traditions of humankind, symbolically grounding earthly reality in the here and now, changing its outer skin to indicate the exit of one state of being to the next."

"And listen to this observation - born of His continual self-examination: 'There is so much I still do not understand,' He once said, 'although I also know that I am and always have been linked to it all.'"

Thoughts Versus Experience

"Let me try to summarize My experiences of Life - including My experiences of My dear Son, Yeshua." said Mother Mary, "reflecting perhaps the different stages of My human and now divinely inspired life. Either way, the process of learning appears never to cease."

"As a backdrop, I often think I know or intuit everything - especially since giving birth to what turned out to be the culminating incarnation of my Blessed Son, Yeshua. And recently that blessing was compounded by My Assumption into heaven. Through it all, I have learned to access and understand the phases of My and the world's development - including the experiences of all the incarnate Souls - now contained in the Akashic Records or Book of Life."

"Of course, it has since been revealed to Me that the entire cumulative record of everyone's earlier incarnations are stored in the base or lower portion of our skulls. The history of our experiences of all our previous lives are always subject to recall - especially during meditation - and thus are available to us as guidance in handing the challenges we currently face during this our latest or current embodiment."

"Such learnings, even if only mental and emotional, can be amazingly insightful. Yet if we delve into them more deeply during meditation, they can also learn to understand ourselves and our world at a truly experiential level, using such recalls to fully comprehend the depth and breathe of the spiritual reality in which we live."

"They even enable us to more keenly experience the happenings of our current incarnation - to actually hear and understand the growl of the lion, the grunt of the camel, the varied calls of birds, the changing facial expressions of human beings, the contours and textures of the earth, the magical insights of children's tales and the myths of all peoples, the pains and delights of the incarnates who pass us by - and of course, the full joys and agonies of being a person in any and all the many phases of life."

"As We experience the seemingly infinite variety of Life, We are blessed to salute and honor it all - be it human or any of other wondrous creatures with whom We share the Earth and the Universe. It is literally breathtaking to realize that Our Lord has now given Us the power to understand and empathize with all the life forms - including the varied human beings that have inhabited this earthly domain. All we need do is give thanks: to bend and bow and humble ourselves in thanks for the prodigious empowerments of the incarnate life. It is thus that I say: how fortunate am I. How fortunate are we each and all."

"I never realized how rich, enormous and sacred is our opportunity to incarnate - until I re-experienced the many incarnations that led to this moment. It is the same for us all. Each incarnation grants us the capacity to experience one more life span up close and personal. So I thank God for the incredible gift of incarnating in living form. Too bad many incarnates seem unaware of their creative power, the gifts they have received just for the asking - the array of precious gifts that enable each of us to learn, to create, to grow in depth and expanse - and to love any and everything we see and encounter."

Chapter IV

Things Change

Life Unfolds

THINGS APPARENTLY CHANGED A GREAT DEAL WHEN YESHUA became a young man.

Here are my notes from my continuing conversation with Mother Mary.

Yeshua was different and He knew it. He played sports with the older boys and was fond of kidding and jousting with them. But He turned more and more to reading – especially the folk tales of the Jewish people as well as the stories depicting the spiritual leaders who had appeared throughout history in the various cultures of the world. Often Mary and Joseph would find Him in the barn or leaning against the fence in the backyard – murmuring out loud to Himself or 'His Father'.

The comments: "Yes, well taken," "Bless Him/Her," "I totally agree' and "To be developed" were among the many notes He scribbled in the margins of His books. Yet His verbal and written reactions also displayed disagreement, reflected doubts and even an occasional harsh criticism: "Emphasizes the negative and forgets the positive," or "No, no, no," "Lacks love and understanding," and "Must be reversed" were among His ways of expressing dissent. He also began to assemble His own writings and recorded them in a bundle of blank pages He carried with Him.

Although He continued His youthful interactions with His friends, He also increasingly sought out the views of His elders, never hesitating to state His own views while volunteering His own comments on whatever topic arose – especially if it was about moral behavior, love and compassion, God's intent or any passage in the Hebrew bible then being studied.

"You are so young: how do you know such things?" was a frequent response He received from some of the elders.

"You are brash, young man: best you should listen to and learn from your elders - those with more experience" - was another.

There was, however, one kind of comment that stung - that Yeshua found insulting. Usually it was some variation on the theme: "Go home. Help your Mother. Leave such matters to those wiser than you." Such insults would bring tears to His eyes.

Note the tenor of His response - which He later shared with Mother Mary. "Please set aside My age; no one, not even you, Sir, is older or wiser than God Himself and His awareness is always subject to expansion and renewal. I appeal only to My intuition and the yearnings of My heart, and prefer to look for a loving interpretation of whatever life brings us. Besides, how else can we continue to learn but to express opinions and raise questions? How else can we emulate God if we don't honor each other as potential contributors to understanding His creations and spreading His word."

In the Temple

"An old story but now the details," said Mother Mary. "There was that first time we went to Jerusalem. We took the entire family so, of course, Yeshua was with us. He was only twelve at the time. Since He was about to enter into His thirteen year, He participated - as was the custom - in what was known even then as a Bar Mitzvah or the ritual of 'becoming a son of the Commandment'. At the ritual He read a passage from the Torah and commented on the text."

"The ceremony was meant to be transformative – signifying that He was then capable of assuming responsibility for learning and observing the law. In essence the ceremony made Him an adult capable of being included in a Minyam – a service for the community requiring a quorum of ten men. It was an exciting time in the life of a young man. We were so proud."

"After the ceremonies, we left Jerusalem, assuming Yeshua was with us as we and many others began the journey home. En route we looked for Him among our family and friends and discovered He was not in our group. We immediately returned to Jerusalem and spent three days searching for Him. Fortunately - but not surprising – especially in context of His recent Bar Mitzvah - We found Him in the Temple listening to and interacting with the teachers and Rabbis."

"As parents – having been so worried – our first instinct was to admonish Him. 'We have searched in vain for You lo these many days. Why did you not tell us where You were going once the ceremonies ended?'"

"His simple answer: 'Did you not realize I would be about my Father's business – a natural extension of the meaning of the Bar Mitzvah ceremony itself?'"

"As parents, we had a right to be worried, protective of our still young son in such a large and busy city. But we had to keep reminding ourselves that Yeshua was more than our son. A human being made of flesh and blood....yes. Yet He was also the divine Son of God! So it was understandable that His entire being increasingly urged Him to give priority and full expression to His divine identity and status."

"Increasingly – but only gradually – did we learn to absorb the impact of this reality. Yet it was difficult – not just to support our child as He grew increasingly independent – a dilemma faced by every parent. But we also needed to learn how to accept Him in His preeminently divine role. In My incarnate role as a Mother, it was oh-so-difficult - for I knew He was growing beyond our parental protection - and needed to express the totality of who He was. Yet on another level, both Joseph and I fully understood so encouraged His growing recognition of His exalted mission."

She sighed. "But It was also difficult, I am sure, for Him to learn how to express the fullness of His divine role yet do so within the frame of also being a human incarnate. To us, of course, He was in our earthly eyes and experience still primarily a child - okay a young man - and we were His human parents and loved Him dearly."

"Now – at least, given the experience in Jerusalem - He knew that the next time He needed to leave us – and we knew those times were coming – He needed – please! – at least to let us know where He was going - and for what reason. Otherwise, as parents: we would worry."

The Cosmos

"As He developed," said Mother Mary, stopping for a moment to take a deep breath before resuming the story of Her life with the young Yeshua.

"Finally," She said with emphasis and an expansive flow of Her arms: "As He developed – oh, my - His greatest interest and concern became none other than the wholeness of the universe, and in particular, the placement of our beloved Earth, or what He called – and here I quote him verbatim: 'that perennial bright blue dot that attracts and bedazzles all the angels and immoral Souls that see it as they travel throughout the cosmos.'"

"He loved, for example, to lie on His back as soon as the sun receded behind the western skies, recalling the works and insights of the 'Greeks, Romans, Chinese and Arabs' - and the grand contributions each civilization made to understanding the expansive nature of the universe."

"'Such stargazers and explorers,'" He would say, "were able to predict the rotation of the Earth and thus the dawn of each new day - as well as the various seasons'. He marveled that they quickly learned all about the various constellations of stars, and the movements of our Earth and other planets as they completed their circuits around the sun."

"'Fantastic,'" He would exclaim each time He focused on humankind's succession of insights into the workings of our physical universe. "'I have seen and understood it all before," He would say, 'but from a much greater distance. Now, however, given My incarnation, My earthy perspective makes it that much more immediate, accessible and vivid.' With incarnation, everything in the physical universe suddenly was also front and center, available to His immediate sight."

"Yet He has continued to marvel at the full range and dimensions of the cosmos - not just in its vibrational dimensions and constant expanse but also in its totality - including the minutia of the microscopic universe - finding it more wondrous and expansive than the one 'above'. It was no wonder He kept using the word 'dazzling' as He opened to and blessed everything He encountered."

"Realize that Yeshua also had immediate access to His capacity to travel at cosmic speed – which is much, much faster than the speed of light. He revealed that He could be on Alpha Centauri instantly - at most in an earthly 'second or two'. And the transit into deep, deep space - to some distant galaxy millions of light years from Earth – would take Him just a few minutes in earthly time."

"He was quick to note, as well, that such powers of relatively instant travel were obviously a natural part of the empowerments granted to all the Souls residing in Heaven as well as those who returned to it following the death of their latest embodiment in the physical realm. All immortal Souls momentarily surrendered such powers, however, during the time in which they served Prime Source as incarnates."

Mother Mary and I looked at each other – smiled, shook our heads, laughed at how incredible - but seemingly normal - were the capacities of the super-natural spiritual realm.

"Of course, that explains how Yeshua can now 'fly by' and be with us one moment and be gone the next," said I, my mouth still slightly ajar.

"And don't be shocked, My dear boy," said Mother Mary. "After I was so-called 'elevated' to the role of Master Soul following my Assumption, I too have been able to travel at will anywhere in the universe and do so instantly and with relative ease."

"But the primary work of My current incarnation centers on the Earth - with some extensions as needed - whereas Yeshua's innate commitment embraces the entire cosmos, which means He normally travels high and wide since His purview and responsibilities include our lovely Earth, the entire solar system as well as the 'All.'"

Putting It All Together

It was through such conversations with Mother Mary and Yeshua - plus the likes of Archangels Gabriel, Raphael and Michael – that I was able gradually to put the pieces together: the empowerments granted in perpetuity by

The Lord to Yeshua and Mother Mary were prodigious, other worldly, far-far beyond human comprehension and ability.

Once Yeshua's status as the Master Soul was fully developed, however, He, in addition to His divine standing, also decided to remain an incarnate in the physical domain in perpetuity, attending to us on Earth yet frequently using His divinely-infused free Spirit to attend as well to the many other realms included in His cosmic responsibilities.

Unencumbered by bodily weight or form, Yeshua could naturally complete a personal fly-through to the Pleiades' and then hover above one or more of the spirals of Andromeda, before switching back again – as need be - to His incarnated or bodily state on Earth. Through it all, He looked for every chance to be on Earth as possible - with the intent of exchanging energy with Mother Mary and aiding the members of His extensive Soul and incarnate families. His divine status enabled Him to bi-locate at will and focus His infinite energy on many different projects spanning multiple directions and complete them all simultaneously.

In addition to constantly serving the needs of others, He would on occasion also enter into the realm of the comparatively small and tiny - revisiting those beloved childhood sites where the creepy, slippery and slimy species dominated. Creatures covered with tentacles and capable of ensnaring others in their gooey webs still intrigued Him. He also used such tours as opportunities to go ever deeper - ultimately as well into the infinitesimal world of atoms and subatomic whirlwinds.

Obviously, He was equally at home and ever the Master in all arenas of cosmic reality – animate and inanimate – combinations of which enabled Him to embrace, adore and become one with each and all of the many beings, particles and energies that comprise the All.

Alas, Mother Mary possessed the same empowerments - yet focused most of them more locally, that is on our more immediate solar system - with special emphasis on our very fortunate Earth.

Attuned

So it was that the universe was completely accessible to Mother Mary as well – although She often willed to concentrate Her energies on the immediate earth-bound issues of our resident incarnates. Her awareness of even the slightest difficultly experienced by others, for example, was truly astonishing. Often She will sidle up to a person – nonchalantly, spontaneously – and offer a word of solace or advice. Once eye contact had been made, She would - in the briefest interaction possible - offer a piece of advice or infuse the type of energy needed - which would work wonders before the other person even had a chance to speak.

"It will be fine, my dear. Just give him time. In the interim, do not overreact. Trust in him, yourself and the Lord - and all will be well," is how She might put it to a woman She just met at the market who was experiencing difficulties in her family. The woman might initially look stunned, momentarily withdrawn and pensive...then as if newly awakened to something important – would simply smile...and say, 'thank you.'

One day, while observing a young girl being angry with an older woman, Mother Mary bent down and whispered, "your Mother looks ill. Surely you will not refuse Her your affection in time of such need. You contain much wisdom – having incarnated so many times before. In those earlier lives you benefited from the kind of patience you now withhold from your Mother. For old times sake – if not to display your great love for your Mother now – best choose to put aside your momentary displeasure. Speak to Her and with love and thanksgiving."

The girl's face literally changed form – and Her features momentarily changed to that of a middle-aged woman. Even Her voice no longer sounded like that of a child.

"Thank you, my Lady. I had forgotten to guide my embodiment - and thus was allowing my inflated ego to overwhelm the counsel of my immortal Soul. You remind me that it is my Soul's mission – while in this incarnate state – to learn how to express love – even under trying circumstances. I have been amiss – but no longer. Thank you."

Then there was the time when Mother Mary befriended a teenage boy with some sharp counsel. After considerable exchange, She finally said: "No. You are better than that. So are they. Let your anger pass, reawaken your natural capacity for joy...and celebrate your gifts. Be your love and not your wounded ego. Be who you are: a spiritual being – a warrior for love and peace. Conquer the world, yes, but first conquer and direct yourself. As an immortal Soul you not only have the ability to forgive others. You are also empowered to make a positive and constructive contribution to all your family and friends."

"My Lady," he finally inquired. "Who are you? You speak so sharply yet with loving care. I've not seen you here before. You do not seem to be Sadducee or Pharisee? They love to judge others. But you do not seem to judge. Rather you offer wise counsel – a very mysterious form of counsel, I must say – one that seems to affirm as it redirects. Are you an angel? If so, I've never met your likes before. I do not like everything you said but I appreciate it...and it will surely empower the better part of me to follow your advice.'

He walked ahead and then returned.

"An angel? Really? May I walk with you! Perhaps fetch you some water or food? At any rate, I hear you – and appreciate your attention to my dilemma. An angel? If so, I am stirred on to greater and more loving thoughts. It's a miracle: how different I feel. Thank you, dear angel: thank you."

Honoring Mother Mary

I had an intense dream last night, one that transported me hundreds of years into the future. The context: I have been wondering about the welfare of Mother Mary in future societies. Would Her words and messages be heeded, respected, be welcomed as wise counsel? She only recently returned to Earth following Her Assumption. How long will this reincarnation last? Will it endure on into the centuries? Will She become like Her Son, ever-lasting in both the incarnate and the eternal realms?

In my dream, I traveled far into the future, accompanied by Archangel Gabriel, and representatives of both the ancient Essenes and modern Gnostics.

The journey consisted of viewing scenes and materials that illustrated Mother Mary's impact – both current and far into the future. [23]

At one juncture in my dream, I explicitly asked Her how She is likely to be experienced by so-called future generations. Oh my goodness: was I ever both delighted as well as 'stunned and horrified' by what was revealed to me. Remember, I received this information in a dream. As an incarnated Soul the insights I received were not the result of some cognitive exploration of Mary's future on Earth. Rather the images and insights I received flowed from what psychologists will later refer to as my 'unconscious'. Understandably, the images I received were both scattered and random as well as organized and sequential. I will now try to put those messages into an organized and understandable form.

First, the images revealed that numerous religious and spiritual groups – as well as individuals representing many different creeds and practices - would have high praise and adoration for Mother Mary. Some of the tributes shown to me emerged in various forms: altars of all sizes and shapes – creative combinations of marble, wood and clay as well as dedicated empty spaces. Various religious structures also featured everything from burnt offerings, grottoes, cascades of water and and images of Her rendered in ceramics of blue and white.

Christian – especially Roman Catholic groups – would praise Mary as the Mother of a Divine Son – and celebrate Her appearances around the world to an occasional adult but most often to children. Such groups would

---

23   I have interacted with Archangel Gabriel ever since and on numerous occasions – addressing him by His adopted name of 'Benu' - which means 'doorway' in ancient Egyptian. His adopted name seems most appropriate given His willingness to listen and give wise counsel. Gabriel was the first Archangel created by Prime Source, and has become known – in Heaven, on Earth and apparently throughout the cosmos - for His roles as 'Divine Messenger' and 'Beloved Guide'.

praise Her for being both the Mother and a guide of Our Lord – and thank Her for Her blessings and interventions.

Too Much

But the list of celebrations grew more elaborate and seemingly detached with each decade, the initial emphasis on simplicity and thanksgiving swerving into highly elaborate praise and adulation. Some of what I was able to foresee in the dream surprised and greatly troubled me: the love and appreciation of Mother Mary's humility and simplicity seemed to deteriorate gradually into mushy and sentimental flattery.

The Mother Mary I had known first-hand, every day - apparently was to be increasingly presented – at least by many - as purely an other-worldly figure, literally divorced from and standing astride the Earth, dressed in long elaborate robes of pastel pinks and blues, looking dreamy and detached, regal and above it all, a dainty and aloof queen who lived very far above and away from the faceless population She purportedly served.

Oh my gosh. I have worked with Mary for years and have always seen Her operating as the servant of the Lord and the average person - in every kind of situation – none of them associated with status, detachment or superiority. I have seen Her work daily in the most difficult of situations – not pontificating from afar while sitting on a queen's throne. Rather I saw Her kneeling with the poor and the afflicted, in the streets and humble abodes, usually guiding and comforting those who were struggling with their moral and physical problems. Her manner was always humble, loving and involved - so unlike many of the statues that featured Her above it all - Her images being placed in the highly elevated niches of churches and cathedrals.

Despite the many who individually and in small groups continued to revere Mother Mary for Her gentle yet empowering ways, there also emerged a countervailing and often dominant adoration that featured Her under bright lights dressed in iridescent-blue mantles and sparkling veils.

Through the centuries, many paintings would also depict Her with a glowing heart of bright red, Her head invariably surrounded by a crown of a dozen stars - not simply walking on the Earth but standing on or above it. And some of Her acquired titles were also over-the-top: Queen of the Angels; Star of the Sea and Mother of All Sorrows.

The continuous praise and adoration was admirable. But need it get so elaborate - and even gloppy? If so, the reality of this blessed and empowering woman would be lost - obscured and demeaned by such unwarranted and unrealistic sentimentality.

A Dream Reflects Reality

Upon awakening, I discussed my dream with my spiritual guides, including Archangel Gabriel (Benu), and my continuing contacts with members of the ancient Essene and Gnostic communities. Those discussions made me realize that the images I received in my dreams regarding the impending depictions of Mother Mary were not far off. My dream accurately depicted a practice of adoration that grew more elaborate with each generation. Special feasts, titles, devotions, prayers, rosaries, pious activities, large canvasses in ornate frames, extensive poems, sculptures galore, musical compositions, paintings, catechisms, honorary titles, processions, shrines, sanctuaries, basilicas, elaborate liturgies and highly decorative portraits - although commemorative - did indeed became increasingly overblown and mawkish.

How much praise and appreciation was appropriate and how much was too much? The term, 'Mariolatry' was coined in the 20th Century by those Christians who thought the escalating streams of adulation for Mother Mary had reached a point of excess and exaggeration, and who appealed for more modest and down to earth depictions and less sentimental and emotional devotions .

Mother Mary's life and being - in my years of being with Her on a daily basis – have always epitomized the humility and love of a devoted Mother that everyone loves and deserves, a friend who honored Her direct linkage to both Prime Source and Her Son yet always served the common needs of the lowliest among us.

Call Her by any of the honorary titles She has earned - as you like. But She is best known simply as Mother Mary – an immortal Soul and divine Incarnate but who also was and still is a full-fledged person - who everyday, whether in heaven and on earth, wears a simple dress, walks barefoot, gives whatever is in Her hands to whoever is present, talks from Her heart, and who is totally at ease with Herself and every situation that arises.

Moreover, She is a real person whose divine Soul is also present in blood and flesh. She loves to serve and to pray. She also loves to sing and play – not just with the children She meets but with anyone who is willing to share in Her spontaneous and joyful nature. Predictably, She also loves to laugh and smiles more than anyone I have ever met.

Long Ago

"Do you remember when we first met?" Mother Mary asked.

We had finished our meal and the fire had burned to a soft glow. Overhead, the stars shone especially bright – the storm clouds of mid-day having blown out to sea.

"The first time?" I asked, searching my memory for even an approximate answer. "There have had so many intersections during our many incarnated lives, and I sense, even during our stays in the heavenly realm prior to incarnating. But I do recall one time here on Earth when an angel of God visited with us – oh, so many years and incarnations ago."

"I remember exactly," said Mother Mary. "It was on a night like this. It was a chilly but we were beside a lovely fire. It was indeed long ago – eons in fact – when strife ruled the land – in an area not too far from where we are sitting tonight."

"The so-called rulers of the land – and there were several of them – were at war again, each fighting for dominance. Those of us who honored Prime Source were discouraged by all the turmoil and were wondering if any of us – no less the entire physical world – would survive. We were – we thought - experiencing what appeared to be the imminent demise of all the God-loving peoples."

"All the progress we had made was being jeopardized by the incessant warfare between these self-appointed leaders - all of whom bragged of their supposed semi-divine status and thus alleged right to rule over others. Slowly but surely, those of us who believed in everyone's innate dignity and our right to live our lives with love and compassion - as God intended - were being eliminated. We had just come from a counsel of such spiritual survivors. We had agreed to carry on – but the mood was far from optimistic."

Familiar Patterns

"I now realize there have been many such dark periods in human history," Mother Mary continued, "some going back thousands and even millions of years, times when wandering groups of nomads were incessantly forced to search for food and even kill large beasts in order to survive. Fortunately, the coming of warmer weather enabled us to mend our tents, tend to our wounds, and prepare to survive the inevitable return of the storms that dominated most of what was to become Europa and the Middle East."

"Finally, we, that is the incarnate homo-sapiens, experienced an amazing new awareness and calling. Slowly we decided to mesh our small bands into larger groups, give up our reliance on hunting and the constant search for sources of food and choose instead to settle in fertile areas, preferably near a water supply - and learn to plant and grow our own food."

"I recall that we humans continued to hunt as needed - but staying put in one place and farming were soon preferred to the constant search of a prey not easily subdued. By learning to farm and settle in small communities, we added another notch to more civilized living."

"Of course," Mother Mary concluded: "We did not realize at the time – or, at least, not soon enough - that such resultant accumulations of land, people and wealth would motivate some to seek control - and attempt to rule over the resulting large congregations of people. Thus the attempted power grabs by self-appointed dictatorial leaders continued - outcompeting the wish of most to live quietly and at peace."

Aha!

"Ah, yes, yes, yes – thank you," I said suddenly, looking over to Mother Mary. "Now I remember the exact time when we had our most dramatic meeting so many incarnate lifetimes ago. We had met many times before but there was that particular time when we both experienced a set of deep personal revelations."

"My memory takes us back to this very land, the northern and middle tiers of what was later invaded by the Jews who soon thereafter organized settlements throughout Israel and Judea. Yes - it was in Canaan when we were visited suddenly by a presence we initially thought was a complete stranger but – as we were soon discovered – was actually our old friend, our most revered guide from the spiritual world, the infamous Archangel Gabriel."

Mother Mary laughed. "Oh what a rogue that stranger seemed to be: dressed in tattered robes, with a long beard, appearing suddenly as if from nowhere. We soon became aware of the fact that His appearance - and His message - was facilitated by the alignment of certain stars – portending a wondrous gift."

"There, now," He said suddenly in a deep voice. "There was indeed a portentous event at the midheaven: Saturn aligned favorably with Jupiter and Venus - signaling that good times were about to unfold."

"God was speaking - and would do so again very soon," He continued. "In fact, Prime Source now sends Me, His trusted messenger, thanking you for your prayers and meditations, and letting you know His blessings will continue to sustain you."

"We were stunned but I remember finally confronting this wondrous stranger," I said in recalling the incident, asking our unannounced guest: 'Good Sir: How is it that you speak with such great authority'". Then I glanced at you, and realized the downward sweep of your hands urged me to just be quiet.

Looking up, I saw the tattered appearance of the stranger transform into a body of glittering light. His features were no longer distinct from His head or body – for He was entirely enveloped in a shroud of golden light.

"Be not afraid," He said. "I am sent by the Lord. You know me as 'Gabriel'. I am here to serve, and relay a message from our Lord on High."

"Please forgive our suspicions," is what you said, Mother Mary. "There are many unsavory characters about - for these are fearful times. But you, Gabriel – of course - are most welcome. And we wish to hear your message from our Lord."

"The Lord simply asks for your continued patience. Dark forces do indeed arise – but will not last forever. You are both destined to deepen and extend your service to the Lord. You, Mary, in particular - shall conceive and give birth to an incarnation of the Son of the Lord."

"Such a blessing may not unfold for several more incarnations," is how Gabriel put it, adding that "during which time you, the future Mother Mary, will continue to be schooled in the ways of the Lord – all in preparation for doing the Lord the great honor of bearing the latest and final incarnation of His blessed Son."

As best I can recall, Gabriel then said something like this: "Your future service will be of the highest order and you will be blessed among all people. So, please, do not let the gloominess of the current situation discourage you. You are blessed - and the Lord will continue to prepare you for this most sacred of missions."

"As to you - young man," Mary interjected, imitating Gabriel's robust voice, and recalling His exact words: "God urges you to continue growing wise in the ways of the Lord. This means you are being trained to assist the future *Mother Mary* and then reveal the record of how Her everyday actions will uplift and transform the destiny of the Earth and its inhabitants."

Smiling broadly, I also recall Gabriel telling me that "I would thereafter serve as the future Mother Mary's guide and protector."

We laughed – knowing how accurate those predictions turned out to be.

I also recall Gabriel's prediction: you would give birth to "the glorious and final incarnation of He who would then serve in perpetuity - an event that would not transpire immediately but unfold on God's timing – in an era greater and more opportune than now."

Mary was then quiet for some time, finally saying: "I also recall His parting words exactly. They are worth repeating: 'Therefore know that Prime Source continues to bless you both and all those who will be involved in your spiritual unfolding. Go forth, then, assured that God's wisdom will forever guide you, and Its love will forever bless you.'"

The light surrounding the angel dimmed - then gradually disappeared – and we were left staring at each other – our wide-eyes filled with tears, and awe - and thanksgiving.

Squalid Conditions

Bear in mind, however, that the world that Mother Mary then and has since experienced - has not been a perfect one. Rather the settings in which She subsequently chose to live would often be squalid and the population She served often lacked sufficient food, clothing and shelter. Even today, as we speak, beggars are everywhere – as are the gawkers who peddle their pots and pans along with allegedly secret elixirs and gadgets. Shade from the blistering sun is still hard to find as we travel over dusty roads. During the hottest of temperatures, people still scamper to find space under the canopies strung up along sunbaked huts and buildings.

Yet – no matter what the external conditions - our diminutive Mother Mary continues to work Her wonders amidst the turmoil. Her small size has always been one of Her assets – for She could literally find a way to fit in everywhere She went. Once attracted by a cry, a voice, an argument, the hint of an opportunity to be of assistance, Mary would reach Her intended goal by scurrying into, around, between, below and even up and over whatever obstacle might temporarily block or slow Her from responding to someone's need and distress.

She would often even bend over, crouch or go on Her knees to be at eye level with the aged, the infirm, a child and of course animals. Inevitably She would engage the other, become absolutely present with them, face them fully and directly and work Her 'magic', usually leaving the other transformed and transfixed: healed, comforted, even smiling and cheerful, dazed perhaps but alert enough to express deep gratitude and appreciation.

At first, I took Her prayerful and transformative powers for granted. Increasingly, however, I began to notice the range of people and breadth of events in which She choose to become involved. It was then that I realized Mother Mary's gentle ways did not diminish but rather enhanced Her impact. Her voice and gestures reflected Her healing presence, seemingly reaching deep into the body, mind and Soul of whoever She was then serving.

How Does She Do It?

What exactly does Mother Mary do to obtain such results?

Her physical healings involve direct application – the blessings, the invoking of God's power, the laying on of hands - each expressing Her capacity to share – even at great distance - the healing energy that emanates from Her presence.

Dealing with lifestyle and attitudinal issues involves a different tact. In addition to becoming completely present with the person, Mary would invariably encourage the person to share - as She listened attentively and learned about the experience and needs of the other before suggesting how that person could best remedy or resolve a given issue.

She also would counsel people directly and specifically, urging them – in the verbal exchange - to understand the context of their difficulty, examine how they may have caused or intensified the problem and then help them learn how to forgive themselves and any others involved. With that basis, She invariably taught the person how to muster the kind of personal attitude and energy needed to both prevent and resolve any future difficulties.

Spiritual Tool Kit

Mother Mary also had what I call Her 'tool kit' of actions and gestures – used in both healing and counseling.

Take for example, the simple gesture of raising Her hands: Mother Mary's greeting might begin – and later finish – with Her facing the person directly and then raising Her own hands shoulder high – palms and fingers up, open and extended. This gesture alone created an enclosed sacred space with which She could develop trust and openness.

Following an initial discussion during which Mother Mary would understand the problem or issue – She would move Her hands slowly and unobtrusively in varying angles in order to deliver nourishing energy to the areas most in need - always emphasizing that She was merely a conduit or channel for delivering the energy that came ultimately from Prime Source.

What kind of energy might that be? Well, it depended on the specific person and situation. Remember now: this woman we know as Mother Mary, always presented Herself in the earthly garb of an everyday Mother and even 'little old lady'. Yet, She was able to help everyone in some way given Her extensive set of capacities: She combined the skills of a psycho-therapist with the empowerments of Her Master Soul and was thus quite capable of invoking the extraordinary energies of Archangels and Prime Source Itself.

Body Postures

That's not all. Upon careful observation, I discovered Mother Mary's full range of what can only be called mudras or body postures. For example, She might bring Her hands together in prayer and simply stand witness with an other. At other times, She would bow – for clarity or emphasis, or in sets of three - to invoke and then speed deliver of the energies desired. And She would often rotate the position of Her hands – beginning with both palms open, then either pointing one finger to the ground or up to the heavens, or joining both hands overhead in either a gradual or sweeping motion.

There are times when She appears to speak directly to Yeshua or Prime Source, or to any number of angels and spirit guides. In such cases, She might hum or move Her lips ever so slightly. She might gently bob and weave side to side. I have also seen Her bend low with outstretched hands as if to scoop sustenance from the earth, or reach up high over Her head as if She was drawing on or calling forth some celestial blessing.

Each of Her gestures were intuitively chosen and enacted with confidence – yet they flowed gently from one to another - unless Her ongoing assessment of the person and their situation warranted Her repeating or modifying Her movements or their sequence.

As She proceeded, She would work with the comments and reactions of the person involved to insure Her approach and its selections had the intended effect. In short, Her approach concentrated on helping the other unlock their own awareness, facilitate the application of their own empowerments and/or recall, deal with and thus resolve the memory of something that had been denied or blocked.

The entire interaction could last seconds or minutes, depending on the complexity of the issue or person. I have also seen one of Her interactions last as long as several minutes or even a half hour. In most cases, She was able to unlock the key to the situation within minutes, attaining what a psycho-therapist of the future might need months if not years to attain.

Some times the same person would be at our doorway on several successive mornings – hoping Mother Mary would fine tune or add to the insights and blessings they received the day before. Never once did I see Her refuse a person who requested Her aid and counsel. And often an interaction would begin when Mother sighted someone in need or came across a situation in which She thought She could be of assistance. At other times She would encourage a person who - for example - might have been following us – to finally come forward.

When approached She always responded instantly – and was especially responsive to the children and animals - whose eyes and sounds indicated a desire to make contact. Amazingly, She simply trusted Her instinctual ability to know what was wanted or needed before anyone spoke, made a request or outwardly demonstrated a need. And there were instances when She would awaken in the night or early morning – knowing we had to proceed immediately to one location or another in order to assist some person or situation.

If you ever experienced a person on a mission to help, who seemed endowed to give wise counsel, who was able to bless and heal with a word, a look or a particular posture – then it was Mother Mary. Her heart was – and still is - so pure and loving that Her mere presence could have an almost instant healing impact on anyone She met.

The Dream

I had another dream last night – one that helped me understand why I was so attracted to and loved both Yeshua and Mother Mary.

I was living in a home that was cluttered and dimly lit. The ceiling beams were low, the rooms below were of varied heights and each shrouded in darkness. And there were so many of them that they crisscrossed each other – making the environment above and beneath me very confusing and very complicated.

The room I was in had a rusty tinge to it - as did the doorway to the adjoining room and staircase. I was standing still – apparently not moving and feeling semi-paralyzed by the heaviness of the atmosphere. I could only see a portion of the upper room because the steps led upward and in the opposite direction. And whatever lay further below was a pure mystery.

Then the scene switched to a huge barn like structure. Actually it was my home but it was practically bare: no furniture, no stairways going up or down – with wooden boards strewn about the setting. Parts of the ceiling were very loose and coming apart; wind coming through the cracks made a rattling sound. The dominant colors were blue and gold.

Apparently I was the son of a carpenter who one day encouraged me to go out into the country that surrounded this barn-home and explore the trails and the sunlit hills. I did not wander very far – so anxious was I to return home. And when I did I saw that my father had started to convert the empty space into distinguishable rooms. He built a room for me – it was small but open, giving me privacy yet full access to the now greatly expanded and well-lite living spaces. Each of the three levels were now open and accessible.

There was a woman – who turned out to be my Mother – standing at the juncture of the three spaces. I was delighted to learn She had come to live with us. I also asked my Father for a peer, a young woman, someone who would be my playmate.

The house was still unfinished so my father continued to re-contour the enormous interior space into a series of discernible living spaces. I especially liked the huge window at one end or corner of the house; it spanned all three floors. Standing in front of it I could see the woods, and trails and the open spaces leading to the mountains beyond. Turning around I noticed that my father had already built a balcony on the second floor overlooking the large family room in which I stood.

He then invited me to help him build or complete our home and promised to teach me the basics of carpentry. I hesitated but his encouragement motivated me to serve as his assistant.

Chapter V

Decisions

So Much

I HAVE LIVED AND TRAVELED WITH MOTHER MARY NOW FOR almost two decades. You may recall that following the staged death of Yeshua, I and Mary Magdalene were invited by 'the Sacred Family' (Yeshua, Mother Mary and Father Joseph) to leave Jerusalem and travel with them to the British Isles – there to found - in Glastonbury, the first of what were slated to be a network of sanctuaries around the world. I kept notes on that journey's interactions and accomplishments and subsequently published them – as already noted - in the book entitled *Yeshua: The Continuing Presence of the Master Soul.*

Once the Sanctuary at Glastonbury was firmly established, each member of the Sacred Family chose a different way of fulfilling the next phase of their respective missions. Father Joseph chose to continue providing leadership to the Sanctuary. Yeshua chose to extend His perpetual presence on Earth to other portions of the universe.

And Mother Mary – after agreeing to be *assumed* into heaven – decided to return once again to Earth, resume Her incarnation and extend Her service to all the souls incarnated in the everyday world. She stayed in the Sanctuary upon Her immediate return from Her Assumption but only for a short time - before deciding to follow the wishes of Yeshua (John 19:

25-27) and both travel with and subsequently live with me. Her role in helping the world attain greater spiritual consciousness was thus also greatly extended and deepened - as was my role and responsibility as Her guardian and protector.

I have had the opportunity to observe Mother Mary in many and varied situations – most of them created by Her spontaneous reactions to the people and situations we met on the road - in Britannia, at the Sanctuary in Glastonbury, and as we journeyed back east to Palestine. As we departed the Sanctuary at Glastonbury, for example, crowds gathered both inside and outside the southern gate. Children sang a chorus of songs celebrating nature, the Sanctuary and, of course, Mother Mary. Adults waved flowers and small tree branches. Men and woman bowed as She passed – followed by continuous flows of applause and shouts of good will.

Signs read: "God bless you Mother Mary", "Hurry Back to Us", and "Blessed Be All You Touch and Encounter." Mary waved – one hand, then both - bowed repeatedly, and even stopped occasionally to hug one child or another.

Upon reaching a large tree that preceded the open road, Mother Mary signaled that She wanted to pray and rest. I quickly spread a blanket for Her in the shade.

"Thank you, thank you," I cried to those who continued to follow us.

"Mother is so very appreciative of your affection - but needs now to rest for a while before we continue our journey."

"Aye, we understand," said the remnants of the once huge crowd. "God speed, My Lady and God bless you."

Healing a Young Boy

And rest we did. Mary slept or at least closed Her eyes as I took the donkey to a nearby stream and returned with enough fresh water to last us for at least a few days.

The next day proved to be delightful: There was a lovely breeze, the sun was full but not too hot, and birds seemed to follow us down every road as we headed southeast. Portsmouth was our initial destination - where we hoped to board a boat bound for a larger port further down the coast. With luck we thought it possible to then board a boat at one port or another bound for any aspect of the northern coast of Europa.

On the third day out, we came upon a large caravan that had pulled to the side of the road. Several seemed to be crying. Mary steered our donkey to the side of the road and then approached the group of people that had gathered under a cluster of trees.

A woman responded to Mary's question at to what was happening: "The baby is hot, too hot for too long. We fear for his life. We have stopped so the son of our leader and his wife – the father and mother - may attend to him. Despite bathing and attempting to feed him, they have not been able to revive him."

Mary immediately slid from the donkey and signaled that I bring some of the water we had strapped to its side. Upon receiving permission from the parents, She knelt at the side of the boy – perhaps three to four years old – felt his brow, removed his shirt, examined his limbs and body – then asked for a cloth.

She then prayed over the bowl of water, dipped the cloth in it, and while holding the boys feet in Her left hand, She wiped the dampened cloth over the boy's entire body.

As the parents and others looked on, Mary prayed silently, periodically pursing Her lips and breathing directly on the boy's chest and face. He struggled, groaned, then opened his eyes. Soon his legs began to push against Mother Mary's hand.

Still She continued to pray in silence as She again wiped the boy's face, body and limbs and continued to blow gentle puffs of air close to the boy's heart and head.

This time the boy opened his eyes very wide, raised his shoulders slightly and then raised his hands. Up he sprang, rubbing his eyes, licking his lips, and crying: "Momma, Momma - where are you?"

The crowd hushed, then began to applaud.

In an instant, the father and mother were at the boys' side.

Mother Mary looked at me, exhaled fully... and smiled.

Messaging With Nature

On rising each morning, Mother Mary would - in addition to drawing a mandala shape in any pond She could find [24] - She would also enact a set of rituals – using them "to awaken my body and my heart" as She put it and "thereby honor our Prime Creator and His wondrous creations." Such movements helped, She said, to create "the perfumed air of life eternal".

She would, for example, shortly after breakfast, saunter out into the open air, listening to the sounds of nature as She intoned a refrain such as: "I honor and sing with the creative sound of the birds." En route, She would also laugh and hum a tune as She imitated the birds and their incessant nods and twists.

Invariably She would then walk with a measured and graceful countenance to whatever grassy or wooded area was available – as if asking for and receiving permission to walk on what She called 'this sacred ground'. Her pace would gradually quicken – becoming at times like a lyrical prance, stopping only to examine a particular tree or flower as She ran Her hands over its texture, stopped to inhale its scents and 'receive its natural blessing'.

She would then take a series of slow and deep inhalations as She moved Her arms slowly up and over Her head, voicing such salutations as: "Blessed be this Earth and the entire Universe", or "Let us give thanks to our Lord, Prime Source" – always ending with the phrase, "May all be open to God's love and blessings."

Rain and wind never stopped Her – and we always had a dry towel on hand in case of a sudden squall. Her 'walks' never seemed to take more than ten or fifteen minutes and was often completed before I had gathered our things and readied the donkey for the days ride.

I ascribed the daily glow of Her face to the energy She created with these morning prayers as reinforced throughout the day by other spontaneous involvements. She would, for example, always pause to pray when

---

24   See 'Morning Rituals' in Chapter II: There - and Back Again.

working with the sick or give counseling to whoever She sensed needed assistance. Bear in mind, She did not seek these people out; they just arrived throughout the day as if sensing someone special was passing through. When not serving others directly, I would often find Her in deep meditation – certainly when we rested, and often while we were walking. On occasion She also meditated while seated on the donkey - swaying gently its relaxed cadence.

We also knew enough not to interrupt Her when that faint halo that always hovered above Her head would brighten and then spread gradually to envelop Her entire body. Such 'total' transformations seemed to occur mostly when She was in contemplation – fully identified, or so it seemed – with an object or image. She would describe such an experience as 'encounters with the divine" – and were often sparked by the sight of a child, a sunset, a stream, a perceived act of kindness or a cloud of some special configuration.

Living with Mother Mary was an adventure unto itself for *She* offered so much simply through Her sense of presence, Her wit and wisdom, Her jolts of insight and shared expressions of compassion, Her continuous display of what could only be ascribed to living gracefully in the moment.

Portsmouth

Some of the days we spent on the road were harsh and wearisome - yet we forged our way forward. One day the rain was torrential but good fortune put us within a swift walk to a nearby barn. The owners welcomed us along with many others caught on the road without means of protection. We had spare clothing with us – and so changed as quickly as we could. A small hearth in the barn helped to reduce the chill as we hung our wet clothing next to it – using two wooden sticks to create an X and placing a third one between them as a crossbar. Once settled, we invited the others in the barn to join us for a moment of prayer and thanksgiving.

The subsequent sharing enabled us to learn about the boats that arrived and departed from the local harbor – bound apparently for such destinations as the seaside towns south of London, the ports of northern Gaul and the Low countries of Europa.

"Where do you wish to go?" a young man asked. We looked at each other and simultaneously said 'eventually.... Palestine'. We left the Sanctuary with the purpose of heading southeast toward Palestine but had not explicitly ruled out the possibility of returning to Jerusalem itself. We were still ambivalent since such a full return meant we would have to revisit the turmoil that forced us to flee it so many years ago.

Before leaving the Sanctuary, however, Yeshua told us that ancient Judea was in the midst of attracting an emerging spiritual community. It was – after all - the place where Yeshua had repeatedly triumphed over the forces that sought to destroy His mission. It was also the place where He fulfilled His destiny to become a Master Soul in perpetuity.

Despite our hesitancy, we slowly came to the realization that it was Jerusalem itself that beckoned to us. It was a long way off and making our way could inevitably involve unforeseen difficulties. But back to the land of Jerusalem we would go - realizing that the completion of the round-trip was not just a return but part of our ever-expanding arc of learning and service.

Following the Lord's Lead

With the decision acknowledged and affirmed, we started to check on the particulars: boats left Portsmouth bound for the Low countries northeast of Paris - every two weeks, raising our confidence that we would be able to sail to somewhere in Europa - or beyond - before the end of summer.

We rechecked our belongings and recounted the essentials we would need to complete the rest of our long and complex journey: for each - two extra pairs of clothing, a blanket, a fork and spoon, a pan and a small pot, metal knife, wooden holder, hat and scarf, book of prayers, writing utensils and a set of bound pages – for my writings and Mother Mary's notes.

Most important was Mary's small purse – a gift from Yeshua – made of leather and tied with a gold and blue ribbon. Miraculously, it always seemed to contain more than the amount of money we needed at any one time.

Thus did our desired destination become more specific. Reclaiming our roots in Jerusalem was at first a buried desire, then something we referred to but did not yet embrace fully. It had now become our clear vision. We would return home – and in so doing follow a route that good fortune, circumstances and the Lord determined. We were destination bound yet determined to be spontaneous as we travelled, bringing love and good will to everyone we met, stopping to serve as needed, never forgetting that as we served those of this world we were also honoring the mystic domain of The Lord.

"It sounds crazy in one sense," Mary intoned with a broad smile on Her face. "But we love adventures – and will surely have many opportunities to create or attract some good and loving opportunities en route. Besides, I - and we both - have reason to affirm the fact that 'the Lord supports our journey and will travel with us, at least in spirit - all the way to Jerusalem!"

"Keep thinking and talking like that, Mother Mary," I responded. "I need to hear such affirmations as frequently as possible."

Yet often I would tease: "Are you absolutely sure Yeshua has encouraged us to take such an arduous journey?" quickly adding, "Sorry, sorry, I forgot: forgive me. After all, we do also have your purse! And I am bound to fulfill my mission to record and write about our adventures."

"Yes – adventures and following the Lord's lead. That's clear," Mother Mary offered. Then with an elbow nudge to my arm She added: "And I am so glad we are doing this together. I have delighted in My return to Earth and now we can both look forward to returning to the Holy Land.'"

Trust

Having talked with every merchant and traveler we could, we thought it would be easier to return to Jerusalem via a northern route. It would be best – or so we assumed - to cross the channel either to Calais, Amiens or Le Havre, then follow one of several rivers flowing south and southeast to a port somewhere in southern Europa – which we assumed would at least lead us to some rivers or pathways that would bring us closer to Palestine.

Apparently we were in the midst of invoking – once again - the time worn axiom: "We plan, and God laughs." As it turned out, we ended up retracing the route that brought us to Britannia lo those many years ago. So it was Bordeaux on the western slopes of Gaul that would again beckon to us – and from there we could again trek through Gaul on a diagonal, reverse our steps of years before and travel south-east all the way to Lanquedoc-Roussillion and Perpignan. If all was well, we could then complete our return by sailing east along the Mediterranean – stopping as needed for short stays in Malta, Crete and Cyprus - and finally landing in Palestine.

But I get ahead of the story. Here are the particulars on how our return to Palestine and then Jerusalem actually unfolded.

Decision Time

The boat at Portsmouth was boarding. Where was it bound?

We asked for the captain. He was busy, not available – so we talked with members of the crew.

"The cargo will be delivered wherever it is supposed to go," was the best response we received. "Everything depends on the weather and the incentives for delivering whatever, wherever it was destined, and by what promised date. It is all up to the captain. He usually makes his decision on the exact itinerary on the morning of the sail – which is tomorrow."

I looked at Mother Mary. "I think we best trust God and the options that unfold," I said. "For one thing, being able to sail all the way back to Bordeaux would be wondrous. We could then retrace or at least approximate the steps we took in getting here. But who knows where the captain will determine to go first - and then next. Apparently so much depends on the weather."

"Bordeaux? Wouldn't that be grand. I suggest we ride with the ship, trust in the captain's decision and the Lord's good graces ...and seize on the opportunity to at least move forward – making the best of it wherever this ship goes."

"Agreed," is all Mother Mary said.

Up the boarding plank we went.

Checking the Addresses

We noticed the labeling on the large crates being loaded on board. Many were assigned to shipping agents and companies in Italia; many, many others were assigned to be delivered to Espania; and last were those apparently destined to be unloaded first - each, as it turned, bearing labels of cities located on the western rim of France.

To growing delight, our desired routing was assured when a few large parcels passed us bearing labels to the channel islands just south of Britannia, Brest and the northwestern provinces of Gaul. There were even shipments bound for cities along the middle and southern ports of Gaul. We were indeed going to be headed west from Portsmouth, sail along the northern shore of Gaul, and then proceed south along its western coast.

Given the apparent routing, we were especially happy to see some parcels bearing addresses as far south as the inlet leading down to the city of Bordeaux itself. Apparently we would be able to retrace our steps after all!

The Boat and the Boy

"Would you 'cus me, my man: I've a young boy here and we want to get a seat for this long journey," said the burly man with a young boy in his arms.

"We do not impede you, sir – but there are many ahead of us, and the line will not move until the captain has completed loading the cargo. We are only some 15 feet up this plank leading to the boat itself."

"Then stand aside – if you wish to drag your feet. I for one will push ahead."

"Ah, the man of strong will – ready and supposedly able to push others aside. We will surely give way as soon as room is available. But your impatience will only push against a wall of others who apparently got on this line before you or us."

The man turned to face us, his face red with frustration, his hand on the hilt of the long knife that hung at his side. "Stay put 'til I handle this," he said to the boy. "I'll not be stopped by this country trash."

He put the boy down momentarily in order to confront me directly – yet continued to hold the small boy by one of his wrists.

No longer held bodily by the man, the boy tugged and squirmed until loose, got to the edge of the railing and began to descend the plank. "Mother, Mother," he called. "Please come get me."

"Come back here you good-for-nothing," said the man. "I told your Mother it was you or the rent. Well, be assured you will work off the money owed me. Now come back here."

The boy – twisting and turning – slowly found his way back down to the bottom of the gangplank – spurred on by the return calls of his Mother on shore.

Mother Mary followed the boy as quickly as She could – excusing Herself back down the gangplank, and reaching him on shore soon after he had reunited with his Mother.

I arrived shortly thereafter – with the man quickly at my heels.

"Now I have two truants to deal with," he said huffing and puffing, his knife now pointing directly as us.

"Put that down," said Mother Mary firmly, "and please do so now. "

Both dazed and jolted by Her quiet command, he dropped the knife immediately.

"Thank you," said Mother Mary. "Now we are in a position to help everyone resolve this issue."

"Yes – we did stay at his inn for a week and we agreed I would work in the kitchen for that week in return for free room and board for me and my son," said the boy's Mother. "That week is up and the boat is here – and we should be free to board it and get on back to the Low Lands and the home of my family."

"As it turned out, however," counted the inn keeper, "one week of work was not equal to free lodging for that week. Besides, the two of them ate more than allotted. I have business in the Low countries myself – so feel free to take the boy as a servant – with the lady here working in my kitchen until we returned in a month or two."

"What sum of money is involved?" Mary asked.

"I've say 20 denai for the last week alone."

"Here's five denai," said Mary, reaching into Her magic purse. "Will you accept it and drop all your charges?"

"I've a right to 20, if you don't mind!"

"How about nothing, then, and we call a meeting of the local council to decide the rate – if anything - and perhaps leveling a substantial fine on you for attempting to cheat a widowed Mother and Her son."

"Did you say five?"

"Yes – and in another moment it will be two!"

"Five it is then."

"Fine – and, I assume, you will not board this boat with us and this fine lady and her son - but now prefer to wait for the boat scheduled for next week."

"Oh, one more thing. To insure you do not run afoul of the law, it would be best for you - and all – that we give your knife to our busy captain. It will help him cut the ropes that bind these heavy shipments and thus load each piece without too much more delay."

Still dazed, the once angry innkeeper stood at the railing fingering his five denai – resigned to the loss of both his captives and his knife. It also dawned on him to be thankful: this tiny lady had some mysterious hold on him. "Thank God," he murmured, "She kept Her temper - and did not cause me any serious harm. Good riddance to them all."

Mary Foresees the Future

Mother Mary's reputation on board was soon established. First, She worked Her wonders by healing several crew members of various ailments, and then was able – miraculously - to calm the seas during a violent storm. Ever since, the captain sought Her out for advice on a range of issues.

"Mother Mary, if I may prevail upon you once again," is the way he approached Her yesterday. "There does not appear to be a need for another healing, but this time I've need your view of the future. As you know, I am a student of history and thus worry about our fate. Surely we humans have evolved over the centuries – seemingly becoming a little less violent, ego-tistical and war-like. But will we ever know true peace – individually and as a society? Surely God wishes our planet well and seeks to protect us from ourselves."

"Oh, my dear sir, you raise such fundamental questions," said Mother Mary. "I will respond as best I can."

The Forces of God

"Please note that I and My Son, Yeshua, and many, many angels - continue to live on our glorious planet now, on this day, at this immediate moment," said Mother Mary to the captain and all those who huddled around us. "All of us on this ship are actually immortal Souls - that is, Souls who have decided to incarnate here on Earth and thus appear in our current embodied state. We do so in order to serve the needs of the individuals in our immediate midst - wherever we choose to be placed. When true to our Souls, we counsel everyone to live in the moment, not for the moment but in *this eternal moment* - now. That means focusing on whatever happens on this fine boat as it makes its way to various ports in Europa."

"Cumulatively, of course, our series of moments stretch far into the future. By staying in and acting within each moment, however, each of us – including you and everyone on board - is able to image and thus help to form the future. Was it not for our combined images and the thoughts and actions that followed them, what we are now experiencing would be very different and conceivably much more negative. That braggart for example, might now be on board having absconded with that young boy, the recent storm would not have been sweep aside, and the sickness experienced by some might now be devastating everyone on board."

"In other words, we, all of us, acting together, must strive always to choose positive images of the future by envisioning the best outcome. We do not control that then happens but we can have a very positive effect on it. Thus it is best that we each do what we can to image the best as the best way of warding off and preventing the worst things that could happen. In the process, we also learn how to handle and resolve whatever problems do get through. If on the other hand, we bow to our fears, we merely help to bring them about as self-fulfilling prophecies."

"So I cannot emphasize enough how significant are everyone's daily images of their desired future for they in turn help us adopt our set of very positive intentions and subsequent actions. We are empowered beings capable of maximizing the prospects for a positive future - helping to steer both our personal lives and this universe of ours in the direction of peace, compassion, thanksgiving and good will."

"It is extremely important – for all of us, including all who now gather around us. We each and all, individually and collectively, need to think positively about the kind of future we wish to create. That means focusing not only on what we desire in particular but on how we together can grow the kind of loving community we wish to live in."

"I realize," She said to Her now dazed ship's captain, "that specific situations and the world at-large do occasionally appear dim and create lots of problems – evident in the cycles of civic, religious and community unrest - fomented by people who betray their sacred trusts – and aided by those who cheat, push others aside and seek ever greater degrees of personal power and dominance."

"So - given the realities we often face — we need to be forever determined, clear on what we want and need, and willing to use our ability to anticipate, image and bring about the kind of future we want and deserve."

The captain looked weary and glassy-eyed. "My Lady: I think we all get your drift - but could you speak just a bit slower."

Mother Mary smiled and simply said: "Of course, my friend, of course."

"So... what God and the vast number of decent, law-abiding and God-affirming people want... is to overcome the intentions... of those tempted to go astray... who are capable of degrading themselves...and everyone around them."

"That's the reality we face - so we need... to persist, to continue creating ands acting on our positive visions of the future - just as our positive and abilities ...protected us earlier from that braggart,... subdued that storm... and cured all on board who were ill."

Continual Progress

The captain blinked, blinked again, rubbed his eyes, looked up the sky – took a deep breathe, then another, and finally looked back at Mother Mary.

"I admit I am dazed. I am overcome. I am overwhelmed and astonished that I am involved in such a conversation – here on the high seas, heading for the southern ports of Gaul – helping you and John gain entry to the lands at the other end of Europa and the great sea. By the grace of God Almighty, may you both overcome any appearance of evil and be able to fill your days with love and joy."

He took another deep breath.

"I'll be damned: here I am even talking like you," he said shaking his head. "I don't remember – or understand - all the things you just shared. But I must admit that I am deeply humbled by your presence and enlightened by what I understand from your message."

"By the way: what caused you and John to take passage on my ship, this very week? It still confounds me that you actually are here and boarded my ship. But I am so very, very - grateful."

* * *

Summary - Thus Far!

Dear Reader: Days, nights, weeks, months – have gone by. Until now, I have not learned how to first allow myself to get engrossed in a given experience, translate it into a written record, periodically reorder my notes and then translate all the separate entries into a continuous and readable narrative. But recently - on the brink of being overwhelmed by my own note-taking - I finally decided to take time out to organize, separate the extraneous from the insightful, revise many entries, clustered many of them together under common themes and reached some conclusions. It appears that I am now up to date! Aha! So - thank you for your patience!

This then is also a good time to review – to think through the meaning of what you and I have experienced together thus far – and bring this record of our adventures up to date. So here, are some insights and summaries of what I - and hopefully you - have learned thus far. The lessons are basic but essential – and need to be recorded and affirmed lest I forget why Mother Mary and I have 'journeyed' as far as we have.

First - the most immediate news is that at long last Mother Mary and I are back in Palestine. Once we left Portsmouth, we did indeed travel first west along the northern coast of Gaul, then south, landing as desired at Bordeaux. From there we hitched a series of rides on various caravans, proceeding southwest through the middle of Gaul – finally arriving – months later - at Gaul's southern seaport of Burdigala. It was there that we were able to find passage on a series of boats that headed eastward across the Mediterranean. It seems impossible - but we just fulfilled the gist of our dream and reentered Palestine – and at the approximate spot from whence we departed so many years ago – at Ptolemais, happy to rest before even thinking of going on to Jerusalem.

En route, we - of course - frequently reminisced about the faithful days that followed our decision to leave Jerusalem – the day after Yeshua created the illusion of His supposed crucifixion. It was a faithful decision – obviously long anticipated by Yeshua — one that then unleashed a series of glorious and often wild developments most of which we certainly did not anticipate.

As noted earlier, We also needed to keep reminding ourselves of our over-riding purpose: to serve The Lord – highlighted when Yeshua avoided the charade of the crucifixion. And He did that for several reasons. One, He wanted to support the prophecy of Isaiah, who in one of his prophecies hinted that some spiritual person or nation would face their demise. As it turned it was to Israel itself to which Isaiah was referring.[25]

Two, Yeshua wanted to nullify any notions that He was the warrior King that many Jews yearned for and who they hoped would overwhelm the Romans and establish a United Jewish kingdom.

And three - and perhaps most important: in avoiding the alleged passion and crucifixion, Yeshua honored His dual - and mutually supportive roles - as Co-Creator of the universe with Prime Source and His being designated as a Master Soul by Prime Source at the time of His latest incarnation. Thus Yeshua was committed to bringing Heaven to Earth by

---

25   As quoted above in footnote 10, 'Isaiah's Prophecy,' Chapter I: "Yeshua Opens the Conference."

safeguarding the sacred role of the physical realm - home to His Mother and partner, Mother Mary and all the immortal Souls who had and would soon incarnate on Earth.

*Perspectives Gained

My notes have also included the following set of observations - the result of long conversations with Mother Mary and shorter but very poignant ones with Yeshua and Archangel Gabriel.

Yeshua's incarnation on Earth was intended to have both an immediate and long-range effect. As the culmination of His development as a Master Soul, it signaled Prime Source's wish to manifest Itself perpetually in the material realm and do so by empowering His Son Yeshua to serve as Its surrogate.

Unfortunately - as noted earlier - the truth of Yeshua's incarnation would continue to be distorted by a long line of well-meaning but confused theologians serving the series of Christian Churches, to wit: the alleged passion and death of Yeshua was needed to explain - and compensate for - the imaginary transgressions committed eons ago by the mythic appearances of Adam and Eve.

In truth, Adam and Eve actually were composite manifestations of Yeshua and Mother Mary. And Their latest and cumulating incarnations - Yeshua when born to Mother Mary, and Mother Mary at the time of Her Assumption - honored the progressive reality of Spirit. Their prime, ultimate, non-sectarian and universal missions - as the male and female aspects of the Incarnate God - were not only initiated and blessed by Prime Source. Their perpetual mandates solidified the role love and compassion would play as the central themes of spiritual life. The phrases "Amen" – "And So Be It" – were heavenly refrains utilized by Prime Source to seal Its mandate to Its - and thus - our twin Master Souls.

It was in furtherance of these realities that Yeshua, Mother Mary and our small party escaped Jerusalem, traveled to the west of Palestine, found our way on sea and land to the western shores of Britain, blessing all we met en route and founding a Sanctuary in Glastonbury. It was there that Prime Source's Lord's loving messages were impressed on its buildings, in its rituals and prayers, in a new sacred ceremony, and communicated daily through the healing work, schooling and community outreach the Sanctuary provided.

Thus - all the immoral Souls that have and will soon join our cause - are per force, citizens of both the heavens and the material domain. We - as are you, dear reader - are here to serve our wondrous Earth - and wherever else we subsequently choose to serve. As such, all of us are bound to uplift and inspire whomever we meet, whatever we encounter and wherever we choose to contribute.

* * *

Yes - Weary

One morning, shortly after breakfast, Mary looked up suddenly and exclaimed, 'that's it"... followed by a long silence. Finally, I asked if She was going to let me - and the rest of the universe - in on Her secret.

"Oh, I am sorry John, I didn't mean for it to be mysterious. I think this idea has such merit that it is time to celebrate – perhaps not now or immediately – but at some juncture, soon – namely, that we get back on the road, continue our journey to Jerusalem itself – which would also give us the opportunity to honor some if not all of the spots on Earth where my blessed Son said or did something special. Either way, it is time - truly - to give thanks and commemorate - and get back on the road."

I was taken aback by Her vigorous declaration – wanted to agree yet urged caution, instinctively honoring Yeshua's mandate that I protect Her from Her own enthusiasm and bursts of energy. (John: 9:25-27).

"Let us also remember," said I, "how weary we were when the boat finally landed in Ptolemais. The port that was officially located in Phoenicia – yes - but near Galilee. We were exhausted and unsure as to when and where to proceed next. We talked about it – weighed our options. The more we shared, the more we realized how tired we were. Setting out for Jerusalem immediately was impossible - and now, such an undertaking is still much, too soon and unrealistic. We have hardly had time to catch our breathe no less recoup our stamina. We have been trekking by land and sea for months – eating and sleeping only intermittently. Resuming our journey now - walking the dusty and uncertain roads of Palestine – at this, the most tropical time of the year – would be totally draining."

"The only realistic thing to do," I advised, "was to stay put and stay quiet for a while. We have been fortunate to find a place to rest – so please, let us take full advantage of this opportunity to recoup our energy before rushing off into the rigors and heat of Palestine."

"Okay," said Mother Mary. "I understand and bow to your predictably hard-headed assessment of our earthly realities. So let us rest – but not too long. I cannot help anticipating. You know how impatient I can become," She said with a soft chuckle.

Recalling Our Adventures

So we used our renewed 'resting period' to recall and rehash the number of adventures and near mishaps we had en route to our return to Palestine. All the details may no longer be important. Yet a record of the highlights of our journey may be important for posterity's sake.

Once we boarded the boat at Portsmouth, the captain did indeed head southwest, sailing first along the northern coast of Gaul and then southwest around the western tip of Gaul – en route, we then realized, to España. So it was that the captain – to our great joy – decided to bring the bulk of his cargo to his most important customers first – most of which lived along western shores of Europa.

Then we ran into a series of storms, one forcing us to seek refuge one day along the north-western coast of Gaul, and then another forcing us to venture off course and far out to sea. It took a few days for the crew to mend our sails - in the course of which the captain announced we had run out of drinking water.

So Mother Mary climbed down the ladders to the hold of the ship and 'just happened' to uncover several caskets of fresh water. The captain and two mates went down into the hold to inspect the newly discovered caskets for themselves. 'Unbelievable' is all they kept saying. "Who did what, where and when? T'mas a miracle" - were the questions and conclusions that dominated the conversations on board for the rest of our journey.

Having regained our bearing, we were able to continue sailing down the coastline of Gaul, and was soon gifted with more good news. When we reached the outskirts of Bordeaux, the captain gave orders to sail down its inlet and unload some cargo at Bordeaux itself and thus the open waters of the Gironde River. Ah – one more step in the direction of Palestine. We quickly made plans to disembark - for 'all' we had to do then was head south-southwest, traverse all of Gaul at a diagonal, presumably use the river as far as it would take us and then hopefully making friends and hitchhiking rides on a caravan or two.

Bordeaux was a busy and raucous port. Unable to find room anywhere we inquired, we retreated to a barn on the outskirts of the city. The hay was dry, the warming stove reduced the chill and we washed in the refreshing waters of a nearby brook.

The next day we encamped by the wayside of one of the busiest roads in Bordeaux - until we finally gained passage on one caravan, then another, proceeding by foot as needed, finally boarding a boat that fortunately was also heading southeast – down the Gironde River, thereby taking us all the way to the Mediterranean. We sensed Yeshua - as ever - or one of His angels - was tracing our every step and need. So it was that we travelled to the southeastern tip of Gaul, in essence retracing - in reverse - our landing at Perpignan many years ago.

This Time Sailing West

We boarded one boat, then another, traversing various portions of the great Mediterranean. En route, we were tossed about by one storm after another, and finally landed in Malta – where we waited several days for passage to Crete. Unfortunately the weather turned increasingly cold as we proceeded east. Many became ill, including the young son of a passenger who boarded the ship at Malta. Mother Mary noticed him immediately, tended to him and by the next morning his illness disappeared. The father, who turned out to be a wealthy merchant – was so appreciative that he offered us the use of a cottage he owned in a small village just south of our final arrival in Ptolemais, a port on the western edge of Palestine – just west of Galilee.

We did not realize how weary we really were until we were back permanently on land. We received directions to the cottage offered to us – paid an exorbitant sum for transport by horse and buggy (even Mother Mary was too weary to work Her magic), and settled in. It was then that we decided to stay put for a while, bought and borrowed some furnishings, made contact with the local Jewish community and its synagogue, got our bearings and settled into a life of prayer, thanksgiving and instinctually – despite our cumulative fatigue – counseling and healing whomever we could.

We never thought of that lovely enclave as a permanent home. But it was so *kind* to us for the several weeks that we literally began to think of it as home. "But nothing permanent, mind you," Mother Mary kept reminding me. "We are not really home - yet."

The thought of leaving now – or soon - and getting back on the road – was in my mind, totally unwise and unnecessary. It continued to be foremost on Mother Mary's mind, however – given Her frequent references to 'our beloved Jerusalem" and "the Holy City".

I too wanted to see Jerusalem again, and knew from experience that we were indeed seasoned travelers. Still – I argued – we needed to rest a while longer. Given our weakened physical health, Jerusalem - in my mind – was still very far away. To resume our travels now - so soon – made me cringe, such that I retreated from Mother Mary's presence for several days.

We were in complete agreement, however, on one thing. We both marveled at and gave thanks for the gracious support we had received en route to our return to Palestine. Yet we wondered: was it just the result of many good people helping us in ways that came natural to them, or did it also involve Yeshua or some angelic force working behind the scenes? We concluded that it must have been a combination of both and frequently gave thanks - to both - for our good fortune.

The Woman Revealed

As we rested in our little cottage in Ptolemais, we also got involved in the life of the village. Thus did our neighbors come to know and appreciate everything about Mother Mary.

When chatting one day with a neighbor woman by the name of Naomi, She spontaneously volunteered the following: "By the way, although I have known your Mother Mary for only a short while - since you both moved into the village only several weeks ago: please know how much we appreciate Her. As I understand it, you arrived from Britain – via a lot of other places - and planned to return to Palestine because you used to live here. Although She is generally quiet in Her ways, there is a continuous and contagious presence about Her that commands respect and yes, love."

"I remember meeting Her for the first time in the course of our moving into our home just down the road. My son – then only some fourteen years old – slipped while carrying water from the well, sprained his wrist, and damaged both knees and hands as he tumbled heavily into a pile of jagged rocks. Worst of all, he badly bruised his self-respect. Your Mother Mary saw the incident and rushed to my son's side. They later recounted exactly what had happened."

"Ah – I can see you are watering this dusty pathway," Mother Mary jokingly said to my son. "It is about time someone had pity on all the Souls who must endure these rocks and the thick dust. And you literally threw yourself into your work: ah the sacrifice. You deserve to be rewarded by the town council."

Nicoli, amidst his tears, began to laugh. "Ah yes," he said. "What a contribution I have made to the welfare of my neighbors. I certainly have made them laugh. I fear I am more a survivor than a hero – a damaged one, I might add. In addition to nursing my ego I must now seek aid for my bleeding wrist and legs."

"We will help," said some young girls who also just happened by. "What must we do?" they asked Mother Mary.

"In my basket – there are some strips of cloth and some cleaning powder. Please bring them to me. We shall clean his wounds, stop the bleeding, and bind his wrist to prevent further injury. And here comes his Mother; help him up, fetch her the water you will need to complete the bandage - there, use this small pot of mine - and insure her that her son is well. He not only lives but laughs - and will soon be restored to good health – and high spirits. I must carry on – for I have another to tend to. Apparently someone else has fallen while trying to mend his roof."

"That epitomized your Mother Mary," said the neighbor. "Cool, calm, efficient, ready and able to help any and everyone - and at a moment's notice."

"And that one story reveals so much," she added. "Ask anyone in this and surrounding villages. She does not preach - as if some know-it-all – and she does not act superior or boastful. Rather she talks with us and is interested in getting to know us. Even in our weaknesses, she acts to revolve disputes, cares for the ill, comforts the lonely, and shares whatever resources She has – be it food, money, belongings or shelter."

"I remember when a wind storm scattered my flock of sheep," said a man who overheard their conversation. "You could hardly see in front of you. She immediately blew the community horn – and a host of adults and older children assembled to the call."

"Listen for the bleating, and bring a rope with you," She shouted. "Take care to protect your eyes. And do go out alone but only with another. Here are some long strands of rope or thick twine. ('Where She found them is still a mystery.') Tie one end of the rope to any fence post you can find and the other end around your waist. Then use bits of the twine to harness each animal you find. Lead your mini-flock back to your post – and then harness them in the barn. Good – now go – before the sheep wander too far, get lost or hurt themselves."

Abiding Love

Such was the universal commentary on a woman whose physical height measured only to the shoulder of the average man - but was recognized immediately by the characteristic orange scarf She worn around Her neck or over Her head. Her voice – even when She shouted – had a soothing effect. When She walked She seemed to glide across the floor or terrain – seemingly unattached to the earth and elevated ever so slightly above it.

Her large blue eyes were magnified when She smiled. Often She would appear at a scene – as if from nowhere - especially if it required either assistance, clear thinking or concerted action. The villagers always knew it was Her, even at night, given the appearance of the violet-gold aura that always appeared around Her. At times She seemed to shine like a beacon; She certainly did so during the time the windstorm shattered the sheep. Her personal illumination has been attributed to the inner light that She naturally projects in Her words and actions - personifying so much inner goodness that it shines through physically.

When asked about Her ability to glow, She would pass it off. "Oh, don't worry about that," She would say. "Perhaps it is God's way of keeping tabs on Me. The important thing on this fine day – is - how are you? Your family? And how do you plan to assist and love others today? It may not be clear to you yet. Just wait: you are meant – this day - to be the strong arm and loving voice of The Lord!"

Things would also just happen in Her presence or shortly thereafter. Bones would heal. Families would reconcile. Money would be found. Houses would be repaired. Children – and animals – would be found. Cupboards were filled. Troublemakers were deterred or converted. Insight arrived - and was heeded. Compassion was extolled and conveyed. Concern, interest, camaraderie – all attributes of Her abiding love - would inevitably emerge – whenever and wherever She arrived on the scene.

Unfolding

It was Mother Mary's habit to disappear periodically – not to return to the purely spiritual state - but to have the time and space needed to think, to pray, to take inventory, to access what was happening both to and within Her.

Her Master Soul also loved being an incarnate, having the capacity to help direct Her embodied thoughts and feelings, voice Her emotions

– and choose what to do when - that would have a positive and long-lasting impact on the people and events She encountered each day.

She had long been known for celebrating the process of birthing – the kind of joy She felt when She presented Yeshua to the world - as well as what She called 'the miracle of birth' that unfolded almost monthly in the villages in our area. Each birth was – in Her words "a blessing, wondrous, awe inspiring". She said it reminded Her – again and again - of "God's love incessantly giving birth to life unending".

"Oh Lord," She has written: "How wondrous art thou to have gifted life to the land, to have sustained it with fruits and vegetables, and so infused the plants, animals and humans with the capacity to reproduce that the world was constantly buzzing with life. The creative force You have instilled in human incarnates, in particular, has allowed them – dare I say, 'us' - to express our capacity to invent farming and all the progressive sets of technologies needed to support the many emerging towns and cities. All of it, of course, testifies to Your ever-expanding capacity to 'grow' and motivate us to help in the endless creation of the ever-expanding spirals of Life."

"I am concerned, however, My Dear God, that as a species we incarnates may become so enamored with external growth and development that we periodically forget to put equal energy into honoring You and the spiritual realm as the source of our lives – and Life itself."

"There is so much goodness and sanctity being expressed on this planet Earth yet I fear for its demise – and even extinction – if some of the immortal Souls who incarnate in the earthly realm persist in serving a series of egotistic goals - forgetting and at times negating their promised and primary mission to love and spiritualize the earth."

"Miscues are one thing. But repeated and serious departures from the spiritual goals of incarnation undercut the capacity of many incarnated Souls to achieve their prime mission: to set an example, use their empowerments to reenergize those who waver, and bring love to everyone they meet - and compassion to every situation they face."

"May Gabriel be ever present - and at our side. May Raphael and Michael always feel free to join in and support our resolve and prayerful intentions. May every immortal Soul who incarnates learn to fulfill their promise to bring God's abundant love to every nook and cranny of this wondrous Earth."

Incremental Steps

So it was that we became integrated into the life of this small community. It was not long, however, until the old and unresolved issues reemerged. Would we stay here in Ptolemais – forever? Are we getting so involved and content that we have forgotten our original resolve to return to Jerusalem?

The issue was rekindled again recently when Mother Mary noted how much She "loved it here" and "how gracious the people were" - but emphasized "how the true goal of our journey is yet unrealized."

I frowned.

She noticed.

"Oh, no, no, no, My dear boy, I do not suggest we consider making an immediate - no less fast and furious advance on Jerusalem. But if we do intend to get there eventually," is how She put it, "then it might be best that we initiate some small, incremental steps, make progress slowly – perhaps going first through Galilee then maybe the northern tip Samaria, leaving Judea and Jerusalem to later, and always being sure to rest a great deal as we traveled."

"We might start with an easy trip, for example, going just down the road to Magdala. It is only a day's journey at the most, the place where Yeshua initially met our beloved Magdalene. Perhaps we can find a horse, and even a carriage of some sort. And, as you know, I always have My purse. For us - experienced travelers - it would seem like a stroll along the seaside."

"Starting with Magdala – you say, which is just down the road, you say," was how I responded. "It sounds like you already have a series of other places in mind – some potentially farther than a day's ride on a donkey. And how is it that you are suddenly confident of finding a horse and carriage?"

"You know I am in touch with everyone – a minute here, five minutes there, in my dreams, sometimes with a chance encounter as we mix with others in the village, even receiving messages and encouragements from those on *the other side.*"

"And, I promise you," She said gently punching my arm, "nothing too strenuous, just one town or locale at a time. Ah, it will enable us to get closer to hugging and thanking all those who made the various aspects of Yeshua's earlier missions so eventful and successful. I get excited just thinking of it. Besides, Yeshua is sure to join us en route – at least He better," She said, shaking Her renowned right index finger and brimming from ear to ear.

"So we would leave here?"

"You know we are committed to getting to Jerusalem. It is inevitable. We have had a good rest. And there will be many opportunities to stop and rest en route, I promise you. Incremental progress is good for the soul, and even better – as you know - for the body. And as our previous journeys testify, we are indeed built for – and glory in - movement and progress."

Limits

"Okay, of course, I agree," was my response, "but only if we do not overdo it. My plea is for traveling to only one place at a time and nothing too far or too strenuous in any one day. Remember by primary role includes protecting you – and that means spiritually, mentally and physically. I concede your latest idea qualifies spiritually and mentally...but I am still unsure about the physical aspect."

"I am concerned about the additional physical and mental wear and tear involved in one more adventure – one taken too soon," I continued. "Just when we are getting fully recovered from the rigors of our long and at times difficult experience in getting all the way to Palestine – which involved, might I remind you - covering an enormous amount of land, traversing several countries, overcoming the vigors imposed by many a forest and mountain, the largest sea known to us and two – or was it, three - horrendous storms, all of them at sea."

"Besides your Son made me promise not to give in to your every whim, to act as a break and even a naysayer on what you inevitably call 'just one more adventure'. Realize, your latest proposal, involves undertaking a series of treks – often through potentially hazardous terrain – so very soon after what we both agreed was an epic 'survival-arrival' - from Britannia to Palestine. We now flourish on consistently firm ground. Getting on the road again – so relatively soon - may prove to be too soon and still beyond our combined health and well being."

There was a long silence.

"I must admit, however" said I, "that the idea of getting back on the road, any road to anywhere, no matter how close, has me caught between two masters. On the one hand, your Son is also sure to love this wild scheme of yours – for the two of you are branches from the same tree. The route to Jerusalem would enable the two of you to relive and commemorate some of your most glorious moments and contributions – and that factor alone might very well cause me to override my concern for your immediate health and welfare. Forgive me for saying so, but you are still so thin and at times look weary when you return from all your involvements - in just this one little village."

"Ah, yes," Mother Mary said softly as if talking to Herself. "I knew from the start – from the time I realized our work at the Sanctuary in Britain was coming to an end – that something would change or at least need to be further clarified. So Yeshua, sensing He was about to leave on another phase of His mission, He did indeed designate you as My protector and companion. But by implication He also entrusted Me to be your pro-tector - and - your companion - in adventure."

"I'm flattered that you think me capable of both protecting you and being your companion and fellow adventurer," said I, "for at times those dynamics can prove to be worlds apart or at least in direct conflict. That is still the case. Even you will concede that my commitment to provide 'pro-tection' is always and automatic. But support for and involvement in your inevitable 'next set of adventures' is not. This time, given the context of our having just completed the journey of a lifetime, my support for another so soon - is limited to timing and the concern that we resume the journey too soon."

There was another long silence as we looked at each other wistfully.

Finally, I said: "why don't we invoke Yeshua's wisdom regarding this issue of 'timing' and 'desired limits' - when we inevitably see or hear from Him next - probably very soon, given your communications network."

Win-Win

We did not have to wait long for both of us to receive a message from Yeshua. He made His presence known later that week. His approach was not direct but nevertheless it was overt and pointed.

We realized He 'was around' and mindful of our request for advice – when one morning we found a note stuffed into the gate outside our cottage. It read: "Is it not wonderful that each of you is honing your respective earthly - and spiritual skills - in interaction with another who loves you dearly. Is it not possible to do what you both want in the long run yet do so at a pace that serves your mutual needs and responsibilities?"

Mother Mary and I smiled at each other. "Seems the message is for you," said Mother Mary, smiling and again wagging that famous index finger at me.

"I was thinking if was for you," I replied with a broad smile.

We laughed and fell into each other's arms.

"Oh how I love and appreciate you," She said, and before I could return the declaration, She placed a gentle hand over my mouth.

"It appears that I am still learning how to be fully human again – that is, overcoming the sense of 'unfettered freedom and invulnerability' so dominant on 'the other side'. Then there are the temptations of My human ego to be overly assertive - a tendency I certainly did re-inherit upon My return. Obviously, I am still learning how to modify the first and work through the latter – to temper My ingrained spiritual energies as I also strengthen by capacity to empathize with My earthly guide - who after all has a responsibility and will of his own!"

"I know this embodiment of mine is now intended to last for the long run. Taking good – if not extra care - in getting there is part of my learning process. You are reminding me of that necessity and I apologize for being so stubborn and insistent."

"So I hereby fuss up to the fact that My incarnate needs to learn how to be ever more patient and not so head-strong – especially when faced with the earthly reality that that is exactly the attitude I need to adopt if I am to attain both My short and long-range commitments."

The moments passed. I could not speak for tears had welled up in my eyes.

Finally, I said: "You overwhelm me with your grace and honesty. How Yeshua ever picked the likes of me to watch over the likes of You shall remain one of this world's greatest enigmas and mysteries."

"Alas, I did receive a charge from the Lord to watch over and protect you – even from yourself - and that charge I will continue to honor. Perhaps that mission is near complete. Some days – at least – I also feel that the need for continued rest and re-creation have passed – and that we are indeed ready and able to travel further south and revisit the earlier glories - and turmoils - of Jerusalem. I must also admit that I too have been stubborn, perhaps hiding behind my rather strict interpretation of Yeshua's charge, not facing the fact that our reality has indeed changed, that you – and we - are indeed much closer to being fully restored in mind and body than we were several months ago."

"So what about the following: give me - and thus us – four more weeks, and I promise thereafter to cooperate in setting an easy schedule – but not a march – to Jerusalem. At that time - assuming our continuing good health - we can work out a plan to get back on the road by – let's see – perhaps by the onset of autumn."

"Does my Son know how to both protect Me from Myself and grant Me the most loving teacher and guide of all?' said Mother Mary. "Thank you, my dear John. Thank you."

On the Road Again

It was not long thereafter that Mother Mary and I made specific plans to visit several villages to the East. Depending on which caravan was going in that general direction, we intended first to revisit a series of towns clustered along the western bank of the Sea of Galilee. I outlined our potential itinerary - and as you can see - did so with growing enthusiasm - all as Mother Mary sat by smiling and simply nodding in approval.

"First and foremost, we should concentrate on the many towns made 'famous' by Yeshua's various *activities*."

"Capernaum, was one: Yeshua's home base while in Galilee and site of several miracles and spiritual events. It was also the hometown of the former tax collector, Apostle Matthew."

"Then there is Bethsaida, also north of the Sea of Galilee but just east or on the other side of the Jordan River. Reportedly it is still mostly desert and uncultivated - yet it is the site where Yeshua miraculously fed the multitude of 5,000 with only five loaves and two fish. Bethsaida was also my hometown and that of my brother James, we being the sons of Zebedee and Salome. It was also the birthplace of apostles Simon Peter and Andrew." [26]

"If so, we might then visit Tabyha, a village on the western and northern side of the Jordan River, and the site of Yeshua's other feeding, that time caring for some 4,000 followers - again through the 'natural multiplication' of a few loaves of bread and a few fish."

"I see you have been doing your homework - and thinking ahead," Mother Mary said - with a nod, raised eyebrows and a broad smile.

"Well - just a little - just in case," I countered with a laugh.

"To continue: Magdala, of course, would then only be slightly west of Tabyha, back over the Jordan River, south of Capernaum, which was, of course, also the birthplace and home of our Mary Magdalene."

"We would then be close as well to Tiberius. Following Yeshua's miraculous feeding at Bethsaida, He and the crowds that followed Him used boats from Capernaum and traveled back to this southeastern part of the sea."

"And who can forget Cana, point east, in the middle of Galilee," said I with emphasis, "the site where you, Mother Mary, prevailed upon Yeshua to participate in His first 'reported' public miracle. Remember: you were

---

26   Mark 6:30-46; Luke 9:10; and John 6:14.

at a wedding festival and You - in your motherly way - urged Him to transform the barrels of water into a brand of exquisite wine."

"Then, of course, we could visit Nazareth, Your early home with Father Joseph and his sons, and eventually Yeshua's home as well."

"Depending on the weather and the particular route of the trade caravans, I estimate we could traverse the approximate 45 kilometers to the Sea of Galilee in three days. The roads were still in fine shape following the deployment of the Roman army to that area in 4 BCE - when they were used to quell the riots that erupted following the death of Herod the supposed *Great*."

"The roads were apparently well maintained by the Army and were reportedly reinforced when a command of the Romans suppressed the Jewish revolt in Judea and Galilee during the years 66-73 ACE." [27]

"I hadn't told you but the tradesmen we met in the port of Ptolemais also estimated that the roads throughout Judea and Galilee were likely to be crowded in the fall given the resumption of commercial traffic and the coming of annual religious pilgrimages. But that could play to our advantage: the better the roads, the greater the traffic, the greater the chance of hitching a ride with some gracious caravan driver."

"The more I talk about it, the more enthused I become," I said finally.

"I noticed," said Mother Mary, again sporting Her broad smile. "I am delighted that you are approaching the prospects of resuming our travels - and doing so with such forethought and enthusiasm!"

---

27   The scholarly designations of ACE, ('After the Common Era'), and BCE ('Before the Common Era') have since replaced the old sectarian acronyms of AD ('Anno Domini') and BC ('Before Christ').

Chapter VI

Rediscovery in Palestine

Bells and Whistles

So WE WAITED ON THE SIDE OF THE ROAD LEADING EAST. By biblical standards it was a good road, not paved with large flat stones as might be the case in some areas of Jerusalem. But the hard beaten soil reinforced with crushed stone enabled both wooden and iron wheels to traverse the roads without much difficulty. Of course one had to be careful: there were no curbs - for there was often the need to avoid sharp declines at the road edges. And any heavy rain – or series of high winds – could quickly create deep crevasses along the road edges as well in the roadway itself.

Even if riding on anything from a donkey, a horse or a horse-driven caravan - one had to be careful and not travel with a high expectation that you could make the desired progress in reaching a particular destination. This reality induced a sense of fate in many travelers: 'it would be wonderful if the gods and the roads worked on our behalf – but we best not count on it'.

All of which got me thinking about time - and the potential distances we might travel that day. Lo and behold, pure luck enabled us to proceed - or was it one of our many spiritual friends, if not Yeshua himself who intervened. As usual, whenever we squatted on the side of the road and waited for good fortune, it was not long thereafter that help arrived – this time dressed in bells and whistles. The horse-drawn wagons were all decked out in ribbons and hand-made flags. A groom-to-be – and apparently his entire family – were en route to points east.

We rose as they neared us, and clapped rhythmically to whatever song they were singing.

"Thank you, thank you," the singers shouted. "How far are you going?" I shouted back.

"To Capernaum, or bust," said one of the revelers. "In three days I do wed the loveliest maiden in all of Palestine!" came the emphatic response.

"May we ride and thus celebrate with you?"

"Just you and the lady?"

"Yes."

"Then climb abroad. You are most welcome."

No Accidents

Many hands were extended to us as we put one foot on a wheel spoke, reached up and were hoisted up into one of the caravans.

"You travel lightly," said one.

"Well, we've not much to carry," I rejoined - to the laughter of all.

The groom-to-be and several of his friends and family introduced themselves with hardy handshakes, and polite bows to Mother Mary.

"We are glad to have you," said the intended groom. "Please help your selves to any of the food and drink you see before you. We've enough for all – in fact – more than enough to last until the wedding day four days hence."

"You are very kind. A ride to the East, good fellowship and now food as well: surely God has blessed us!"

"So you know of God, do you?"

"A bit, yes."

"Well one of the people we are to pick up in Chabulon – which is just down the road toward Capernaum and Bethsaida - has a daughter who has been possessed by a demon. If you can be of help, we would appreciate it."

"Mother Mary is adept at such things," I said. Looking over to Her, and getting Her consent, I continued with the assurance: "I am sure She will be willing to help."

"Ah, I knew there was a reason for inviting you to join us. There are no accidents."

"I assure you – kind sir - the feeling is mutual."

Spiritual Progress

"I sense you are both about bigger or deeper things than merely traveling the countryside," said the older man holding the reins.

"Yes sir, Mother Mary and I would like to think so," I said laughing. "In fact, we travel with and for the Lord."

"We, and our young man," he replied, "have been reveling for most of the day – in sheer joy for our groom-to-be. Perhaps it is time we gained a wider perspective – and something our comrade here - may take with him to the ceremony. So, please – if I may speak for all of us - tell us more. I sense it is time to listen and learn."

"Thank you, sir. With Mother Mary's consent and your invitation, I accept. I will outline what we consider the joys and contributions of our belief system."

"First and foremost, we believe our Souls in heaven agreed to incarnate or embody on Earth in order help make this material realm become more and more loving and spiritually oriented. We believe we are each - all of us - incarnations or physical embodiments of our heavenly Souls."

I looked around, saw only nods and curious faces, so continued on.

"We believe our hopes and desires – both material and spiritual – act like natural magnets and repellants. We attract the opportunities we need to live fully and the energy we need to fulfill our spiritual desires. In the process we are also empowered to avoid any person or situation that might undermine our spiritual progress. Through it all, we are led to seek out and connect with those of good will and situations in which we may be of help. Witness, for example, your instinctual kindness in picking up two strangers on the road, and now our desire - in turn - to help your friend undergoing some difficulty."

"Ah – both aspects of those interactions certainly seem to be true in our meeting," said the caravan driver. "Please go on."

"Well, we also believe there is no guarantee that our Souls will overcome all the negative and selfish tendencies that could mislead our all-too human egos. So we are fortified with strong wills, a life-commitment to some fine intentions and goals, and the determination to spiritualize our material involvements while here on Earth. We all have a common life purpose: to become more authentic spiritual beings, honor our Lord God – and to help everyone we meet become ever more loving and compassionate."

The groom to-be and his fellows seemed intrigued. "Good stuff, certainly relevant for a wedding," said the woman in the group. "I'd like to hear more. Assuming all the others agree," she said, looking around the caravan. "Seems like they do. Please go on."

So I asked them to think of their lives being created by four kinds of decisions.

One, what you want to achieve in life; what's most important.

Two, how you prefer to act throughout life – for example, either take advantage of another person or negative situation for personal gain, or treat that situation as an opportunity to be of help.

Third, strengthen your instinctual ability to remember and keep account – as best you can: comparing what you actually do in comparison to what the deepest part of you - your conscience - tells you is your abiding goal and destiny. This last part involves a great deal of hard work. But it is doable - and soon becomes a very helpful and enlightening exercise. Though self-examination we learn how to be honest with ourselves - and then make the adjustments in our attitudes and behavior that then enable us to behave as the loving and compassionate persons we wish to be.

Then the really hard but essential part – the most challenging, perhaps difficult to understand - but essential. As immortal Souls we adopted a life-contract while still in Heaven - that would guide us once we incarnated or became the physical beings who sit here in this caravan.

I checked the facial expressions of our gracious hosts, and spotted some blank faces yet others who seemed to express keen interest. So I took a chance and continued on, saying in essence that once here on earth, we quickly realized that we were capable of either living up to the guidelines we adopted in heaven, or rejecting them - in part or completely. Such is the daily struggle: will we be at our best and thus earn the support of friends and love of our Lord God, or degrade ourselves and hurt our loved ones by succumbing to the evils and temptations of the world.

Fearing that I had talked too much, or that the subject was too difficult to understand or absorb, I stopped, took a deep breath and waited for reactions. There was a long silence until someone said: "You've got our attention," and several others nodded in agreement.

Self and Other

With that implied vote of confidence, I reached for a conclusion.

"The process of self-evaluation is - of course - made difficult by our human tendency to forget the intentions and desired practices we outlined in the spiritual realm before incarnating. But the decision to monitor what we intended to do in comparison to what we actually do - does keep us actively engaged in evaluating our behavior, being ever reminded as we live each day of our ingrained desire to be the best person we can be - despite the many temptations to compromise our standards. Continual self-examination is the best way to achieve that goal."

"One last reminder, if I may. We are not necessarily referring to the declarations or teachings of any official religions or philosophies - but if they help, so much the better. The best standards come from deep within ourselves, from our identity as a Soul and child of God - naturally and instinctually committed to both giving and receiving love and compassion - as you naturally did earlier today when you extended your loving hands to help two strangers on the side of the road."

Day and Night Dreaming

Slowly the celebratory mood settled into a modulating hum. One by one the revelers allowed the darkening sky, the wine and perhaps the weight of my comments to take their toll. Yawns replaced songs and the repartee gave way to salutations of 'thank you', 'good night' and 'sleep well.'

Ah – the perfect time for me to think of the larger scheme of things, and what actions *I* needed to take in order to realize my desired intentions and experiences. Mother Mary has often chided me – gently of course – on being a bit too philosophical. "Stay in the moment, my dear boy. Think of how best to attain your goals. But then be sure to get on a horse and actually ride it to your desired destination."

"Simply choose to act in the most spiritual way possible, and then choose the way to obtain it," She consistently advised. "I am not suggesting that anyone act precipitously without being clear as to what they want to attain or contribute. But it is crucial to follow through, to act in order to actually experience what you want."

I like to think of myself as capable of blending it all – as I did what I was capable of doing while chatting with the good people of the caravan. Perhaps in talking with them – actually 'lecturing-analyzing' but with their consent - I was also talking to myself: namely, my need to clarify my own purpose and goals and how I would attain them.

"Well," said Mother Mary. "Why not first chose the restorative and the clarifying aspects of sleep? Perhaps when we awake, we can share what was communicated to us in our dreams. Actually, I find both day and night dreaming to be very helpful and stimulating – for they often tell us what is missing in our incarnated lives, what we may need to do more or less of, and thus clarifying what we really want – or need - to do next."

Joining Forces

The recent convergence of events seemed to defy rational explanation: so much has happened, so fast, involving a diverse series of events and a wild range of situations and characters. The combination of lessons delivered and hopefully learned is a bit overwhelming - invoking in me an awareness of their connectedness, the aligning of one experience with another, each one supporting the unfolding of still another aspect of the emerging theme. Perhaps it is all the work of some angel who walks with or just ahead of us, using both carrots and sticks to lead us in the right direction.

Did all my recent experiences and adventures come together by chance, or was their some inner template that first attracted them and then fit them into a mutually supportive system? And if so, should I not continue to trust the process, the natural progression of one thing opening the door to still another related opportunity, each one complementing and building on the one before - and culminating in a series of successive outcomes that exceeded - yet mysteriously fulfilled - the potential of the original axtion. Is this not the story of what happens for each of us - every day, month, year - and lifetime? And does not such a progression of outcomes for any one individual involve and impact on others - both one's casual acquaintances as well as one's significant others?

Such surely is the case with the long string of *happenings* that have unfolded in the life of Mother Mary – not just impacting those She encountered overtly but also all the millions of others who were and are indirectly affected by Her life and teachings.

The cumulative and cascading alignment of the pieces and aspects is now clear: Her early life in the Temple, the marriage to Joseph, giving birth to Yeshua, the years of parenting, guiding of Her Son through the triumphs and difficulties of Palestine, witnessing of the mirage of Calvary, the subsequent departure for Britannia, the founding of the Sanctuary, the Assumption into Heaven, Her return to Her mission on Earth and the physical realm, Yeshua assigning Us to each other's care, leading Mother Mary and I deciding to leave Glastonbury together, completing our complex and at times dangerous journeys through Britannia, Europa and the Mediterranean, which then returned us to Galilee, whereupon we negotiated and resolved our differences as to when and how quickly we would make our way to Jerusalem, leading now to our decision to commemorate the places immortalized by Yeshua - as we make our way to back to the Holy City.

Ah - 'tis easy to view the convergence of these events - or those of any person - as the result of a random set of decisions – momentarily forgetting that the parameters of Mother Mary's - and each of our respective lives - are carefully set by each of us before we incarnate and are thereafter carefully monitored, guided, nudged and facilitated from above - always with the same abiding love and compassion.

To quote Mother Mary: "Oh – myy...oh myy...oh myyyyy...."

Cause and Effect

Surely there was a pattern here, an underlying template that connected and made sense of this sequence of events. Aha: this very theme gives me the opportunity to indulge my love of systems and philosophy, and in this case, apply Aristotle's four categories of causation to our lives. Do not be discouraged: it is not as dry as you might think. In fact, the distinctions are quite illuminating.

Aristotle had a fascinating way of defining the cause of events. There were four of them. We can illustrate each by applying them to our recent experiences. The results are illuminating - but not surprising.

The *formal cause* is that which is responsible for the overall design of what happens, which in turn sets the stage for a series of related events. The formal cause for making a table, for example, would be a plan or blueprint. It seems clear that both Mother Mary and *Prime Source were the formal cause* of Mother Mary's life. She chose Her life pattern - using the system of incarnation instituted by Prime Source.

The second type of cause discussed by Aristotle was the *material cause,* the matter or issue that was the subject of the activity that then unfolded. In the making of a table the material cause would be *the wood* itself. Surely the material theme of of the sets of events described in this book are a combination of the incarnation of Yeshua and both Mother Mary's Assumption and return.

The third causal or *efficient factor* is the agent of change. In making a table, *the carpenter* would be such an efficient cause. Clearly the most likely agent of change here is *Mother Mary*, given Her over-all commitment to reach out to others, Her decision to re-incarnate following Her Assumption, and then also becoming the driving force behind our epic journey back to Palestine and Jerusalem.

The fourth or *final cause* refers to the purpose or result sought. For our proverbial wooden table, the final cause would be its intended use for dining and being the center piece for family or group get-togethers. In our case, there is but one nominee as the final cause, namely *Prime Source*. Behind everything, everything, everything - from instituting the system of incarnation, the Annunciation, the Assumption and Mother Mary's string of healing interventions were all centered on and outgrowths of Prime Source's desire to spiritualize the Earth.

Intentions, Guidance and Adjustments

Now I admit the aforementioned subtitle is a bit wordy and points in several directions. Yet it also feels right, true and helpful for understanding how everything fits together. When I shared this entry with Mother Mary She simply smiled and said, "I have been saying that all along: each and everything that happens unfolds through God's love and Its attention to details."

Well, She obviously knows more and possesses more direct access to the cumulative record of Life, the workings of the Lord and the ways in which the spiritual realm envelops everything we think or do. Yet I obviously still need – and secretly enjoy – the comparatively complex ways of human reasoning. Such mental and emotional 'finger pointing' is one of the best tools we incarnates have for making sense of our experiences, although hanging around with Yeshua and Mother Mary has convinced me there are easier, more direct and more complete ways of connecting the developments on earth to the intentions and actions of heaven.

At least it is nice to know that Mother Mary and I usually end up agreeing and reaching the same conclusion, although it is me who appropriately ends up leaning heavily in Her direction. It just takes me – and seemingly every other - everyday incarnate Soul - a lot longer 'to get there' - even with the aid of prayer and meditation.

Let us hope and pray that Yeshua, Mother Mary and a series of angelic influences continue to help all of us. Whatever the number of years still remaining in our respective and oh-so-brief incarnational lives, it appears that the scene is always being reset, the living realities and arena constantly changing, new factors always entering as old ones slowly evaporate.

With hindsight, the central issues were always definable if not predictable: when the new day inevitably dawns and new factors and situations are introduced – sometimes within days or hours - the continuity of the overall thematic seems to continue if not elongate.

No matter where our personal sagas take us, we continue to be personally responsible for choosing what we desire - and then experiencing what we choose to create. If we temporarily miscue, we find that help is always en route - for God loves soft landings and thus sends whatever guide books and maps we need to at least choose a remedial response. God even helps us recoup from a sluggish or erroneous start by sending us a sudden intuitive awareness, one that invites us to redirect or respond to a new call to adventure, any one of a set of 'somethings' that puts us back on the path of making one more contribution to the annals of love and compassion.

How Magnificent the Commitment

Unbeknownst to us, the wagons had pulled aside at dusk – allowing our hosts to obtain fresh water for the next day, feed and groom the horses and make ready for an early start. We slept through it all and only awoke to the rustle and bustle of morning breakfast.

It was a cheerful group: soft singing and friendly jostling was in full swing. We were not sheltered, however, from their joyful barbs.

"Well, look who has finally awakened. There we were beginning to think we had picked up two dead bodies," said one. "Oh, leave them alone," said another. "They are not farm folk - used to working all day, partying all night – and still rising early and ready for the day's chores."

I looked at Mother Mary.

"They're right. We didn't do much but pack a small bag, walk to the main road and get abroad this fine caravan. Surely something else has contributed to making us weary...or perhaps we are still recouping from the arduous days of old."

"It must be the cumulative wear and tear, the worry and fret of a lifetime, especially the last few years," Mother Mary teased. "Maybe we should have rested even longer in our lovely little home in Ptolemais – as you suggested!"

She laughed and shook Her head – making me ever so aware that this immortal Soul, this heavenly being, this Master Soul who gave birth to a divine Son – was also like me and all of us: also an incarnate, a mortal human, a person who works and worries, who obviously loves to joke and jostle, yet who simultaneously is capable of facing this earth's everyday challenges with the empowerments of incarnation and a set of exalted blessings from heaven.

Toiling as She did throughout Her many earlier incarnations, [28] She was formally - and historically - honored and recognized as the Divine Mother and a Master Soul at and during Her Assumption. As you know, He did not rest on Her laurels, but decided to return to the material realm and continue Her commitments as Mother Mary. Like Her Son, Yeshua, She thus decided to serve humanity in perpetuity. The reality of it all still astonishes me. Surely Her heavenly status must make Her daily life on Earth especially burdensome: it would for a mere soulful incarnate. Yet here is this divine being choosing to live each day in the material realm - facing all the restraints and burdens of a greatly reduced human embodiment. Amazing!

I – like us all – am an immortal Soul, blessed by the opportunity to serve God here on Earth and contribute as I can. I have chosen to adopt a series of spiritual norms and practices and infuse as much spiritual energy

---

28   As noted earlier, in footnote 17, in the sections on 'Realities' and "Evolutionary Progress', *Chapter 1: Yeshua Opens the Conference,* Mother Mary has been incarnated throughout our history - hundreds if not thousands of times - appearing as such mythic heroines and spiritual contributors to civilization as the feminine Eve aspect of Adam-Eve, Nut, Astarte, Hathor, Inanna, Isis, Hera, Istar, Asherah, Circe, Kuan Yin, Athena, Artemis, Hecate, Maya and Sophia. See in particular, *Myths of the Female Divine Goddess,* by David Leeming and Jake Page (New York: Oxford University Press, 1994).

and purpose as I can into the material situations I deal with. And that – for me, and all of us - is a lot.

Yet the depth and expanse of transitions it takes to become an incarnate is nothing in comparison to what Mother Mary has done, having been assumed into Heaven and ordained the Queen of Heaven, yet choosing to return once again to the inert and at times stubborn and cumbersome challenges of the physical domain.

I smile and marvel in deference, deeply appreciative of this incredible being sitting beside me, who at this moment is stretching and yawning and rubbing Her eyes like the rest of us. Yet it is She who has agreed to carry the enormity of Her divine nature while relying primarily (with some well documented exceptions) on just Her human equipment – expressing Her divine intentions through the meager energy available to Her everyday embodiment.

I gazed at Her in astonishment. How horrendous - Her personhood. How magnificent - Her status. How enormous - Her contributions. Yet as a return incarnate, She has volunteered to a massive reduction in power and status in order to honor Her commitment to work for us, with us, and as one of us.

Commitments - Continued

One more thought: Mother Mary was obviously right about my love of philosophizing - trying to make human sense of the workings of this divinely inspired universe and its impact on our everyday living.

In particular, how can we explain to other earthly beings who as yet have not fully awakened to their soulful identity and thus not realized what is really going on - namely the blending of such extraordinary opposites as the following:

- the heavenly or divine reality has been and will exist forever and yet everything in material reality is of limited duration.

- divinely endowed and perpetual souls like Yeshua and Mother Mary have chosen to incarnate in the physical realm in order to serve along side billions of other immortal Souls – many of whom in their incarnate form are still not aware of their heavenly identity and heritage.

The whole thing is utterly amazing – especially for all of us who know we are integral extensions and expressions of God or Prime Source. Yet the stunning nature of the Divine is still in great part an awesome mystery to us who honor It yet work to fathom the fullness of the workings of The Lord.

I realize that I - in particular - have been blessed to be an earthly every-day companion of Mother Mary. I have learned so much from Her - as Her physical guardian at the same time She serves as my spiritual guide. So I have many, many - perhaps silly - but significant questions.

1. Why – in first journeying all the way to Britain, then returning recently all the way back to Palestine, and now moving from town to town along the shores of Lake Galilee – doesn't Mary choose to use Her divine powers to transport Herself (and me!) to 'wherever' She (and we) wish to go versus continuing to walk and ride on a donkey or in a hay-strewn wagon, over bumpy roads - for days and weeks at a time?

2. Why has this Queen of heaven and Mother of the Divine Yeshua chosen to live a relatively harsh life as an incarnate living on a tiny planet that is itself only a minute particle of rock circulating around a distant and very local sun, as part - mind you - of a spur of the third rung of a relatively obscure galaxy – and is - after all - merely a tiny blur on the map of an ever-expanding cosmos?

3. How can so much divine love and dedication be packed into such a tiny, five-foot four human frame that probably weighs – in today's terms - no more than a 103 pounds?

4. Surely Mother Mary - given Her divine status - naturally invokes assistance - not only from Yeshua and ubiquitous set of Angels assigned to watch over Her - all at the behest of Prime Source. Put is all together and we are also forced to realize that She – like Her Son – has the capacity to be present in multiple places

- simultaneously – something She now admits - even appearing each time in a configuration and costume that matches the standards of the given culture and situation.

5. Is it not possible then to meet Mother Mary – as well as Yeshua – in any one of a million different appearances: on a street corner, at a wedding, anywhere - She posing as any number of characters - each time posing as an ordinary human being yet still emanating divine energy, capacity and powers?

Surely – and hopefully – I will have the opportunity to experience then describe many of Her infinite variety of appearances as I continue my travels with this incredible enigma known as Mother Mary.

Uplifting

We were awakened on the second night by a loud thud and a pronounced rocking of the caravan. What must it be?

Most of the men were out visiting neighbors and family members throughout the towns of mid-Galilee – just north of the city of Cana - and were not set to return until morning.

The only others in the area at the time were the driver of our caravan - himself an older man but the reputed head of this band of travelers – plus a woman with two children and two burly male helpers who had not yet completed their assigned tasks at the encampment.

Earlier the driver, his assistant and the two helpers had strapped some lumber to the sides of the caravan, to be used the next day to erect a covering for the forthcoming wedding celebration. The lumber held but the caravan did not; the load turned out to be too heavy for its wooden wheels and it listed badly to one side. The spokes of one wheel finally collapsed - causing it to break in two. The left side of the rear axle now lay on the ground - such that the entire caravan swayed to a considerable tilt - making it both impossible to sleep that night no less move the caravan in the morning.

"We might as do what we can – now – before it gets any worse," said Mother Mary. We climbed down the ladder, bemoaned our fate and exchanged ideas with the others on what to do next.

"I have a spare wheel stored under the seats up front," said the driver. "But with most of the fellows away, we've not the manpower to lift the corner of the wagon high enough to hoist the new wheel into place."

I looked at Mother Mary. She skewed Her mouth to one side, rubbed Her chin, squatted down to examine the broken axle, looked over at the proposed new wheel, and said - loud enough for all to hear: "Not necessarily. We do have a combination of godly and people-power," She said with a smile.

"Okay – I am certainly willing to try," the leader concluded. "There – Simon: you can grab and lift the wagon here at its outer side. One of your helpers can grab and try to lift the axle itself. The other one can guide the new wheel into place. And you, John: you have the pivotal role: affixing the screws and bolting them into place."

"And the boys and I can lift the wagon from this side. But that would still leave us without anyone to lift the other crucial part, namely the middle of the wagon."

"Oh, I can do that," said Mother Mary. "Logically it should be me because I am the shortest and can easily fit under the wagon and push upward from there."

"Besides, this fine woman and her two sons stand ready to help me if needed."

"My Lady, I mean no offense...but are you daft?" said the leader.

"Oh, I forgot to mention or did not make myself clear," said Mother Mary. "The very powerful arms of the Lord will also assist Me – and all of us."

"Really, not to worry," She assured. "I can already kneel upright here, and so will be able to push upward, slowly inching My grip along the axle to a point where the new wheel can be put in place. No problem."

Everyone raised their eyebrows, shook their heads, but assumed their 'assigned' positions - yet remained skeptical regarding the role Mother Mary said She was ready and able to assume.

"Heave-ho" was the cry – and at the count of three – lo and below, up came the wagon. The new wheel was then quickly affixed to the axle and bolted in place.

We all cheered, yet the men were still wide-eyed - and kept looking under the caravan for Mother Mary.

Suddenly, She cried out: "Thanks be to God" and re-emerged from under the wagon – dusting off Her slacks, then moving about to shake everyone's hand.

Her appearance was greeted with three rousing choruses of "Thanks be for Mother Mary" - and then a giant hug for each from the leader.

The Sacred City of Capernaum

On the third night of traveling we stopped on a hillside just outside the town of Capernaum, the destination and site for the forthcoming wedding. The revelers were now quiet, anxious to enter the town the next day with reverence for the wedding ceremony. Reputedly the bride's family home was but a short distance along the northern wing of the town's crossroads. The ancient synagogue was in the opposite direction but also only a short distance away, just down the southern wing of the intersection.

Simon, the groom to be, as well as his wedding party of parents and friends, used the ensuing morning to bath and put on their best clothing. The air was electric – alive - more expectant than tense.

We took our leave - with great thanks for the group's hospitality – and promised to attend the wedding ceremony later that day.

"This is indeed a sacred city, made so by all the miracles My Son performed here during His frequent stays," said Mother Mary. "The mood is reminiscent of all the loving energy He affirmed while in this hamlet – which included feeding the five thousand from the baskets filled with only five loaves of bread and a few fish." [29]

"I also remember Him teaching in the synagogue and afterward healing a man who reportedly was possessed by an evil spirit. Actually, the man had caused his own right side to become paralyzed after he struck a peasant girl who begged at his door."

---

29 Mark 6:30-44.

I also realized that it was here in Capernaum that Yeshua healed Simon Peter's mother in-law as well as the servant of a Roman centurion who pleaded for His help, the same centurion, mind you, who - it turned out - was one of my soulful extensions.

You may recall that I also later posted as the centurion who served with the Roman Army on the Mount of Olives, the one who 'guarded' and then followed Yeshua into the City. I later resumed my primary presence as John, standing with Yeshua, Mother Mary and Mary Magdalene on the Temple mount as we observed the appearance of Yeshua's mock passion and crucifixion.

Obviously, I was not only learning about Yeshua and Mother Mary's ability to extend themselves. A bit of their inspired empowerments had apparently rubbed off on me - although I now realize that making an extension of my incarnate status - in this case as a Roman centurion - was also my birthright as it is of any immortal soul who believes in and affirms their capacity to invoke any number of extensions or aliases.

I also remember the incident that took place in Capernaum that involved the paralytic who was lowered from a building's roof to be healed by Yeshua, thus circumventing the huge crowd that was blocking the front door - events since recorded by both Luke 4 and Matthew 8. Ah – what a glorious town, known subsequently 'as His own', indeed the center of much of Yeshua's public ministry in Galilee.

I noted – as well - how close Capernaum was to Bethsaida – scene of the second feeding of the multitudes – situated as it was just on the other side of the northern bend of the Sea of Galilee.

"And let us not forget Gennesaret," said Mother Mary, "where Yeshua came ashore after walking on the sea waters in order to save the disciples threatened by a storm. It was at that time that Yeshua also uttered one of His most poignant phrases, "Be Not Afraid." [30]

---

30   Ibid, Mark 6:50

"Then, of course, There is Magdala," said Mother Mary, "just down the road from where we stand. I am so glad we came this way. Magdala is the birthplace of our beloved Mary Magdalene – and the arena in which Yeshua spent many of His most vivid and glorious days," She said with a sigh, raised eyebrows - then a broad smile.

Reunited

"Thank you, dear Mother," said a deep voice seemingly out of nowhere. "Those were indeed significant days for bringing both God's words and His works to this beloved world."

Mary and I looked around; There was no one there by a workman squatting on the ground under a tree. We looked. He laughed.

"I did not mean to frighten you," said Yeshua. "I have been sitting here for what seems like hours. Perhaps I had fallen asleep but suddenly there you were mentioning these towns as if their aura had faded. The blessings bestowed on them, however, linger still today – in fact, they permeate the very grass and hillsides of the entire area."

"In recalling those times, I realize now that I may have expressed initial disappointment with Bethsaida and Magdala – along with Chorazin – lo those many earth years ago," He confessed. "Although my latest embodiment was by then in Its thirties it was obviously still young and thus susceptible to My ingrained incarnate impatience - wanting everything to unfold 'immediately'. Yet I do recall spending much of My early ministry here in what subsequently became known as the 'Evangelical Triangle': the sites of some of My greatest inspirations from Prime Source - which then enabled Me to make some of My - and Its - greatest blessings evident in physical form."

Slowly the external appearance of the beggar was transformed into the full appearance of the Christed One. It was indeed Yeshua Himself. We rushed to His side, embracing Him with both tears and cries of joy.

"Oh, how I have missed seeing – and hugging you – every day," said Mother Mary."

I then stood aside as Mother and Son whispered endearments to each other, Mother Mary at once stroking His face with one hand and massaging His shoulders with the other.

"And has this one - not been worthy of his titles," He exclaimed, pointing in my direction. "Apostle and Guardian of Mother Mary - he is and always will be."

"And stubborn and playful ... and as inquisitive as ever," said Mary. "I could not ask for a better companion and protector. Gentle...and strong... is what he is."

"Well then," said I. "Tell Our Lord the story of the caravan and who was both gentle with the drivers yet proved to be the strongest of all."

"Ah, yes: I sent kudos to you from Heaven, My dear Mother," said Yeshua with a hardy laugh. "Hundred of angels watched those scenes with Me, every ready to assist and even 'fly' to your side. But I urged them to relax, knowing full well that you are after all 'Mother Mary.'"

The Wedding Revisited

We had just spent a morning in Cana – a delightful experience since the town was filled with memories and evoking recalls of the time Yeshua performed His first public miracle. The similarity between the wedding event that took pace in Cana and the one we witnessed here in Capernaum was uncanny.

Those of you familiar with the stories of the New Testament will remember that Cana was the site at which our Lord activated "the first of His signs" or miracles. I wrote about it in my Epistle. It was the time Yeshua turned water into wine - after the original supply of wine ran out in the middle of a wedding feast.

You may also recall the sequence and cast of characters. Yeshua, of course; Mother Mary, of course; me - as the witness and scribe; the steward, the bridegroom, a few servants – and all the invited guests. Allow me to quote from my own epistle, namely John 2:1-11.

"...There was a wedding in Cana of Galilee, and the Mother of Jesus was there [along with] Jesus and [a disciple]. When the wine ran out, the

Mother of Jesus said to Him, 'they have no wine.' And Jesus said to Her, 'woman...My hour has not yet come.'"

"His Mother [nevertheless] said to the servants, 'Do whatever He tells you.'"

"Now standing there were six stone water jars...each [capable of] holding twenty or thirty gallons."

"Jesus said: 'Fill the jars with water.'"

"And they filled them to the brim."

"'Now,'" said Jesus, 'draw some out and take it to the chief steward.' When the steward tasted the water that had become wine, and not knowing where it came from, called the bridegroom and said: 'Everyone serves the good wine first, and then the inferior wine once the guests have become drunk. But you have kept the good wine until now.'"

And so the passage concludes: "And Jesus did this, the first of His signs...and [so] revealed His glory."

To say that this subsequent wedding in Capernaum exactly mirrored the earlier story of Cana, is to claim too much. But witness the similarities.

Again the wine caskets were dry – no surprise given the appetites and thirst of the hardy and enthusiastic group from Ptolemais. So once again came the laments of the wedding party and guests. Fortunately, Yeshua had agreed to accompany us to the wedding.

Yeshua looked at Mother Mary. "Will you again insist?"

"The opportunity certainly seems to present itself. Why not make the gift willingly – without My having to nudge you once again? Besides this is the bridegroom and it is his family who just gave John and I a ride from Ptolemais."

Yeshua smiled, then laughed. He then spoke quietly to the servants.

A few minutes later the wine steward was seen congratulating Simon, the bridegroom - then pointing to our table.

Simon asked his bride to join him as they came to our table.

"My dear Mother Mary and John: forgive me for not realizing at first how fortunate we were to welcome such wondrous souls onto our caravan.

You certainly had that aura about you – but it was not conclusive in our minds until we had time to ponder your words of wisdom, John - and then the incredible incident of you, Mother Mary, lifting the wagon from underneath! Needless to say, we are long overdo in telling you that we were - and are now again - greatly honored to greet and know you. If there is anything we can do for you as you continue your journey south, please do not hesitate to call upon us."

And turning to Yeshua, the bridegroom and bride bowed.

"Dear sir: we did not expect You to be here – but we can never thank You enough – for the wine, of course, but primarily for blessing our humble wedding with Your Presence. We shall never forget You – and hereby dedicate the love of our marriage in Your name."

In Search of Mary M

"If we may, Simon," I finally said to the groom, "we do have an additional request."

"Anything, anything at all," he said.

"We will resume our travels tomorrow, wishing to go south from here, revisiting grounds sanctified by members of our spiritual family. For example, we now go in search of the original home of one Mary Magdalene – which may very well be located in the town of Magdala. We were fortunate to ride here with your caravan from Ptolemais but lack such transportation now as we proceed toward Magdala and eventually Jerusalem. Do you know of any caravans that will be going in that direction relatively soon - and would be willing to help us?"

"I can do better than that, I assure you," said Simon with enthusiasm. "How about a horse and small caravan of your own – to carry you as far as you wish...and serve as shelter each evening."

"Oh, my - that would indeed be wonderful. But can you spare them - given your need to return west to Ptolemais with your new bride?"

"Well, remember my bride's endowment brings two more horses and caravans into our family's holdings - plus a set of donkeys. We can at least spare one horse and wagon for those who literally 'walk with God', and who so enhanced our wedding reception - and blessed our union!"

"Oh my, how generous you are," is how I responded. "I can tell that Yeshua, in particular, with His broad smile is already indicating how pleased He is by your support of his Mother and disciple. We cannot thank you enough. Walking we are able, but riding is much preferred. We can now proceed feeling both safe and protected. Thanks be to you...and the Lord."

So it was that we were in Magdala by evening the next day.

There – At the Doorway

As our continued good fortune would have it, we found the former home of Mary Magdalene almost immediately. We neared the town at dusk, and having no clear indicators, decided to proceed as best we could - toward the only light we could see. A side road led to the left. Around the bend we spotted the outlines of a barn. We pulled to a halt, hitched the horse and wagon to a fence and headed to what appeared to be the main house.

"Hello. Is anyone home?" we shouted.

Our call was greeted almost immediately.

"Thank God – it is you: I have been waiting for days. Where have you been?"

At the doorway – with open arms - stood the one and only - Mary Magdalene.

The exchange was fast and furious.

"Oh, Mother Mary – and you, Brother John. I have been expecting you. Yeshua was here a few days ago – just a short visit – and He told me you would soon be at my doorstep! How delightful to see you – and to hug you both again."

"Yeshua was here? My, how that Son of mine does travel. He visited with us recently too – when He helped a couple fortify their wedding wine. I almost had to urge Him to do so again – but this time He quickly volunteered and everyone ended up having a wonderful time - as usual."

"And you – you look so grand. We have not seen each other since our work together in Britain. It took us quite a while to get back here to Palestine – with the aid of a few boat rides, a set of caravans through Europa and more than one long boat ride along the sea. How did you manage the same distance - and so quickly?"

Maven and Leader

"I really cannot explain it. Yeshua motioned to me as He too was about to leave our community in Glastonbury. 'I will return in a few days and will then help you return to Palestine in record time,' is all He said. My plans for the next phase of my mission were still undetermined – so I was more than willing to hear and heed Yeshua's promise – as unusual as it seemed - yet knowing nothing is ever really unusual with Yeshua."

"Well, He did indeed return by mid-week, and bid me a sudden 'lovely good morning' as I strolled through the flower garden.

'Good Mary Maven' was what He said. I was and am still honored by His greeting; between us, however, it did sound a bit over the top."

"Actually," He continued, "I have two surprises for you – both well earned. First, a formal recognition, an honoring. And then an invitation to help you get to Palestine and your old home - in record time."

"First, and most important, the honor and special recognition."

"I must have looked startled for Yeshua immediately took my hand and said:'You stood with me, Mother Mary and John as we watched the apparition of the passion. Then days later - having heard that Joseph of Arimathea had reserved a tomb for someone who had allegedly been crucified - you rushed to investigate. You were the first to go to and enter the cave – but were not in any way surprised to find it empty; you knew – having watched the illusion of the passion with us - that I was still very much alive and well - still very much an incarnate living in My newest embodiment."

"Then you were met by an Angel – which you now realize of was Me - in apparitional form. I urged you to go to the other disciples, then gathered in Emmaus, and to tell them the alleged tomb was empty - and that I was indeed as alive as ever." (John 20: 11-18.)

"Actually – as you know – since you witnessed the events with Me and the other members of our sacred family - I never died on a cross or otherwise: Prime Source staged the entire passion, creating a mirage through the use of lights and lasers. The clerics, the soldiers and the crowds saw what they wanted to see. Of course, We knew better." [31]

"Your subsequent testimony to My disciples at Emmaus also fit your consistent pattern," He said. "You have played a crucial role in supporting My ministries – even causing silly Peter to become jealous when he heard that it was you who talked with Me first - at the cave site.'"

"And so Yeshua thanked me for having spoken so 'forcefully and lovingly' of His continuing and everlasting gospel. 'Despite Peter's provocations, you gave them wise counsel on how to deal with My supposed death - affirming My - and thus their - continued ministry.'"

"And," said Magdalene, "The Master even thanked me for contributing to what He called our subsequent and 'sacred retreat' through Palestine and Europa - and then helping to establish our spiritual community in Glastonbury. At that juncture, I started to feel overwhelmed and self-conscious, uncomfortable at being singled out for what was always a group effort - with Yeshua, and you, Mother Mary - always being our primary guides and inspiration."

"I was then totally overwhelmed by what happened next."

"He thanked me for my dedication and devotion and then... then He proclaimed: 'Saint Mary Magdalene: Devoted Maven and Leader' - quickly adding that henceforth such a title would be so inscribed in Heaven.'"

He ended our meeting with these words: "I was sure even Peter will agree that each word in that appellation is totally true and long overdue."

"Stunned, overwhelmed...I could hardly move - for many minutes - or was it hours? Oh Mother Mary, can it all be true?"

'God Speed'

"You have earned the honor, My dear Magdalene," said a joyful Mother Mary. "Brava, a million times over: brava. We are so delighted for you."

---

31   See Sturner, Yeshua: The Continuing Presence of the Master Soul, op cit.

After a series of group and individual hugs, Mary Magdalene - with a deep sigh - asked if she could help us unpack our few belonging and get settled. After showing us to our sleeping quarters, she prepared some lunch, and told us again and again now happy She was to see - and share - with us again.

"So tell us the rest of the story of your encounter with Yeshua," said I brazenly, "something about a second surprise He had for you as you prepared to leave the Sanctuary at Glastonbury."

"Well," she said after inhaling and exhaling deeply, "you can well imagine how intrigued I was by His promise to help me return to Palestine 'in so-called record time.'"

"If that meant less walking and not having to wait on the mercy of passing caravans and the fortunes of long boat trips, I was all for it!"

"As it turned out - He was then away for several days. Frankly, the suspense was a bit unnerving. He then suddenly reappeared and waved to me while I was gathering firewood one morning shortly after breakfast."

"Mary," He said with the stern look of a father figure. "If I may continue: the open road is no place for a single woman. And Palestine is a long way from here. Do you still intend to travel alone? Well, we'll have none of that; the roads are too dangerous these days - even as a member of a friendly caravan."

"I propose you come with Me."

"I am delighted to do on, my Lord," I said with enthusiasm.

"Now," He said – again with a serious look on His face, "I want you to realize that traveling with Me – this time - might initially be a bit frightening, certainly unusual. We will not walk very far nor will we have need of a donkey or a boat or even the appearance of fellow-travelers - no less their wagons and horses."

"I'm listening, my Lord," is all I could say, adding only that "I am ready to undertake any means of travel you propose. I would love to return to Palestine – if any all possible - and join with Mother Mary and John who headed in that direction so many months ago."

"Well," said He, stroking His beard, "That itinerary and its routing would, as you know, take a very long time. Besides, the roads are now likely to be very crowded and at times difficult to traverse. So I think it is best that We fly – getting you there in plenty of time to greet your dear friends."

"Excuse me, my Lord, but did you say 'fly'?"

"Yes I did – not literally like a bird, but by temporarily suspending the laws of earthly nature, amplifying the magnitudes of the mind, setting a clear destination, invoking the support of Prime Source and the heavenly airwaves - and off we go - proceeding, 'God Speed' – so to speak. We can transport ourselves and proceed to wherever we wish, which in this case, would be Palestine. You need not do anything but simply follow My advice and directions ... and then, of course, just 'hang on.'"

Hanging On

"I must have looked dazed, my mouth wide open. I even sensed my eyes were bulging. Yeshua then offered to teach me some breathing lessons: ways of controlling my mind and breadth - such that I could automatically flow with Him and what He called 'heavenly empowerment.'"

"I listened and tried my best, and before I could complete the third round of rehearsals I felt the air suddenly turn warm, very warm. Then I heard birdcalls, and in opening my eyes I could see waves of water rippling across a huge lake, then flatlands alerting with mountains, then more water, finally hearing Yeshua saying, 'Easy, easy, mind your limbs, that's it, beautiful, you did it, and with a perfect and graceful landing indeed.'"

"There now, that was not too bad...now was it," said the deep voice of the tall man standing next to me.

It was Yeshua – again or still in the flesh. And we were standing on the shore of Lake Galilee. The sign read, 'Capernaum' and we were wading into the shallow water just down the road from where you, Mother Mary and John, placed your horse and wagon but a few hours ago. Today begins the Sabbath. I arrived - with Yeshua - from Glastonbury - six months ago - and have been waiting for you ever since."

It All Depends

"I am so very happy for you," said Mother Mary, 'Is not traveling with Yeshua just so awesome and wondrous! It is the divinely intended way."

"Oh Mother Mary – you know of such things - for surely you have experienced them," cried Mary Magdalene.

"Oh yes, my child, often – but not frequently enough. Remember – and please forgive the phase - My so-called 'elevated status' also enables Me to access some greatly enhanced or heavenly empowerments. I am, as you know, very human - an incarnation of an immoral Soul like you. Yet I am also divinely endowed, something My pregnancy with Yeshua and subsequent Assumption confirmed and consolidated. So I am able to use the visions I can activate during meditation - to, like My Son, disembody and move freely amidst and around the curvatures of time and space. I must admit that the physics are all too complicated for My mortal brain. But the infusion of divine-like powers in My enhanced 'being' does enable me to respond at will to My visions and activate My capacity to make all sorts of extensions of My endowed heart, mind and body."

"I am sure it is Prime Source's intention that – sooner or later - all immortal Souls will be able to take their 'heavenly' empowerments with them when they incarnate in human form," She added.

"So why did Yeshua and You not travel initially to Britain by using such powers? Why didn't you return here to Palestine by invoking your endowed capacity to fly?", Mary Magdalene asked.

"Why indeed?" I added, shaking my head and smiling broadly. "Personally I would have jumped at the chance to forgo the rigors we just endured – although I did enjoy and profit from all the things we did en route."

"It relates directly to our rights and responsibilities of also being human incarnates in the material realm," said Mother Mary. "Our Souls are honored to be incarnates – for we then get to serve directly in the physical sphere – despite all its human limitations. It is only as incarnates that we're able to learn what it is like to be human and then learn how to imbue the experience with as much love as we can muster and thus help to evoke the spiritualization of the created world."

"I know I am now known as the 'Queen of Heaven' and 'a Master Soul'. But following My Assumption, I knew My destiny was to put My heavenly status on 'hold' - so to speak - and once again assume the responsibilities of being an incarnated being - destined to serve the average Soul living in the physical domain."

"My early experiences as a Mother and wife of Joseph, the many years of raising of Yeshua, being an integral part of His mission, then everything we encountered en route to and then living in Britannia - were all invaluable for learning how to operate with love and compassion in the so-called 'real' world of everyday reality. My mission was to focus on learning about people's issues and problems first-hand. Fying over them would have totally undercut the reason for My being here."

"The same is true for the journey John and I just completed. Yeshua made it clear that He placed John and I in a reciprocal relationship, guardian and protector of one another. Our journey back to Palestine created the opportunity to do just that – and I must say – we have not only proved it was possible; our interdependence and mutual support has more than exceeded our expectations. Our connection was always close yet we have since proven we can disagree yet bend, compromise and uncover new creative ways - always choosing, above all, to cement and even grow our relationship - forging it into something special as we each nurtured it with unconditional love."

Special Empowerments

"Yet – to get back to your original question: as the Mother and the servant of the Lord, and as the female equivalent of His Master status – I am also entitled, as envisioned, to call upon My special or greatly enhanced empowerments. They include – for example, being able to overcome the physical laws of the earth, something I have chosen to invoke only on very special occasions, preferring - most of the time to live by the norms of being an incarnate in the material realm."

"Witness, as well, the miracles performed in My name," She continued, "divine counsel enabling Me to interact with and thus impact how people think and act. I do not surrender My divine powers when I am an incarnate...but rather choose to use them discretely and with focus. I honor the combination of both soulful and divine identities - for they each contribute to My empowerments and ability to handle My responsibilities. I hold all the 'divinity stuff' in abeyance much of the time so I may experience and learn from both the delights and the difficulties of living as an incarnate - on this extraordinary planet - in this most remarkable physical realm."

"So does Yeshua also convey Himself as needed - in order to express and implement His remarkably complex, awesome and both mundane and cosmic mission. This time He took Mary Magdalene with Him on one of His divinely inspired fly-overs. Who knows where He went - unbeknownst to Magdalene - before and after He dropped Her off here Palestine. I have learned since day one, however, not to question His intentions, His goals or His purview. I do nudge Him on occasion – as you know in such certain circumstances as transforming the wine for a wedding or two. Otherwise I know enough to stand aside and just view Him with awe and wonder - and unconditional love."

"I do know, however, that He is always, always, always motivated to serve Prime Source and in so doing help all of us learn how to love without conditions - and that includes Angels, incarnates, and every one and every living thing in the cosmos."

"I know that His instant transport from Britannia with Mary Magdalene indicates some big time 'heavenly' power to the inhabitants of the Earth. Yet don't forget that all incarnates are also endowed with sub-stantial powers – healing power, loving power, power to motivate and forgive - the depth and extent of which depends on the kind of person one is and wishes to be become."

"I assure you Yeshua's powers of instant flight and awareness are as essential to Him as they are to Me. Yet in the great scheme of things such empowerments are mere trifles in the heavenly domain. Remember Our responsibilities include not only caring for the many creatures who inhabit our beloved Earth and planetary system. They also include *all living energies* that exist throughout the universe - each of which is also helping Prime Source to create and transform our ever expanding cosmos."

"And that includes each of us - with you, Mary Magdalene and John, being prime examples of service through love. As your Souls' latest incar-nations, you have become perfect examples of the loving and compassionate prototype, wondrous manifestations of the glories of the immoral Soul;

perfect examples of what it is like to be fully endowed spiritual human beings."

Let and Allow

"When I decided to leave the Sanctuary in Britain," Mary Magdalene replied. "I was worried that I would never contribute very much and be on a 'a fools' errand', if you will. I prayed for direction and meditated on visions of contribution and the privilege of helping others."

"I spoke with Father Joseph a few times before I left. He stressed only that my life was sure to be gifted with insight and courage. I believed him – in principle - but still wondered when such gifts would ever appear and in what form. I tried to obtain the counsel of Yeshua Himself before leaving the Sanctuary – but that was a very busy period for us all - especially Him."

"So when I got the opportunity to travel with Him, I seized on the opportunity to chat a bit first - before we obviously broke the speed and light barriers en route to Palestine. It was glorious!"

"First and foremost, He urged me to trust my inner counsel and affirm that I was already everything I wished to be. I, Magdalene – like us all, said He - had the power to create our desired reality. So it was especially important for me to monitor the visions I - and we all - consciously and deliberately create and invoke. Each moment apparently presents such an opportunity to indulge our 'flights of fancy' - no puns intended."

"Yeshua told me that it was right, for example, to trust in our day dreaming, our instinctual desires to follow our hunches and the images of potential we receive - especially when we pray and petition God for guidance and blessings. All of our intuitive images of our potential take us deeper and deeper into the realm of Pure Spirit – where the purest and most powerful images are honored and supported."

"In meditating, for example, we need to trust Prime Source and the angelic forces that serve to energize our intentions. We also need to open ourselves to our strong and repeated impulses – trusting in their counsel even if – and especially when - such counsel arrives without our having asked for it!"

"Then there the insights we receive in contemplation; by focusing on the virtues and the depths of the spiritual world - in essence 'bathing in' the natural beauty of inspiration – we enable ourselves to learn directly from the myriad ways in which divinity expresses Itself through us – reflected in what we suddenly begin to notice, what we hear amidst the din of social interactions, and what we then envision, attract and evoke."

"So my insight into the multiple ways I can help to create my future and fulfill my destiny were confirmed as I traveled with Yeshua over the many miles of Europa and the Mediterranean. The time passed was to me, apparently very short - but it was in a spiritual sense so very intense and enlightening."

"After He dropped me off - so to speak - I began to think anew: I realized my human or incarnate identity had been frightened by the prospect of leaving the Sanctuary and going out on my own. Yet Yeshua reminded me to counteract my fears and hesitations with affirmations of my direct contact with Spirit. I could also reach out to my guardian angel and other spiritual presences and request their assistance - as I seized on whatever opportunities emerged in the here and now."

"I realize more than ever that our receptivity to love is a force waiting to be utilized - propelling us to seek out, discover and actually do things that demonstrate our love. It is our attitude, our sense of purpose, and our visions that both attract then fulfill the images we nurture. Choose hate and distrust and that is what happens. Choose love and compassion and those energies inevitably unfold by the force of our commitment."

"So, Yeshua said: 'meditate, contemplate, envision and act'. But do not push or be impatient with any of them. Rather - allow. Don't try to make anything happen. Just let – your vision of your contribution and your future – emerge – as a natural consequence of what you want and the specific images you choose to nurture.'"

"Meeting you and John – here - so soon after receiving such insights and anticipating our re-union – surely was the result of my increased ability to trust in myself – and thus enable my latest vision of my future - to unfold on God's timing."

Questions and Answers

There was silence for a long time.

Finally, I said: "That was beautiful Magdalene. Thank you, thank you." Mother Mary concurred, saying simply: "Brava, my deal Magdalene. Fantastic. Beautifully described" - then sealing Her enthusiasm with a big hug.

All this sharing made me very much aware that I too had something to say, something that had been troubling me for some time. It was nothing monumental, I muttered - but thought it was a good time to raise it while in the company of trusted friends.

"Well, perhaps this is silly, but the most important question I have at the moment is this: what is the correct name for God Almighty and the immediate members of the divine pantheon? I have heard many names used over the years. Personally, I have used 'God' a lot along with 'God Almighty'. Then there are the pronouns like 'Him and Her and It', and the salutations of 'Father', and you 'Mother'," said I, looking over at Mother Mary. There are even the titles borrowed from royalty, and even the military - like 'King' and 'Queen' and 'My Lord.'"

We both looked at Mother Mary. "What say you - fair Mother Mary?" And we all laughed.

"Complex questions. Easy answers," is how She began.

"The salutations of 'The Lord' and 'Our Lord' are right on. Some refer to 'Our Savior' but that is based on a false theology: Yeshua is here to enlighten and guide and love us – not save us from any silly misrepresentation of the supposed actions of Adam and Eve; besides Yeshua and I were petitioned by 'Prime Source' to serve as that initial composite - as described in the biblical or Middle Eastern version of our earliest incarnations."

"The affirmation of God as 'Prime Source' is the most accurate for It subsumes God's unity of masculine and feminine attributes, thus possessing the attributes of Father and Mother. The name *Prime Source* is thus all inclusive and signifies The One - the loving 'creator' who exists both beyond time and space and yet - as the philosophers put it - is both transcendent to or beyond everyday life - yet is reflected or immanent in every aspect of it."

"The appellation of Prime Source also correctly implies that Its universal and conglomerate energy consists - in great part - of an infinite number of 'cells' or immortal Souls. Add in the Divine Hierarchy – as well as their assisting angelic figures - and you in essence have the *All* that continually creates, guides and expands the universe."

"Okay?" She asked.

"I recall hearing this before," said Magdalene."but this time I think I got it."

"I certainly agree to that as well," I said smiling - yet still shaking my head.

Names Plus Context

So Mother Mary continued: "My additional comments may go beyond the issue of 'what to call Our Lord', but here are some observations that set the context for all the issues we face as incarnates."

"For example, some of the interpretations now emerging - regarding the new religion of 'Christianity', assumes – as noted earlier - that Yeshua came into the world in order to repent for the alleged sins of Adam and Eve. Thus Christianity's use of the term 'Saviour'. That's a silly term, however - since as noted earlier - the tale of Adam and Eve actually refers to the system of incarnation created by God to encourage immortal Souls like us to leave the heavenly 'garden of Eden' and literally *incarnate* in the physical domain - in order to uplift its spiritual fortunes."

"There also was and is no such thing as 'sin', or 'the need to be saved' - since Adam and Eve - actually Yeshua and I - helped to initiate the system of incarnation - a system specifically designed by Prime Source to spiritualize the material universe. Nobody was kicked out of Heaven: we volunteered as surrogates of Prime Source to manifest ourselves as Its creative male and female energies. We thus set the stage for the generations of Souls who serially followed us into the incarnate domain, 'people' the universe and help to imbue it with love and compassion."

"Each incarnating Soul has -ever since - infused a portion of its soulfulness into a new born at the time of its birth. If the resultant incarnate did not follow the 'contract' or agreement its Soul adopted prior to incarnating, it would - upon the death of its embodiment - be counseled when it returned to the heavenly sphere. Then, if a given Soul wished to incarnate again – as most do (and as the two of you have also done thousands of times), then it would be counseled on how best to avoid or overcome the difficulties it may have experienced during it's the previous incarnation."

"So if a Soul's incarnate succumbed to temptation and badly inflated his or her ego while in the physical domain, then the returning Soul would be counseled on how to turn such situations into opportunities to exercise love and compassion during its next reincarnation."

"Let me repeat for emphasis," said Mother Mary continued. "When We - as the twin or male and female aspects of the Master Soul - symbolically ate the fruit of the 'knowledge of good and evil' - We followed Prime Source's request and enacted the incarnational system - the universal and creative means by which The Lord's heavenly energies of love and compassion are infused into the physical world."

The Difficulties of Incarnating

"I assume," said I, "that this obviously makes incarnating both a glorious and a difficult process – one we know that is filled with all sorts of opportunities to contribute as well as overcome its many challenges, seductions and difficulties. Incarnation is a wondrous process but also one that challenges us to be ever on alert not to overindulge our free will and allow our egos to act in ways that are detrimental to our soulful intentions."

"Right," said Mother Mary. "When Souls choose to incarnate on planet Earth in particular, they take on one of the toughest and roughest placements in the universe. The process of living on Earth is filled with many, many temptations that can easily induce or seduce an incarnate Soul to inflate its ego, lose sight of it soulful heritage and negate its original intentions to display the love and compassion it outlined in its original contract."

"Too many incarnates – for example - even some who subsequently assumed leadership roles in ancient civilizations as well later in Jewish and then Christian communities, proved to be self-serving and even corrupt. They became susceptible to the counsel and edicts of a series of self-appointed hierarchies, using their earthly powers to adopt a series of restrictive rules and regulations that misinterpreted Prime Source's ministry of love – and even succumbing to violence, lies and misinformation in order to attain selfish goals."

"All that Prime Source wanted for this world was that it serve as the grounds for the sets of incarnates who wanted to demonstrate love and compassion in the material realm and so support the spiritual evolution of the physical domain."

"Prime Source always encouraged the likes of Yeshua and I - in each of our many incarnations - to develop and display our capacities as designated Master Souls. Thus It serially placed US in every type of civilization and culture - spanning the generations of time and the broad range of Earth's geographic and cultural areas."

"Apparently, those hopes and desires worked only in part and for so long. Many of our early appearances did make contributions to the various cultures, and many have become parts of the world's evolving spiritual evolution. Others initiations, however, faced rapid decline while others were temporarily stymied. No one of the appearances by Us and all other incarnates were able to realize Prime Source's full intent. But together We did make substantial progress in many areas of spiritual belief and practice."

"When Yeshua and I completed our apprenticeships - as occurred during the second or new biblical period - We, working with and through thousands of other incarnates, were empowered to influence the adoption of more enlightened behaviors and policies in many of the world's cultures. Such progress included the founding of several culturally-based religions and ecumenical movements that served the growing spiritual community well by supporting enhanced standards of love and compassion for all."

United As Ever

There was silence for several minutes. Each of us sat down near the campfire – obviously pondering the impact of what had been shared.

Finally, Mother Mary reached over to clasp our hands.

"See how love becomes the binding agent, the life blood of Prime Source's presence and Yeshua's teachings and perspective. Here sits one called 'Mother Mary' - for I am indeed the Mother of Yeshua. And there sits My guardian and protector, the one who Yeshua called 'beloved', the one who on the night preceding Yeshua's staged passion, was invited to physically lean on the shoulder and thus embrace Our Lord during what is usually referred to as the 'Last Supper.'" [32]

"Actually – as Mary Magdalene has informed us - that meeting turned out to be Yeshua's next to *The Last Supper*. Two days later, after She discovered Yeshua's alleged tomb to be predictably empty, He appeared to her once again, this time revealing that He would soon dine with her and the rest of the apostles in Emmaus for what turned out to be His *'last supper'* with that group of Apostles."

"So thank you, Magdalene. I am also very grateful for this opportunity to reunite with you as well - thus making our blessed traveling-trio to be complete once again. You were – and still are - integral to our combined missions. And you were as interactive with My Son as any of the men subsequently designated as 'Apostles' by the newly formed church."

"And you were one for whom Yeshua openly displayed and confessed His love, the person who stood with us on the hill overlooking the enactment of the staged crucifixion, the one who was the first to seek and talk with Yeshua at the site of the empty tomb – and thereafter also played a central role as we traveled across Palestine and the Mediterranean and helped us found the Sanctuary in Britannia."

---

32   See Leonardo da Vinci's late-1400's mural painting of "The Last Supper": now housed at the convent of Santa Maria delle Grazie, Milano, Italy.

The other apostles and hundreds of disciples, Mother Mary explained, have since scattered and are making their contributions throughout the world. "The spirit of each of them hovers around us this day: every one who contributed so mightily to Yeshua's mission was and still is a continuing member of one extended family, individually unique in idiom, mission and life style yet united in common devotion to the life and work of My Son."

Multiple Trinities

"Is it not apparent - as well," said Mother Mary, "that we three now manifest one more reflection of the eternal and ubiquitous Trinity. Has not Prime Source taught to us to revere the unity and power of the trio. The dynamics of the three are activated when any one person invites another person or two to join with them in focused sharing - vocally or in silence."

"Once a two-some is formed, the third party may be invited to appear in person or simply have their Soul invoked. That third person - like the second - could be a friend, a loved one, or someone you just met. The duo could also invoke the presence of Prime Source, Yeshua, a particular Archangel, Angel or a spirit guide to form the Trinity. Either way the essence of Trinity is present. A trio is a trio - and once formed, present or invoked, its loving intentions enable each of the three participants to operate as a sacred Trinity."

Taking a deep breath, I then applied that approach to our own threesome, a natural trinity if there ever was one. "So look at the three of us," I said. "Together we are a natural trio. Any of us can - at any time - invite the others to create a trinity - replicating what Mother Mary and I have done frequently as we invoked your presence, Magdalene - or someone we met but a few days ago. Either way we comprised a Trinity – even though the spirit of the second or third party may not have been physically present with us at that time."

The Need for Community

"And I must thank you both, as well," said Mary Magdalene. "I have been lonely since leaving the Sanctuary because I not only missed the camaraderie. It has been especially difficult not having anyone to talk with, some one with whom I could share a basic linkage to spirituality. I did arrive here - extra fast - with the help of Yeshua but thereafter I have been on my own: folks have been friendly yet I have not met another with whom I feel totally simpatico, totally at ease, free to discuss and affirm matters of spiritual depth, to affirm Yeshua or anything meaningful regarding love and compassion without sensing I would excite opposition or a blank stare."

"So - my glorious friends – if I may refer to you, Mother Mary, in those terms as well: I thank you for being here, for coming here and reawakening and reaffirming the basic moorings of my life."

"For months now," Magdalene continued, "I have been able to discuss the various developments in the village, even the latest stories of the struggles the Jews continue to face while living under Roman rule – all assuredly themes of great value."

"But to have been a devotee of Yeshua for so many years and then deciding to go off on my own - has faced me with a difficult transition. Having traveled and lived with Him and each of you for so long, and then suddenly departing from the loving environment of the Sanctuary – has been very difficult indeed. Yet I felt the need to leave the Sanctuary in order to fulfill the promise I sensed I made when I incarnated, namely to initiate spiritual communities wherever I wandered - as we did in Glastonbury. I must now admit that this most recent time – the months that have passed between my leaving and your arriving - have been very lonely."

"And so I say, over and over again: thank God you are here and that I am here with you!"

"Our deepest spiritual work is often initiated and accomplished alone," said Mother Mary. "Yet we all need tangible as well as psychic connections with those with whom we can share our experiences, dreams and desires. How the monks of past and future generations survive so less thrive – Anthony and Paula, for example - while serving in isolation in the desert - of all places - is a mystery to me. They have a spiritual fortitude I as an incarnate do not yet possess. God love them."

Alone - Yet in Community

"As you may know," said Mother Mary, "soon after my birth and then throughout My early years, I lived as a virgin in a busy synagogue. I had regular meals and regularly saw and interacted with others. I had what can only be described as the best of both worlds: alone - yet in community – a combination which enabled me to focus and thus deepen my spirituality through my relative solitude while at the same time taking advantage of the opportunity to interact and share with kindred spirits."

"I do, however, also recall periods of deep loneliness. What I am trying to say is that a sense of aloneness can also enable us to cultivate a deeper understanding of and commitment to our life's mission. I realize as well that after a while too much time spent alone can create a sense of loneliness – signaling that it is necessary to seek company and reclaim community and sharing with others – which is exactly what you - Magdalene - are not only recommending but also now doing!"

"Much of My own work with others unfolded once I left the synagogue to become Joseph's bride, experienced the Annunciation with Gabriel, and then gave birth to Yeshua. My interactions intensified further – of course - given My caring for Joseph's four boys."

"Judging from My own experience, we all need and seek periods of both aloneness (for focusing and depth) and interaction with others of spirit (to feel affirmed and enhanced by such communal sharing). The combination of both is what enables us to deepen our personal spirituality as we also serve The Lord in community."

"The proportions of spiritual solace and interaction with others on our needs for and experience of the spirit - of course - change over time. I apparently now need a strong dose of both - when earlier as child I may have initially needed more aloneness. Both are involved in fulfilling one's mission. Yet there is no formula that fits all - or for any period of our earthly incarnation. Each person should feel free to seek and attain the evolving emphases and proportions their Souls encourage and circumstances invite."

"I sense, however, that one of the most difficult situations to handle is the kind you describe, Magdalene: a social setting in which you feel lonely because you have yet to meet anyone who speaks and acts with your sense of reality and identity. So you value your aloneness yet yearn for a fuller spiritual interaction with others.

I am delighted to know that sharing with John and I is now helping you – and We – camaraderie we all seek.

Everyday Miracles

"Well," said I, "I now wish to share as well. My theme concerns the related issues of appreciation and giving thanks. I have meditated deeply of late and have been given insights that have helped me better understand the role we wish to play in helping to enhance the spiritual potential of the Earth."

"I refer to the incredible link between intention and behavior. Barely a mini-second goes by, for example, between my spontaneous decision to - say - raise my right arm - and miraculously - my arm is raised. I'll do it again now - and voila: I simply wished to raise my arm and then did so. I may also express a desire to speak – as I am doing now - and obviously - out comes what can hopefully be described as a series of understandable sounds."

"What is it that connects my - and thus anyone's intentions - with the ability to follow through in actual behavior? This applies to everything we say and do: we simply choose an intended action, give ourselves the hint of a command, and voila, some fantastic connect happens - and we are literally able to lift our arms, say words, compose entire sentences - even write some of them down by using the presumed dexterity of the hand to 'automatically' imprint our thoughts on paper as it spontaneously grasps a stylus and dips it in ink? Is not that an incredible series of events?"

"Apparently the will-mind-body connections are such that to wish becomes the intention to act, and that implied, gentle yet internal command immediately activates the desired and complementary behavior. It's miraculous. Behind every thought and wish and intention lies the potential of activating the action desired. All linked, all unfolding in a moment, all seemingly spontaneous. Amazing. Simply amazing!"

"You are both looking at me as if I was silly or insane. Have you never thought of this basic empowerment before? Taking it for granted, are you? Denying yourself an awareness of one of life's most incredible and basic miracles?"

"Convert water into wine? Surely a miracle. Heal the fever of a child? Another miracle. Talk with the Being who created the heavens and earth and then summoned billions of immoral Souls into existence? Of course - totally miraculous."

"Exercise the Soul's power to incarnate and thus transform purely heavenly or spiritual states of consciousness into a physical embodiment that can walk and talk while living on a planet that is whirling around a central sun that is part of a planetary system that exists on the edge of a seemingly minor galaxy. All of it: truly, truly remarkable!"

"Thus once we incarnate on this earthly planet we can intend or choose to say or do 'something' – deliberately and consciously, or even 'automatically' and unconsciously – and voila – the related actions unfold. Sound incredible? Impossible? Yet miraculous. The only difference between the millions of actions we incarnates take every day - and the miraculous reality of the incarnational process itself – is that we take our everyday actions for granted. But the intent-action connection is the same as agreeing to and actually incarnating on Earth: namely, they are each examples of a dynamic that is not only creative but miraculous."

"What else can we call such transformations but miracles? Once here in the physical domain of the Earth we replicate the powers of the heavenly domain: we perform hundreds if not thousands of mini-transformations every day – each of our intention-action connections displaying how the mind and body coordinate to make things happen. How one body part - like the brain - can evoke a series of bodily subsystems into automatic synchronization - and thereby effortlessly and continuously create a life of experiences - is surely incredible."

Continual Support

"In fact, much of our ability to transform internal energy into external action follows automatically once the initial intent activates the process.

Once born with the capacity to breathe freely, the lungs automatically take over. The scientists of the future tell us – that in order to sustain life, we naturally inhale air into our lungs that fortunately is mostly oxygen. Upon exhalation, however, we naturally exhale the nitrogen and carbon dioxide needed to sustain plant life. And lo and behold the opposite is true: plants in turn convert carbon dioxide into oxygen – thereby completing the mysterious yet miraculous system of 'give-and-take' essential to the creation and sustaining of both individual and planetary life."

"Science has or will soon reveal that the rhythmic beating of the heart and the 'natural' circulation of the blood make for another automatic life-sustaining exchange. The oxygen that is carried into our system through the process of 'automatic breathing' is also conveyed 'automatically' by our arteries to our various organs and cells. Once that exchange is complete, the veins carry the blood back to the heart for an instant refill of oxygen. This process repeats itself over and over again, sometimes - if we incarnates are fortunate - for eighty and ninety - and even a hundred years or more."

"Obviously the heart continues to circulate our blood through the body throughout the entire day - without any of us having to consciously remind it to keep beating. We don't even have to wake up at night and periodically command it to keep pumping our blood throughout our entire system."

"The living body we have adopted is in good part already on automatic as soon as the body is born and we infuse our soulful essence into it. Breakdowns in the system unfortunately do happen occasionally throughout life - with the brain, the heart and every other aspect of our bodies. But it takes a severe illness or an accident to interfere with the automatic regularity of the body's timing, natural connections and continual self-maintenance."

"So even if any of us do feel temporarily alone and even unsupported, we have our incarnated bodies to thank for their continuous capacity to activate, sustain and enhance our embodied lives. Our incarnate minds and bodies are always at work automatically as they also mirror and achieve our conscious and unconscious choices. Amazing. Simply amazing!"

There was a long silence. First Mother Mary hugged me – rubbing Her head on my shoulder. Then Mary Magdalene kissed me – one side then the other, then laughing as she acclaimed: "Suddenly I know I will never feel lonely – or alone - again."

"And I," said Mother Mary, "am so grateful to be traveling with and guided by a person - who so perfectly grasps the blessings of being an incarnate in the physical realm. Your insights are phenomenal - the stuff of great spiritual wisdom. We are indeed - truly and *outrageously blessed.*"

Declaration

"That desires a toast - and a hug," Mother Mary continued. "How fortunate we are. We are often faced with a long slog during our many incarnations but we often forget - or fail to recognize - the wonder of it all and the advances we make with each appearance in physical form. I for one am overwhelmed with how deeply you, John, understand and embrace the glories of what it means to be living on this planet. Heaven, of course, is delightful - the little I now admit I remember of it," she said laughing. "But this earthly everyday life is nothing to sniff at. It is in fact to be honored as truly remarkable and endearing. Oh my goodness. Thank you my dearest John. Thank you so much."

"I concur completely - for the wisdom of your sharing and the joy of witnessing such a grand affirmation of life. May I - oh, I must - hug you as well." said Magdalene.

"Hmmm. Where do we go from here? That's hard to follow but certainly not impossible - and I predict the best is yet to come," said Mother Mary looking over to Mary Magdalene.

"May I say again, how delightful it is to be united again. Yet, as you know, Magdalene – John and I intend to continue traveling south – slowly mind you - yet advancing ever onward - for Jerusalem, as usual, calls," is how She put it with a smiling glance at me. "There are many people to see - there and en route - and many epic events to commemorate and renew. We would love it if you decided to travel with us but understand you may have other plans."

"Indeed, I do," said Magdalene. "First, I now realize I was once called 'Magdala' - named after the town that was my home for most of my childhood and early adulthood – a natural occurrence, I suppose, since it is has been common to identity females with their place of origin. Now that I have traveled and learned so much from all of you – before, on the way to and during our stay in Glastonbury – I am ready to assert – or as they say *own* and assert my individual identity."

"'Magdalene' truly is a woman's name yet it also infers and pays homage to my beloved 'Magdala'. So it not only links me to my past but also honors who I have become - a full grown woman empowered by God to make Her own contributions, in my own name."

"By the way - you may also recall the story of my being allegedly freed of seven demons during my childhood. [33] I have since recalled and now know those disturbances of the mind were not caused by so-called external demons but by childhood traumas caused by atrocities forced on me by male relatives."

"I honor the number 'seven', however, for it symbolizes the alleged demonic realm from which I have been released - and the new spiritual one to which I am now committed. Since meeting Yeshua by the well and then meeting all of you, I have come to realize I am not only able to foresee events but can now increasingly anticipate the needs of others, take preventive action and especially help those recovering from their childhood traumas."

"I know such developments are difficult for folks to understand. They unknowingly tend to attribute my turn to spirituality to some external religious force but I – with the help of Our Lord - have turned the energy of the number 'seven' on its head - not for any religious reason but to honor my innate spiritual being, an identity that Yeshua and you-all have helped to awaken and develop."

---

33   Luke 8:1-2

"Whatever the cause of the initial blockage, my history tells me that I have been freed of any obstacle to embracing my new set of associations and identities. The name, 'Magdalene' is now an affirmation of my mystic and healing capacities – especially evident when I am working with children - a calling that has been fully awakened since living with all of you at the Sanctuary. Therein lies my destiny: as in Glastonbury, I will help to found a school in Palestine - and I sense that I am destined to do so in Jerusalem. So - if you will have me - I would love to travel with you to the place where we all first met and together redeclared our common commitment to Our Lord."

I could not help myself and immediately shouted, "Yes and thanks be to God. What lovely news," as I rushed to embrace Maggie – I mean *Magdalene*. "I promise to help," I said with enthusiasm, "and with your permission, build on the work – and the relations - we achieved in Britannia."

Mother Mary simply looked at us both and smiled – sensing – as did the two of us – that there was more than just a spiritual affinity that attracted me (now a most energetic young man) to the very creative, effervescent and lovely Magdalene.

Ubiquitous

So the three of us decided to proceed south - and take our time – which fortunately turned out to be our only alternative: there was no destination-bound caravan, no revelers, no jolly bridegroom and bride, and no Yeshua in sight. So we slept late, had a grand breakfast and then packed our few belongings in the horse drawn caravan gifted to us by the new bride and groom.

Mother Mary - in homage to Her status and presumed relative fragility - rested in the back as Magdalene and I agreed to take turns at the reins. Ever since She lifted the wagon with the broken wheel, however, there was good reason to assume Mother Mary was hardly frail. Still I was concerned about the cumulative wear and tear of the journey and reasoned it was best not take any chances. So She agreed to rest – without complaint, I might add.

Just as we finished our preparations to get on the road - south-south-west to Nazareth, perhaps some ten to twelve miles away – we were met by a group of children.

One of them, a girl of six or seven, walked directly up to our caravan and was quite direct. "Are you the people from....from...a far away land?"

"Britannia," whispered one of Her companions.

"Yes. I had almost forgotten. Yes: Britannia."

"That is exactly where we have come from," Mother Mary answered.

"Well, a man came to our school this morning – and taught us some new ways to pray to God. Not that our current ways are bad. He just thought we might learn some new ones as well."

"And before He left He asked us to bring you these flowers and this note."

"How thoughtful of Him – and you – to bring us such lovely gifts."

"Oh – and one more thing," said the girl. "He also asked us to sing you a song. He taught us the words. It is easy and we love it."

She signaled her three colleagues to come closer.

"Go in peace,
go with joy,
the way before you
is filled with love.
Revelations await you
adventures galore,
they are for you
as ever granted
from above."

"That is lovely indeed," said Magdalene. "Thank you," quickly adding: "May we ask who this gentleman was who taught you such an inspiring song?"

"He did not say," came the reply, "but we'll never forget His blue-blue eyes; they seemed to sparkle. He had a long, dark beard. And His voice was gentle but strong. We really liked Him, even asked Him to stay but He said He had other children to visit."

"And His note to you. Do you like it?" asked the little girl.

Unfolding the paper, Mother Mary read aloud.

"Ubiquitous am I,
ever loving
ever protective
always watching
over you."

It was signed in bold letters:

YLovesYou - N&Forever

Nazareth

Nazareth was a small town, nothing more than a hamlet of several hundred people. Donkeys could be seen here and there. Rarely was there a sight of horses - and in this case, the people we saw were surprised to see one of them carting a small caravan - instead of pulling a plow. There was a stir as our threesome wandered into town late one afternoon.

"What's your name?" asked a young boy, probably a ten-year-old and measuring all of four feet tall.

"Well, My name is Mother Mary."

"What is your name?

"I am Sarah....Sarah with an 'h'."

"And what's your name?"

"My name is also Mary, but more specifically, my name is Magdalene."

"So I suppose your name is Mary too?"

"No, no, no. My name is John."

"Thank goodness," said the boy. "I was beginning to get confused."

"Do all of you live around here? I have not seen you before."

"No, I am afraid we are just passing through - on our way to Jerusalem."

"Oh, the big city – where God lives?"

"Well, you could say that – although we understand that God moves around a lot...so He ends up living in many different places."

"Hmmm. Sounds like you might know God. Do you?"

"We certainly have met someone who loves God - on many occasions, and in many different places," said Mother Mary.

"What does your friend look like? They must be nice – as least that is what my Mother says."

"Well, your Mother happens to be right. I must say our friend is very nice – at least He is to Us," said Mother Mary laughing.

"Could I ever meet such a person?" came the next question.

"Sure you can – and perhaps you already have. The holy one we know gets around."

"How would I know it is Him?"

"Well, a good sign is that He is usually helping someone – like helping an elderly person if they are ill, or a child who has been hurt, or an animal that may have fallen into a ditch. Sometimes He poses as a beggar – and just waits for people to approach him."

"He must be strong – especially if He can help an animal that is – say – as big as a donkey, a sheep or even a camel."

"Yes – He is indeed very strong. He is also very kind – and you can see that in His eyes - which are big, and round and very blue. And they seem to create a light that shines directly on you as He smiles – which He does a lot."

"Hmmm. I think I have met Him. He may have been the man who helped at my cousin's wedding last week."

"What happened?"

"Well, everyone was all excited about something – like the man my cousin was marrying was accused of not being circum-something, and everyone was yelling and many were getting up to leave before the cere-mony, and then this man – was it God or your holy friend? - who appeared with what He called 'testi-gomy' or something. He called the groom a good and loving person - and that seemed to settle things down."

"Wow, that must have been quite something. Were you frightened?"

"No – I just hung onto my flowers and had some extra cake. But the man with the testi...?"

"Testimony," said I. "Well, after everyone calmed down – my cousin got married after all. It was fun. There was a canopy and they stepped on some glass and there was an exchange of rings and something my Mother called 'vows' and then there was music – even dancing."

"Is that man – the one you thought might be God: have you seen Him recently?"

"Oh yeah. He is helping my father start a school. A real school would be wonderful. I love to learn and read everything I can – which in this village is not very much. But the man you asked about calls Himself 'a teacher'. I hope He brings lots of books and stuff when He visits next."

"I don't know where He sleeps. Maybe my father knows. The nice man - with the extra big eyes – the one who got everyone calmed down at the wedding and everything – well, He comes and goes - a lot."

A Transportation System

Amos was a carpenter, one of the elders of the village of Nazareth, a man who was quick to laugh, to sing, to go out of his way to help others. Starting a school was only one of his projects; he was also working on plans to build a bigger cistern to insure the village had sufficient water throughout the year.

We met him the next day as we wandered through the village, and were delighted to learn that Yeshua was indeed in the area. Amos reported meeting Him earlier in the day when Yeshua offered to help unload the rocks and wood Amos had in his cart.

Amos told us the story of how this man appeared suddenly one day. He simply asked me: 'why I was working so hard?'

"I told him I wanted to complete a small building where we could teach the youngsters of the village some skills, some trade. The religious school up the road was fine but we needed to create employment for the young people or they would continue to move away to the bigger towns."

"Besides," I said, "we can attract more people to our town if we had more skilled labor available to help them get settled and perhaps build a house of their own. A few parents got together and so here we are," is how I answered Him. "Maybe you will be one of our volunteers," I suggested. "Have you a particular skill?" I asked. "If not, we still need helping hands of any and every sort."

"Well, I was happy to hear that He said He learned a little carpentry from His father but 'not enough', as he put it, to put a real carpenter out of work. But, He said, He could help by moving and lifting things - so He then and there volunteered to be part of what He called 'our transportation system.'"

Amos laughed: "I liked that: a transportation system!"

"We don't have a school – yet – but we might soon have *a transportation system!* So I told Him: if you are serious, please know You are hired. I have no money to spare but I promise to share my lunch with You - every day."

"'Please, sir, know that I am well fed,'" is the way He responded. "'I fact, I may know where to find food for your volunteers, and even get you some building materials that could be conveyed to you every morning or whenever you liked.'"

"Frankly, I was stunned - and let Him know we would graciously accept anything He could provide. We shook hands – which for me always included a hug. Then I invited Him to inspect what we had accomplished so far. By the way," I asked Him, "do you live nearby? I have not seen you before."

"His response: 'I am a bit of what you might call an itinerant. I've relatives throughout the area and so usually spend My evenings with them. Not to worry. I am well cared for."

"So I showed Him what we had completed so far," said Amos, which consisted of a large portion of one wall, and the placing of a heavy cloth cover over the entire area – giving us protection from the sun, the cumulative dust and the occasional rain."

"Then I invited him to join us on the next day – as soon as He could, noting emphatically, however, that although we have made progress – we obviously still need a lot of help."

"The very next morning there was a pile of wood and bricks sitting outside the construction site. There was also a note: 'I was up early so gathered some things together for you. See you soon. It was signed: 'Y'."

All Sorts of Connections

As you can imagine, Mother Mary, Magdalene and I also went to the building site the next morning.

We found Yeshua, head bowed, praying silently as we neared the benches along the nearby synagogue. Mother Mary knelt next to Him, and soon they were praying aloud in unison: "Our Father, Who art in heaven, hallowed be thy name..."

A school? Children? Others needing help? – that meant there was work for all of us. At the construction site, Mother Mary immediately paired with Amos's wife. Magdalene and I gravitated to the cluster of teenagers who were hovering about - apparently interested in checking out the rumor that might soon be opportunities to learn a trade.

Amos's wife wanted to make sure there would be options for both men and women - since it seemed everyone was looking for work. Despite the suspicions of some parents, some of the taller and apparently older children - both boys and girls - immediately voiced interest, hoping they might even get paid 'something' to help their families.

Yeshua apparently had resumed His conversations with both Amos and his young son, both of whom were increasingly curious about the materials that kept arriving every day before dawn: wood, bricks, straw, iron bars, even heavy cloth for the roof covering. And there always seemed to be food, lots of it – greatly augmenting Amos's ability to attract more workers.

"Let us say we have angels working overtime," said Yeshua, looking from son to father. "They work while we sleep. When they discover a heart as big as yours, and the will of your strong and dedicated workers, they not only show up but work through the night. They also eat well, very well – although they obviously cook more than enough. So by morning they are able to leave lots of food for everyone else."

"Poppa: is Yeshua fooling us?"

"I can't tell," his father answered. "I admit it all sounds a bit crazy – but it is such 'a good crazy' that I am for willing to give Yeshua the benefit of the doubt."

"'A good crazy.' I like that," said the boy. "Sounds like a lot of that started happening to us once Yeshua became our friend."

Handling the Resistance

I could not help be reminded of all the people who helped build the Sanctuary in Britannia. Only this time construction was not impeded by the local command of the Roman Army.

But other obstacles soon arrived. It seems some people complained – supposedly about the noise – but mainly because the construction allegedly was not in strict accordance with some imaginary rules governing an educational facility – especially one that supposedly violated some equally mysterious building codes. There was also the accusation that we were violating some restrictive interpretation of the Sabbath.

One morning, four men arrived – each extending their necks to see and supposedly figure out what was going on.

Their question: "Why do you build so close to the synagogue?"

Our answer: "The local rabbi has given us permission to build here – knowing full well that the synagogue owes this property and thus made the rabbi its overseer. Besides the synagogue itself is far away and is built of brick. What noise can travel so far and penetrate through its walls?"

The next question: "Do you also realize then that it is the Sabbath – when all work should stop?"

Amos's response: "We work all week as it is permitted. And now it may be close to the Sabbath but not quite. Daylight still has three more hours...and so we labor on."

Question: "We notice some men are doing the work of those who have already been certified to do such work."

Answer: "We are trying to work through those details. We are now suggesting that the skilled workers constitute themselves as a guild - which would entitle them to teach their trade to newcomers and their young children."

"In the meantime," came the next comment: "Please be informed that you make a lot of noise – with all this banging and shouting – interrupting those who come to the synagogue to study and pray."

Answer: "That we can understand your concern and are doing everything we can to build as quietly as possible - even though, as we have already noted, services are not offered until later in the day, and are actually held in a brick building which is some distance away. In the meantime, please realize that progress can be a bit noisy. We apologize, but please know what a great contribution a new school like this will make to the community."

Ever the tease, Amos added: "Perhaps you yourselves might be interested in contributing your labor? We have many openings for more volunteers, and your labors would help to make our work go that much faster. In the meantime, your capacity to pray aloud with such gusto would also help to muffle the sounds of our progress."

Mary: Can It Be You?

"Mary, can that be you – and led by such a fancy horse?" cried a woman, now aged - apparently once the neighbor of Mother Mary and baby sitter to Yeshua.

"Yes – it is me, Zelda. Oh - my dear friend. Wait - and I will get down and give you a proper hug and kiss. How fitting it is that you are the first person I recognize from the old days."

"So where is Joseph?"

"He is well, far away - in Britannia of all places: a long story," said Mother Mary as She opened Her arms to Her old friend.

"And these are my fellow travelers – Magdalene and John – really my guardians and companions. Another long story."

"Well, tomorrow we will talk. Tonight we must find you lodging. It so happens that my son, Joshua, is out of town – bringing his wool to market. You can stay there for a few days until you get settled. Come - I will show you. By the way, where did you come by such a magnificent animal? Okay - I know: 'we'll talk'. Sounds like we'll need at least a few days just to catch up."

There was a small barn – and hay – near a stream, so we fed and groomed the horse before wandering into an attached two-room house. There was a kitchen area, and another room apparently used just for sleeping – obviously for a single male not yet beholden to the finer things in life.

I was relegated to the barn for privacy reasons. But I loved having my own space – in this case it was almost too much. I would have shared – under different circumstances – but as they say, 'that too is another story'.

Zelda brought food and we supplied the wine. We lit a fire, sang a song or two, laughed and thoroughly relaxed. Our accommodations were basic but dry, cozy and warm, making us realize all the more that another day of bumping along the dusty roads of Galilee was now behind us.

Becoming

"Come," said Mother Mary, "we must visit the home we once occupied - when I was a young bride, Joseph was plying his trade as a carpenter - and Yeshua was only a youngster. If Yeshua is indeed watching - as promised – perhaps hovering over us at this very minute: He is also sure to enjoy this glimpse into the past."

It was a one level mud-brick home – similar to the one Mother Mary said they built so many years ago. But She quickly pointed out that it had been greatly expanded. In addition to the traditional two rooms, the new occupant had since added a third one, a covered work area out back, a small kiln for baking pottery and making bricks, and a large fenced area that enclosed a large barn that housed sheep, chickens and a few donkeys.

We knocked on the door and who should appear but another set of Mother Mary's old friends, the man and his wife for whom Joseph made furniture, and with whose children Yeshua played with for years.

"No – oh my God – can it be you?" the woman named Phyllis, exclaimed. "We remember when you moved away – on a mission of some sort I never did quite understand. At any rate, come it, come in. Abraham, come see who is here!"

And so Mother Mary and the couple reminisced. "Remember, this", "remember that" – on and on they shared amidst much laughter and tears. Magdalene and I listened intently – for the exchange revealed so much about the early years of our Lord Yeshua.

No Denying Reality

The conversation between Mother Mary and Zelda revealed all sorts of fascinating details. Apparently Yeshua once walked a long distance back to a friend's house in order to return a marble He inadvertently left in His pocket. And then there were the many times a child would get hurt – and it was always Yeshua who quickly attended to His playmates - using soothing words and a gentle stroking of the wounded or troubled area - all of which then restored His friends to full health.

Rumor had it that He was able – more than once - to stop the bleeding of a badly damaged body and later even reset a broken limb. In fact, so many stories were told about His healing powers – He was at the time, mind you, still only eight or nine – that adults with all sorts of physical problems started to knock at their door asking for His help. Mother Mary said there could be as many as five or six villagers waiting at their door each morning.

Yeshua's reputation grew rapidly – such that Mother Mary and Joseph took Him a side one day and asked if it had not become too much. Was it causing Him to neglect His studies? Was He not draining His energy? Was He not assuming some portions of His mission and revealing His divine identity too soon – issues better left to His teen years if not His adulthood?

"It is more difficult to hold back, to hide, to be the opposite of who I am," He would stammer. "Please do not ask me to stop doing what I am here to do. I realize My body is still young – yet My very being cries out to help any and everyone who needs it – doing only what Prime Source has empowered Me to do. This is the work of My Incarnation – to help and heal and save in any way I can. Helping and curing are central to who I am, something I can neither ignore, deny or refuse."

Yet, Mother Mary also reported Him saying – on at least one occasion – that He promised to temper the pace and expression of His spiritual calling since He realized He was - in His embodiment - still a young boy. He also admitted He needed to spend less time interacting with others and more time alone - reflecting on the full range of experiences that constituted being a human being - now as a boy, soon as a teenager, and later as a young man.

Yet He also found it 'impossible' to give up the joy of playing with the other boys and girls of the village. Still Mother Mary and Joseph counseled Him not to neglect the lessons prescribed at school and the synagogue. When cautioned, He merely smiled - and with His boundless energy promised to complete His lessons, His counseling, His reflections and mediations as well as His healings without curtailing His play time with the children of the village. He avidly believed He could easily balance it all and proceeded to do so. And He did: no problem!

Affirming His Mission

Mother Mary noted that the older He became, however, the more He faced and embraced the fullness of His destiny. He continued to scurry about and play games, and He loved His studies. But He realized more and more that He reincarnated on Earth again - primarily to understand and teach, to heal, to present and to demonstrate a way of life built primarily on – in His words: 'the principles of love and compassion'.

"That process," said Mother Mary, "the process of becoming who He was and was destined to become - was already upon Him - and us. He tempered the expression of His overriding purpose during His early years as best He could. But delaying, stopping or denying His divine mission was impossible."

"I remember one scene in particular as if it was yesterday," said Mother Mary. "One day, after listening to Him affirm – again – what He referred to as His 'calling', Joseph and I looked at each other, sighed, drew in deep breadths, then shook our heads in acknowledgement. Reaching over, We hugged Him as the full and amazing child that He was ...and the full and amazing man He was becoming."

Family Affairs

Phyllis and Abraham then asked, "What has became of the others, Yeshua's brothers and sisters, Joseph's children by an earlier marriage?"

Mother Mary recalled that Judith and Deborah had both married very early and had moved away prior to Her marriage to Joseph. Unfortunately, She noted, they did not choose to stay in touch. Joses did the same. Distance plus the growing awareness and display of the controversial nature of Yeshua's powers and avowed mission – added to the breach. Shaking Her head, She noted: "Joseph and I were heartbroken."

"But James followed Yeshua's or His step-brother's lead - and helped to organize groups of disciples. And, Simon, subsequently did the same."

"James, for example - later called 'James the Just' - became a leader in the early years of what has since become known as the Apostolic Church. He came to revere Yeshua and subsequently died of martyrdom in his late sixties; 68 as best we can determine. We were still in Britannia at the time. Yeshua grieved the loss of His step-brother, many years His senior."

"I got to know James well," I added. "He was strong willed, opinionated, the spokesman for that portion of the emerging church that emphasized Yeshua's Jewish roots – that is, the role he thought Jewish law and practices - including circumcision - should continue to play in the emerging movement."

We also came to know that Yeshua's cousin, Simon or Symeon, the son of Clopias (Father Joseph's brother), was selected by a congregation of apostles to succeed James in that leadership role. That apparently happened sometime after the Roman conquest of Jerusalem (in approximately 70 ACE). Simon then served as its presiding bishop until the approximate year of 107.

As to Jude, Yeshua's other step-brother: he became known as the 'patron saint of lost causes', the man who was always willing to assist anyone who sought his help, however dire the circumstances. He too was martyred – with a club or axe - around 65 ACE while living in Beirut in the Roman province of Syria. He was variously called Jude of James, Jude Thaddeus, Judas Thaddeus or Lebbaeus in order to distinguish himself from Judas Iscariot. He has since been depicted with a flame around his head, representing his presence at the Pentecost when the spirit of Yeshua appeared to Us approximately fifty days after His staged crucifixion.

Mother Mary also noted that many other Souls - incarnated as members of Yeshua's informal family of followers – served Yeshua faithfully; many subsequently also faced violent mortal deaths. Apparently several of them are slated to reincarnate soon, choosing to continue their service through a new or different form. Like most things, Mother Mary said that too was another story.

Zelda said She heard that Yeshua tried to mediate between James and the comparative new-comer, Paul of Taurus – when those two giant personalities reached opposing interpretations: James thought the new movement should follow Jewish law – including circumcision and the dietary restrictions - while Paul's advocated for an outreach to the non-Jewish population.

I voiced our combined sense that Yeshua supported Paul - since Yeshua hoped each new spiritual gathering that emerged thereafter would be ever more inclusive and be based ever more thoroughly on the universal principles of love and compassion.

Best Leave It Alone

Phyllis and Abraham blinked, trying to absorb all the information about their children's former playmates and acquaintances, and then our references to which approach seemed to dominate relations among Yeshua's many and diverse followers. The biggest obstacles to their understanding – they confessed - were the implications regarding Yeshua. Apparently such references as 'Disciples of Yeshua' 'Serving their Lord, Yeshua' and 'Martyrdom' - were, to them, so new as to be utterly confusing.

Why, the couple wondered, would anyone be referring to Yeshua with such high-sounding titles? He was - in their experience - an admittedly bright and God-fearing child and young man. But our more lofty references - they admitted, "were - to them - very new and even strange".

They had known Him initially as 'a bit different - even strange' - apparently reasoning that they 'best not' make a fuss or bring up concerns about Him - especially since their old friends spoke of Him with such sincerity and vigor. 'Best let it go – at least for now,' they seemed to think. 'Perhaps things will clarify later'. In the meantime, they reasoned, they were not anxious to learn much more about a set of beliefs and occurrences that - if the rumors were right - could warrant one's arrest - if not execution - by the authorities.

Sharing and Learning

Mother Mary became quiet, and looked pensive and perplexed - as we left the home in which She raised Yeshua and tended to Her extended family.

I touched Her arm – asking if She was okay.

"Fine, oh fine – it is just that I thought I had worked through all the memories, integrated them – no longer needing to revisit and ponder My experiences during all those years - at least the major ones: like living in relative isolation in the Temple, the support I received from my Mother and Father, being betrothed to Joseph, and, of course, that most incredible visit by Gabriel announcing I was with child – spiritually impregnated with Yeshua by Prime Source Itself. And to think all that was followed by My visiting cousins Elizabeth and Zechariah, then Joseph and I later traveling to Bethlehem, and, of course, Yeshua's actual birth into incarnation.

"Oh my: the images and so many reverberating voices, the many visits to and from afar, the myriad aspects of nurturing and raising Yeshua. How can a Mother ever forget such extraordinary events. Oh my, ooh my, oh myy," She sighed.

I looked at Magdalene. We nodded in apparent agreement.

"Mother Mary," said Magdalene, "we do not have to be anywhere else than where we are: no rushing, no appointments or expectations. The weather is grand and we have food and drink with us. And we even have a blanket to spread on the ground."

"It seems you need to talk. If so, we can simultaneous learn more about your and Yeshua's early years."

Looking up, Mother Mary said slowly and deliberately: "You are very kind. Apparently I do need to share a few things. Perhaps if I do talk about them now - at some greater length - I will uncover the clarity and resolution I seek."

"If you need another reason," Mary Magdalene answered: "think of how much we need to learn, how much we continue to learn from You each time you share Your experiences. Alas - You would also be teaching us – at the same time You find resolution within Yourself."

"You know me too well," Mother Mary answered with a broad smile. "Okay: where shall we begin?"

Living in the Temple

"My earliest memory as a child was seeing a bright white light at the base on My bed in My parents small home here in Nazareth. I doubt if that little home is still standing but perhaps we ought to look for it. At any rate, the light appeared almost every night for weeks and finally it spoke to Me. I remember its message as if it were yesterday: 'the Lord blesses you and invites you to participate in some special training. You are but a child now but in years to come You will bear great honors and responsibilities. This training will greatly assist You in understanding and fulfilling all that awaits You.'"

"I asked what it would involve, and if I could tell my parents?"

"'Certainly you can tell them,'" came the reply. "'In fact, they will be delighted to hear You are blessed in the sight of the Lord, and will soon begin to assume a special role in the revelations of the Lord.'"

"That is how it all began. I was happy and a bit nervous. Over the weeks that followed, the light revealed that I would soon leave My parents home and go to live in the Temple - where I was to receive special training in the nature of God's love."

"Initially I went to the Temple for only a Sabbath weekend. Then I stayed for a week. Then there was this big meeting between Me, My parents and the chief Rabbi – to decide on what to do next. The issue and the recommendation by the Rabbi that I live permanently in the Temple, with visits – as desired - to and from My parents every other week."

"My parents agreed - as did I. It was no surprise that I flourished as a resident in the Temple. Among other things, I learned to pray and meditate more fervently and for longer periods of time. I even learned to enter directly into long conversations and contemplations with The Lord. There were also two special encounters, both with an apparently high angel - one I came to know and revere as the same Gabriel who visited Me much later with news of My pregnancy. Then - as later - He appeared as or enwrapped in a brilliant white light – usually during the evening and even in my dreams."

"Gradually but then whole-heartedly - I realized that living in the Temple was something my Soul needed and desired, that it was meant to be, and it actually reflected aspects of the life contract I apparently agreed to as a portion of My Soul crossed over and was embodied in Me and My new incarnate." [34]

"I continued to cherish the love of my earthly parents, of course, yet thereafter saw them only once a year on high holidays. They – in turn - seeing how much I grew in resolve, strength and stature - supported My decision to continue living in the Temple and absorbing all its blessings."

"As it turned out, all that was preparation for the dramatic return of Archangel Gabriel years later - when at His prompting - My life began to focus on conceiving and nurturing a Son we named *Yeshua*."

Again - The Light

"In the meantime, the growing maturity of My body indicated that it was time to think of My betrothal. An elderly man – Joseph - having lost his wife years before and seeking assistance in raising his family - including four sons – found himself chosen as My suitor. He emerged as my husband after the rabbi summoned tens of unmarried or widowed males as eligible candidates to be My husband. Joseph was deemed 'blessed' and deemed My rightful suitor when a living dove emerged from the head of his staff – the

---

34 Archangel Gabriel (Benu) has revealed that the Soul infuses approximately ten percent of its Being into Its incarnate; the remainder of the Soul remains in the heavenly realm. The figure of ten percent may seem minor but the wholeness of a full Soul is prodigious - given its integral role as 'a cell' in the limitless Life of Prime Source. Ten percent of such a cosmic being equates to a momentous amount of soulful or spiritual empowerment that is infused into the new incarnate.

last one drawn in the competition. All agreed it was a sign from God and Joseph and I were married."

"Oh dear God – following that - as you know, I had another life-changing encounter when 'The Light' appeared to Me in My bedroom. I remember Him – Archangel Gabriel - appearing in a luminescent outline of a large flame - a figure contained within or surrounded by a tall column of light. His exact word: 'Hail Mary, full of grace, blessed art thou among women and blessed is the fruit of thy womb Jesus' – meaning, of course, that I was with child - with My pride and joy: Yeshua. 'He will be great,' said the deep voice coming from Gabriel's column of Light. 'And He will be called the Son of the Most High'".

"I was stunned. Archangel Gabriel said other things as well – incredible, unbelievable things - among them that My Son 'would reign over the house of Jacob forever, and that there would be no end to His kingdom.'"

"I expressed inner doubt, then disbelief, shaking My head, noting that I was still a virgin - to which Gabriel replied: 'The holy Spirit will come upon you and the power of the most high will overshadow you.'"

"Then, then – to my total disbelief, he revealed: 'the child you will bear will be holy. He will be called 'the Son of God.'"

"I am not sure what I said – if anything - but these are the words that I apparently uttered – for they kept coming back to me: 'I am the servant of the Lord. Let it be with Me according to your word.' Then I remember the Light gradually fading - and Gabriel was gone."

"I realized then, of course, that the Light that appeared in My bedroom was a return of the Light that had visited Me in the Temple so many years earlier. This time, however, it was brighter, fuller and as elongated as a full person, and consisted of a broad band of pulsating yellow-gold, white sparkles shimmering at the edges - all embedded within an aura of radiant red.. From its center came the voice of Gabriel – at once magnificent, over-whelming - yet deeply, deeply humbling."

"The presence of Gabriel thus presented Itself as a layered figure of fire; it is the best way I can describe it. All this happened so fast, but I do remember His revealing Himself to be Archangel Gabriel, who I knew to be the first and foremost of the Archangels, and apparently the spokesperson for the Lord."

Joy Overcomes Confusion

"It was such a wonderful yet confusing time. The Soul in Me was both calm and periodically ecstatic: pregnant, a Mother-to-be, visited by the servant of the Lord - announcing that I would bear the 'Son of God.' I was literally beside Myself - joyous and happy yet also instinctively guarded, careful not to do anything that would harm or damage My precious baby. 'The Son of God' forming, emerging within Me. And I to be His Mother. It was utterly fantastic and unbelievable – all at the same time. Oh my, oh my, oh my."

Mother Mary continued, "There was that other more mortal, incarnated, everyday part of Me that was also frightened. I was of two minds: trusting, affirming, constantly giving thanks, assured that everything was true. Yet I was also fearful: can I really do this, carry and bear not only a child but a child who was the incarnation, the embodiment, the very manifestation of a divine being?"

"Even though I had great faith in My immortal Soul, I realized – again and again – that My bodily incarnation was still very mortal and subject to being overly confident, potentially misled by the prideful yearning of my overly active desire. So at some point - perhaps it was days later - that I was finally able to express full confidence in the words of Gabriel and fully accept and celebrate My new reality."

"As an incarnate with a human body, however, I then struggled with the realities of morning sickness, back pains and a constant desire to eat any and everything that was not necessarily good for Me or My child."

At that, Magdalene and I began to laugh – not at Mother's incarnate woes - but at Her 'oh so human' and humorous way of sharing Her experiences: Her alternating facial expressions, Her tendency to bob and weave Her body as She spoke - at one moment clutching at Her heart then waving Her arms wildly over Her head. She shared Her wide range of emotions - seemingly not withholding anything: tears, giggles, crying aloud, the widest of eyes, the most horrendous of grimaces, sheer explosions of joy - interrupted by interludes of deep sobbing.

The three of us sat in silence for several moments – reminding each other to breathe – to relax, to wait and let everything settle and evolve - and, of course, to give thanks.

The Rest of the Story

"It's time to finish the rest of the story," Mother Mary finally said, "at least the parts I still remember."

"As you know, I visited with My cousin Elizabeth. That was crucial and helped Me reach a point of inner calm – despite having to deal with the bodily realities of being pregnant. Elizabeth was also now six months pregnant with John – the future 'John the Baptist'. Upon seeing me, Elizabeth exclaimed in a very clear voice: 'Blessed art thou among women, and blessed is the child You will bear'. She then reported that the person, soon to be known as John the Baptist - while still in Her womb - 'leaped for joy' when he heard My voice at the door." [35]

"Elizabeth has since reminded Me of My reaction to their greetings. I apparently - and now fully recall - responded with a long and poetic affirmation. I will never forget the words that mysteriously emerged from My mouth:

"My Soul magnifies the Lord
And My spirit rejoices in God My creator
For He has looked with favor
On the lowliness of His servant.
Surely, from now on
All generations
Will call Me blessed,
For the Mighty One
Has done great things for Me
And Holy is His name." [36]

---

35   Luke 1: 41-44

36   Luke 1:46-149 ff.

Finally - the Birth

"Then," said Mother Mary to Her two very attentive companions, "I gave birth to Yeshua during busy times. Apparently, the Romans – in order to take a census - had decreed that everyone had to register in their towns of birth. I have told you about it already - probably a few times. But here perhaps is a more detailed version! Besides, for a Mother - there is no end to telling and celebrating the story of Her blessed child!"

"So off we went to Bethlehem, just south of Jerusalem in Judea. It was a long and weary journey, during which time I went into labor. We looked for an inn but none were available - given the number of people on the road trying to respond to the decree to register. At last we found a home which allowed us to use their barn. It was here that Yeshua was born."

"You can imagine Joseph and I were utterly focused on the pending birth. And unbeknownst to us, the world – and indeed the entire heavens – seemed busy preparing a glorious reception. Shepherds reportedly saw a sign in the heavens as did three royal embassies from foreign lands. Angels hovered on and around the barn. Scores of townsmen arrived from farm and field. The animals in the barn stirred and bellowed. Birds chirped - seemingly coming from everywhere. We heard the resounding voices of an invisible choir. And there we thought we would be alone – traveling as we were at night on a small road near Jerusalem."

"I tried to relax despite the labor pains – and half bewildered – I finally looked up and asked Joseph: 'My dear, what is happening? I was hoping for peace and solace – an atmosphere that would enable our baby to arrive with ease and in a mood of quiet thanksgiving.' Joseph, of course, was as puzzled by all the fanfare as I was."

"Yet - in terms of the universe, the birth of Yeshua was the greatest - and the pinnacle, We realized later - the culmination of a long list of incarnations. But this time He incarnated as the Son of The Lord on High, the final manifestation of Him as a Master Soul and perpetual guide and presence. Yeshua's arrival was exactly what the world needed, was looking for and would learn to heed and trust. Thus it was only right that His birth was anticipated - and then celebrated by all sorts of earthly and heavenly powers."

"So, my dear husband," I remember saying, "we were now faced with three ways of honoring this sacred event. First, there is our experience of greeting our newborn child. Second, We are personally witnessing His latest incarnation. And third, We can henceforth celebrate His birth as the perpetual presence of a Master Soul."

"And what a night it was. The stars seemed so round and bright that they sparkled until the sun rose the next day. The animals never did seem to sleep; they kept wandering around - nudging everyone they could, complete with grunts and bleats and moist animal kisses. As to the birds – they chirped and squawked until day-break."

"Presents galore – flowers, incense, containers of oil – were assembled and presented in His honor. We finally realized that Prime Source - and seemingly the entire universe - was deeply invested in and delighted by the birth of Yeshua."

"He was our Son, of course. Yet He was so much more. His birth signaled the re-manifestation the personhood of God, who once again had ascended to Earth as a divine incarnate, this time as Prime Source's perennial representative – this time as Its personal presence in and gift to the entire physical realm."

"Yeshua had been preceded, of course, by a string of embodiments who served as Master Souls-in-training. Witness the host of biblical and mythical characterizations He assumed earlier while en route to His full development: Adam, Seth, Odysseus, Adonis, David - on and on through every age and in every culture of incarnated life." [37]

"Presents galore were even assembled on and around the gateway. Kings mingled with peasants, and ladies bedecked with jewels chatted

---

37   As noted earlier: for a complete list of Yeshua's (and Mother Mary's) earlier incarnations, see the sections entitled 'Realities', and 'Evolutionary Progress,' in *Chapter I: Yeshua Opens the Conference.*

avidly with women in scarfs. The repertoire of both visible and invisible choirs proved to be endless; fortunately the roof of the barn held strong! And Yeshua proved to be the most joyous and delightful of babies - constantly wiggling in His make-shift crib and grinning ear to ear."

"Joseph and I held hands throughout the night as we greeted and thanked Prime Source, Its enormous and heavenly entourage, the local people and animals and the endless flow of celebrants from seemingly every culture and corner of the world."

Bedazzled

As Mother Mary was sharing, the sun began to set and cooler air was soon upon us. I quickly gathered some wood and made a fire.

Not one of us spoke for a while – allowing Mother Mary's words of the incarnate birth of Yeshua to both percolate and resonate deeply within us.

Mother asked for some tea – then sat slightly to the side, seemingly both reminiscent and peaceful – after having relived and reprocessed some of the most vivid and vital aspects of Her life.

Finally – and suddenly - She resumed, alternating between looking at us and then into the distance.

"We watched Him – Joseph and I – bedazzled by His every movement, each gurgle, each bout of heavy breathing as He suckled My breast or tossed in His sleep. It was a miracle unfolding, one we helped to create and could now witness in person – minute by minute - and even millisecond by micro-second: noting each sound, turn and facial expression He made. His features gradually took on a more precise definition and His body seemed to elongate with each stretch and giggle."

"Having monitored His every movement so closely, you would not think us capable of being suddenly surprised. But every few days we witnessed another demonstrable leap in His development. At two weeks – can you imagine? - He was clearly mouthing, 'Momma', and 'Poppa'. At six weeks – and for many weeks thereafter - He seemed to be carrying on a progressive conversation with Prime Source Itself - first enunciating such words as 'Him and Her', then 'sent and carry', then 'blessed and forgive'."

"Within a month He clearly articulated several words at once – then full sentences: 'Thank you dear Father, thank you. Love and blessings to all' - often repeating such phrases - each time nodding His head and raising His arms as if to heaven."

"Now listen to this: on His very first birthday, He – without any coaching or encouragement – recited lines from the Book of Genesis: 'And God said: Let us make humankind in our image, according to our likeness.' Just before His second birthday, He absolutely stunned us by proclaiming: 'I am the Way, and the Truth, and the Life. No one comes to the Father except through Me. If you know Me, you know My Father as well. From now on - please realize that you know Him through Me - and have seen and witnessed His presence on Earth.'" [38]

"The first statement was from the Hebrew Testament, of course, and the other – I sensed at the time, were in essence transmitting the essence of the words you, John, would later include in 'your eventual Gospel.'"

"In subsequent years, His insights, energy, and what we best described as 'His divine presence' – seemed to transform His every intention into manifest action. 'Miraculous' is the best way to describe it: He was increasingly able to use any and everything in the universe as the basis for realizing His intentions. It was as if some small creature – a being already possessing total integrity in Itself – was before our very eyes intentionally transforming Himself into a cosmic and sacred butterfly or eagle - a magnificent being who has and will continue to soar with the dazzling wings of The Lord Itself."

"As He grew older, there was no issue or subject was outside His purview or power. Witness even now: His capacity to cure, His ability to suddenly evaporate and then reappear at will, His dominance of space and His capacity for instant 'flight', the immediate effectiveness of His gentle commands that cure the ill and revive the dead."

---

38   John 14:5-7

"As a child, He too would occasionally tumble and fall and injure Himself, yet when He did, He seemed to heal instantly. He needed only to a wave His hand to realign the broken bones of a child or adult. He would breathe along with those who had breathing problems – inhaling and exhaling with them until they recovered their ability to breathe fully on their own. He would simply dampen His fingers with His own spittle to cure a fever or erase a debilitating rash."

"And He would talk endlessly with the other children – and parents who were inspired to sit with Him – telling them stories of goodness and compassion – as drawn from the texts of the spiritual sages of the pagan world, the ancient orient, the varied spiritual texts of the East, the Hebrew Bible and an array of sources that would later emerge as the Christian Bible and the writings of various cultures including those of Native America."

"It was like watching all the power and talent of the universe being expressed, magnified and perfected – and then bestowed on anyone or thing in need, a stream of bounty gifted to the world that continuously helps it resolve its sorrows as it also celebrates its enormous empowerments and innate spiritual potential."

Continued Growth and Development

"His development did not stop there, of course," said Mother Mary. "I've told this story before, of course, but to a Mother it is always worth repeating. When He was about twelve years old, we went to Jerusalem as usual for the festival. When it was over we joined the crowds returning to our respective homes. Yeshua was not at our side; we merely assumed He was traveling with friends. At the end of the first day, we still did not see or hear from Him and He was nowhere to be found. So we immediately returned to Jerusalem."

"We searched for three days and finally found Him in the Temple, sitting among the teachers, listening, asking questions, contributing His own observations. Everyone participating in the dialog appeared to be demonstrably astonished by His understanding."

"Relieved yet still concerned, we asked Him directly: 'Child – why have You treated us this way? We have been very anxious, searching for You everywhere.'"

"He looked at us – seemingly understanding our concern yet simultaneously feeling the need to assert the primacy of His mission: 'Did you not know I must be in My Father's house and be about His and Our primary business'?"

"Knowing the nature of His incarnation, we of course accepted and understood His explanation. As parents dealing with the disappearance of our Son, however, we were naturally concerned with what seemed to us as His relatively cavalier attitude toward His responsibilities as a member of our very human family. So we told Him that in the future He needed at least to let us know where He was - or needed to be - before disappearing as He did."

"Fortunately, He understood our anxiety, turned and bid goodbye to the teachers and rabbis - whom He seemed to treat as colleagues if not His students - and promptly returned home with us to Nazareth."

We talked very little en route home. Upon our arrival, however, Joseph and I thought deeply about the experience, inviting us – no, really forcing us - to realize how much Yeshua had increased in stature, not only in terms of His innate wisdom but mostly in terms of how much He also needed to embrace the fullness of His divine identity and mission.

Enter The Fearful

"And all was well until news of His empowerments spread throughout the land," said Mother as She continued to reminisce. "Initially He attracted the curious and the seekers, the elderly and the youth, the apparently rich and the outwardly needy. But then His fame attracted the opposition of those who has a vested interest in maintaining the status quo, who held and continually reaped power and profits from their current roles and positions.

Some of the more myopic clerics and ideologues refused to acknowledge no less honor anyone they considered 'silly amateur and delusional newcomers'. They resented anyone else speaking of the holy and the sacred

– realms they considered were reserved to them exclusively. They were especially appalled by the words and actions of Yeshua – for they initially considered Him a young, presumptuous and inexperienced youngster – whose parents were undistinguished and whose small band of followers were rabble, uneducated and of no consequence."

Mother Mary sighed deeply. "As the Temple officials continued to hear of Yeshua's words and actions, they also became fearful – concerned that His message, demeanor and growing sense of authority would eventually disturb the peace they they promised their Roman overlords. Many of the very conservative Sadducees, some of the Pharisees, and some members of the Temple hierarchy came to consider Yeshua a potential usurper, a threat to their own authority, and soon labeled Him 'the enemy.'"

"As far as the Romans were concerned, peace and quiet and the right to collect taxes were all they wanted or needed. Disrupt the peace, the flow of traffic, the financial tributes - and they too were ready to emerge in force, arm and arm with the most fearful of Temple officials. The religious and the military thus joined forces out of fear of losing their respective positions of dominance and acclaimed eminence."

"Forgive Me for speaking so harshly – but as the parents of our remarkable son, We began to feel increasingly protective. Fortunately, the final clash was averted for years. Then – as we know - in took only three years for the twin-headed dragon of religious and civil authority to emerge from its lair. Deeming itself superior, it entered into a fray armed with scorn and swords. Little did they know - or care to know - who they were dealing with."

Mother Mary let out a sigh. Her usual rosy complexion had turned pale and shallow. Her words of anger and frustration turned to tears and deep sobbing.

"And then," She finally said, "and then" - repeating the phase over and over until She could hardly be heard.

"Mother, please: enough, surely that is enough... for now."

"Okay," She sighed. "Agreed: that surely is enough - for now," She said with a grimace and finally a smile, adding wistfully: "But to be continued – as needed – at a later date."

The Gift of Rain

By morning, Mother Mary, Magdalene and I were back on the road to Jerusalem. Our horse was fed, watered, and our little caravan packed with our few belongings. So off we went, intent on crossing the Great Plain and reaching the hills of Samaria in no more than a day and a half.

We were also mindful of the saying: "It is good to have plans. But please realize: they often cause God to smile - if not laugh."

First it rained, followed by intermittent mixture of drizzle and sand storms that lasted all morning and into the afternoon. There was nary a place to seek shelter so we trudged on until the air cleared and we came upon a thick line of trees surrounding the village of Scythopolis. It was there that our damp slog was rewarded.

We saw smoke, we heard laughter and drums, we even smelled food being cooked over an open fire. Gradually we came across a group of people we assumed were gypsies, dressed in colorful clothing, dancing within a circle of wagons.

We hesitated, stopped, and momentarily watched. A few of the dancers soon motioned to us to join them, one yelling "Come on in. Don't be afraid. Come - you are most welcome."

Funny thing: most of the dancers gloried in the intermittent drizzle – and the bouts of renewed downpours. Some even chose to gallop about wherever they could find the biggest puddles.

"We have had no rain for weeks," said one. "Now we can fill our pots, feed our plants, wash and water our animals, bath ourselves and our children, quench our thirsts, sooth our sun-burned brows – and yes – dance for the joy of it all."

"Even the River Jordan has run dry – but not any more," said a tall man who had literally danced on over to us. Water ran down his face and his arm was draped over the shoulders of his partner as he shouted to the skies: "We give thanks – for now we are being gifted with God's bounty."

Wiping the rain from his face, he cried: "Dancing in the rain is now part of our liturgy."

Simplicity

"How wondrous for that gypsy man to celebrate the rain," said Mother Mary, "not just because it feeds the plants, fills the reserves and supports everyone's cooking and health – but simply because it is wet and cool and oh-so cleansing after days of our very hot and dry weather."

"May all the people of this earth, all those who have chosen to incarnate at this time have the opportunity to so celebrate life. We should never forget that everyone we meet is an immortal incarnate - an embodied being who has given up the relative comfort of heaven in order to work hard and toil long hours as an incarnate," said Mother Mary. "Seeing so many delight in the simple joys of the Earth is so gratifying - even heart-warming."

"Seldom do many incarnates in this land have reason to experience no less express joy, and then have the good sense to enjoy the natural gifts of heaven. I am thinking of such natural expressions of joy as childlike enthusiasm, falling in love, the birth of a child, the opportunity to contribute to the welfare of others – and, now, here before us, to freely express the joy of getting absolutely drenched while dancing in celebration of this precious rain."

Magdalene and I looked at each other with broad smiles – marveling at Mother Mary's capacity to overcome the rigors of our journey and all the difficulties and intense emotions She just recalled in being the Mother of Yeshua. Despite it all, She always seemed to muster the capacity to see and experience what was in front of her, to put first things first, to admire the primary virtues, to seek and appreciate the precious nature of simple things, to thus praise God for the natural blessings of everyday living.

Laments and Intentions

"And yet these gypsy people are often forced to retreat," said Mother Mary, shaking Her head, "forced to move to the outskirts of a town, for example, because their ways do not conform with the so-called sophisticated ways of those with presumed superiority or greater wealth and authority. Many of our customs and rules do help the varied groups to get along more smoothly with each other. But too many other regulations and customs are restrictive and punitive, adopted by too many narrow-minded groups taking advantage of others while hoarding the rewards of their personal situations."

"And I do not know if it gets any better," She continued. "Barriers and restrictions galore will continue to trample on the basic rights of others to live as they please. I don't know if our work here will ever be done. It seems there will always be another set of incarnates - who apparently lose their way and allow cynicism to enhance their own position at the expense of their spiritual brothers and sisters."

"In a more complicated situation, look at the constant prevalence of violence and war. Worse: look at how many of our brethren enter unto incarnation and then choose to succumb to greed, avarice, violence, and even war as their preferred way of passing their limited tenures on this earth. Seemingly, very generation will have its share of the poor and the destitute, much of it is created by the few who in gaining authority choose selfishness and aggression over others."

"I know that many incarnates have the capacity to live up to their agreements and adopt personal credos that champion honesty and goodness. We sense more and more of them will adopt lifestyles that further the practice of love and compassion."

"When the force of love and compassion are fractured it leaves society open to the power seekers - with their multiple levels of alleged distinctions, long lists of don'ts than do's, and posted suspicions and condemnations. That's when neighbors are susceptible to being labeled as foreign, when slight bodily variations are viewed as strange and inferior, when Our Lord's standards of universal acceptance are frowned on – when the aspirations of those falsely designated as 'other' are blocked by the negative judgments and deflating regulations adopted by many - not all- who assume positions of power and dominance."

"That's it: the next time it rains, I propose we not seek shelter either - but rather go out into it, revel in it, and like the gypsies – dance in it - for the very joy of being alive."

Basic Goodness

I thought to myself: Mother Mary is able to lament the difficulties experienced by others because She constantly sees things through a spiritual lens. Someday there is bound to be a book composed of just Her profound comments and thoughts. Actually, that might make for a series of books - since She and Her Son will romp the Earth and the rest of the cosmos long after we temporary incarnates have surrendered our bodies - and resumed a less challenging but far less exemplary lifestyle on *the other side.*

Take for example the additional comments Mother Mary made while talking to some of the female gypsies.

"You seem to live such a simple life," She observed. "You live and travel in the same quarters. You apparently teach your children not only the basics of life but their letters as well. You carry your sacred traditions with you – even knowing how to cure certain illnesses and maladies with herbs, cactus and flowers."

"You also naturally observe – and celebrate - the changes in nature that you experience throughout a day and year: the movement of clouds, the changes that occur in the constellations of the sky, the speed and direction of the wind, the waxing and waning of the moon, the changing seasons. I especially marvel at the ingenuity you express in devising ceremonies that celebrate both your ancestry and the energies manifest in nature."

"How could anyone be critical? Should not all of us bow to your ability to capture the essence of living: simplicity, love, acceptance, ease – literally attracting what you need on a flexible basis - versus trying to view everything from a sense of neediness and alleged deprivation. It is also a great joy to behold how engaged you are with the cycles of life – all the pronounced stages that emerge from birth to aging and death. In short, you have learned to live with whatever unfolds, be enlivened by it as you honor the divine cycles and energies that guide us all."

"We obviously have had different immediate experiences than you and thus have slightly different ways of doing things. Our combined - albeit varied ways of operating - are united, however, around a common core - one that displays deep reverence for the variety of ways we are able to embrace and appreciate the act of living fully."

"We are honored by your recognition," said a tall woman who had wandered into the circle of people now gathered around us. "We know others choose to live by different codes and practices – many of which seem to us – garrulous, unnecessary and very complex. But the variations and differences are fine with us – as long as we all show mutual respect for each other."

"The problems arise when others judge us - rather than just seeing and accepting us as different – which we are. Dismissing and punishing us for our differences, however, seems very much at odds with their professed belief in a loving and tolerant God."

"We do not suppose to know God completely. But we do know enough to revere God and so accept all the varied forms of honoring Him or Her. However, some of our detractors love to brag that they know their God so well that it demands that they ignore, berate or defeat us – even though such actions ignore what we consider to be the universal norms of compassion and tolerance."

"Some new interpretations now reportedly revere a God who allegedly died for their sins, a deity who allegedly was buried and then resurrected within three days. And there is an even older religion - very popular around here – that condemns activity, even intended acts of contribution and mercy - if it occurs on their Sabbath. There are all sorts of variations on that theme. So be it, say we. Long live our differences. And may God enable all of us to respect each other and honor our unique variations on the great themes of life - and do so with zest, honor and thanksgiving."

The three of us stared at each other - then bowed to this obviously holy woman - realizing once again that Prime Source endows every incarnate with great spiritual wisdom - whatever their group, race or earthly heritage. Wet, invigorated, informed and uplifted, we bid our hosts goodbye as we gave thanks for the opportunity to meet with still one more reflection of the face of God.

Chapter VII

Jerusalem Bound

Soul Groups

"THIS ALSO SEEMS TO BE THE PERFECT TIME TO REMIND OUR-SELVES THAT THE THREE OF US HAVE BEEN TOGETHER MANY times – during countless incarnations," said Mother Mary, "in fact, more times than the gray hairs on My head. The three of us – and many others - have met frequently during an untold number of incarnations - just as we are meeting here again now. And we are bound to do so again – perhaps countless times in the future."

"The facial and body configurations our Souls have chosen for each of our many earlier incarnations have surely varied slightly to a great deal – including as major differences in the role we played and types of energy we conveyed. But the inner resonance and aura of our various incarnates have tended not to change markedly with each incarnation, enabling us - through our different outer appearances - to at least recognize, be attracted to or just sense an affinity with one another as well as other members our *Soul Group* – a grouping that could very well total 40 to 100 Soul members."

"My sense is that we three have been members of the same *Soul Group* for eons of time. And some members – and I again sense the three of us in particular – have also been members of even smaller group called our *Soul*

Council that consists of approximately ten to fifteen Soul-mates, the incarnations of whom tend to appear frequently in each other's incarnational lives – in whatever role a given Soul requested and the others agreed to."

"In other words, we - in our Soul groupings and councils - often agree to help each other achieve the goals outlined in our respective contracts. Thus we may appear to each other as a friend, loved one, antagonist or play any other role that helps a given incarnate overcome its challenges and achieve its goals. We fellow group and council members always try to play the roles requested - whether that means our being helpful or the worst of irritants."

"Often it is only after we have returned to the heavenly domain that we recognize and understand the reason why our compatriots played certain roles during a particular incarnation. It is only then, for example, that we may realize that some allegedly 'negative' person in a given incarnation was actually a Soul-mate helping us to attain what we wanted."

Gabriel Arrives

"I certainly do not remember all our past encounters," Mother Mary said with a laugh. "But I do remember one in particular, perhaps because it was at a turning point for all of us. In was in the ancient times. We were sitting by a fire, the three of us – countless thousands of Earth years ago. We were each discouraged by one thing or another – and generally regretted the ability of the overlords to trick our people into thinking that they, the overloads, were so holy and powerful that they should be treated – and addressed - as gods."

"It was then," She recalled, "that a tall figure wearing an elegant robe wandered into our campfire. He listened, said He understood our situation - yet advised us not to be discouraged. If so, He reasoned, 'the bad guys win', and their views and actions would continue to rule the day."

"To be an immoral being who incarnates does not mean the obstacles to clarity and spirituality automatically disappear or lose their power," He advised. "Agreeing to incarnate does not mean our intentions become self-executing. We agreed to incarnate into the physical domain in order to work at whatever we lovingly intend for the world; were it any easier, we would not need the training we go through with each re-incarnation as we learn to overcome a given set of challenges and achieve what is desired - in personal traits as well as professional and spiritual outcomes."

"Were it easy," said this mysterious presence, "Prime Source would not have instituted the process of incarnation. One of the reasons our Lord created immortal Souls was to enlist us in the essential task of transporting what you know as Souls living in heaven and enabling us to use those skills when transferring to the material realm. By incarnating, we quickly learn the material world can offer obstinate resistance to our heavenly energies. The tasks of incarnation can be wearisome and the rewards few and far between. But we are empowered with each incarnation to not only survive but help to bring about the kinds of changes which contribute to the welfare of both individuals and society."

"When we volunteer to incarnate we become Prime Source's agents of progress and transformation, thereby doing what we committed ourselves to do when we incarnated, thereby infusing as much spiritual energy into our worldly interactions as possible. The actions we perform on Earth are thus intended to mirror the intentions we outlined in our heavenly contract. Our ability to follow through and thus further spiritualize the physical world are greatly celebrated by Prime Source and earn the deep respect of our colleagues in heaven."

"So our incarnate roles - although not easy – are essential."

"Unfortunately, some of our colleagues may go astray in the process, succumbing to the temptations of the earth and indulging in some of the vulnerabilities inherent in the human organism. If so, those Souls return for more training once they surrender their latest embodiments - thereby enabling them to reincarnate once again, take on their next earthly assignments and make their next set of contributions."

Agents of the Lord

"As I recall we were silent for a long while after that robed figure spoke," said Mother Mary. "Each of us apparently just stared at the fire, trying to absorb the advice of that shimmering figure - and think of something to say."

"Finally, it was you, John, who spoke up."

"May I ask, dear sir, by what means do you come by such wisdom and offer such advice. Are you an angel of the The Lord."

"Well, I am indeed an angel of sorts" said the figure. "The Lord sends Me to you in your time of difficulty and apparent doubt. I am indeed from the other side, the heavenly domain. I am none other than Archangel Gabriel, at your service. Perhaps I will have some advice. But first I must listen to you, hear what it is that troubles you so."

I remember it clearly. Stunned. Gabriel in our midst - the same Gabriel that later was a to appear to Me in My dream and then, of course, as the Spirit conveyed The Lord's news that I was pregnant with Yeshua. His sudden appearance always had both a startled and energizing effect. It was no different this time. You, John, were particularly awestruck, finally sharing that you gradually came to feel very much at ease – and wanting to share or admit to some shortcomings. And so - with a nod from Mother Mary, Magdalene - and Gabriel - you shared in ways that surprised us, being in your words, "totally honest".

"I have to admit how disappointed I am - with myself," is how you put it, apparently unable to complete your "grandiose intentions".

"This place has its own set of laws and I don't think I have yet figured them out. Was it any wonder that I thought myself only a so-so incarnate. The appearance Gabriel obviously touched that nerve - for in essence striking me with a metaphoric lightening jolt."

"Last week sometime I was awakened from a dream with a blaze of understanding: 'We were empowered' – I was told - as all incarnate humans are – 'to love and heal through words and actions.' But during our stays as incarnates, we could no longer call on all the capacities our Souls possessed innately while in heaven. Now we had to navigate the difficulties of the earthly world by using our considerable but still greatly reduced human powers to effect the changes we promised. So we could and should not expect to create instantaneous and wondrous breakthroughs. As incarnates we were enabled only to contribute what we could, learn to be very, very patience - trust in The Lord - and wait on divine timing."

"Somehow I had buried that insight; perhaps it is Gabriel's appearance that allows me to recall that dream in vivid detail. No matter how difficult the circumstances. I am at my core an immortal Soul, of course, but I obviously need to be reminded that I chose to serve Our Lord as a human incarnate and thus work with my empowered but still limited human hands in a human environment. Living on Earth, in particular, is the opportunity of a lifetime to contribute what we can, knowing that we work in partnership with the Lord and trust - unconditionally - in Its wisdom, design and timing."

"I also realized anew - that all incarnates go through negative periods and occasionally doubt themselves. Yet with prayer and meditation – and, in this case, a fortunate visit from a sacred being, I am able to come to the crucial realization – once again: there is much work to be done, the purpose our lives is to contribute what we can, and in doing so we need to be patient and work on God's not our all too-human timetable."

Guiding the Powers of the Ego

Having listened to my 'confession' – Magdalene joined in - freely admitting that She too suffered from mistakes, mistakes that still resurface now and again. The issue: dealing with what she called her behavior of "occasionally being overly assertive and presumptuous" as She put it, "rather than trusting in my Soul and allowing God to set the pace and the impact of my efforts."

"Initially, I too thought I was going crazy," said She, "because the world seemed so inert, so unresponsive to my intentions. So I gave up on subtleties and adopted stronger intentions powered by sheer will and the full power of my human ego. We incarnates now refer to that temptation as 'ego-inflation'. As you can imagine – and have experienced - how my very willful approach often got me into a lot of trouble."

"Rather than using the very powerful dynamics of my very helpful human ego to guide and energize my spiritual intentions, I too often allowed it to inflate and run wild. Somewhere along the line, I am sure I heard my Soul say, 'watch out', 'be careful', 'the powers of the ego are not be trifled with', and 'time to restrain your assertiveness' and 'best just trust

God'. Eventually I heard, 'opps, now you've done', 'you best go back home to heaven, pick up the pieces, retrain and start over again.'"

Spiritual Missionaries

Mother Mary laughed. "Oh my dears: it is indeed quite a job learning how to be both modest and humble and assertive and robust, surrendering our relatively privileged positions in heaven and learning how to use the different but still immense powers of embodiment in this entirely human - and at times - hostile Earth. The ability of our human ego to 'go crazy' certainly is not to be underestimated by any young incarnate who naively assumes their work here is best likened to a cake-walk - thinking 'we are – after-all – immortal Souls'!"

"Yes, we all attended the courses on modesty and humility. But demonstrating that spiritual mindset while simultaneously governing the powerful energies of human nature is always a challenge for both the naïve newcomer as well as the so-called seasoned veteran who has incarnated many, many times."

"Gradually – or eventually - we learn how to use Earth's tools of empowerment on behalf of our Souls' objectives: our human capacity to act on loving intentions, the joys we experience through the simple acts of kindness and honoring, the care and attention we can muster and focus on specific issues – and, of course, marshaling our human emotional and cognitive strengths to attain our goals. We can – and indeed are able – to create a series of delightful experiences while also making a series of very loving contributions to the very physical domain we volunteered to serve."

"Besides, while here on Earth, we are still immortal Souls, able to call on our inherent powers - not in full soulful or angelic proportions, of course. Yet the residual force is still substantial. The combined impact of our Soul investments in our human empowerments certainly do not equal heavenly portions or intensity but they are nevertheless sufficient for handling the temptations we face on Earth – that is if we temper our overanxious egos and allow our love to shine through."

"I look, for example, at the marvelous work completed by millions of incarnates who will choose to act like St. Francis and Helen Keller - who fulfill their difficult missions with love and compassion despite the temptations to do otherwise. Unfortunately there are millions of other incarnates who waste their own and our Lord's time as they denigrate their identities as immortal Souls and allow their human embodiments to run amuck."

"Then there are those utterly 'lost Souls' like Hitler, Mussolini, Genghis Khan and the generations of corrupt politicians and swindlers of the world – who unfortunately incarnate in every generation - who literally sell their Souls in exchange for continual binges of power and greed. Realize as well, such incarnates – unless they mend their ways, may have a difficult time clearing their negative traits and records when they return to the spiritual state. They can, course, choose to retrain and fortify themselves against such repeat performances in future incarnations. But such transformations have proven to be extremely difficult. Thus the continual reappearance in each generation of those incarnates who seemingly are unable to change their ways - despite their Soul's promises - and remain bent on raising hell and denigrating the wondrous opportunities of the incarnational process."

"Alas, it is always possible that instead of becoming true spiritual missionaries, such degraded Souls could again, upon re-incarnation, relinquish their opportunity to contribute to the spiritual welfare of their human and spiritual communities – and choose to reactivate their propensity for self-aggrandizement and selfishness. Do not be fooled: there have been and will be many such negative repeats among every set of new and renewing incarnates. Unfortunately, we apparently will always have those Souls who despite their heavenly intentions end up wreaking havoc – morally and physically – on almost everything they touch and everyone they meet."

Burning Issues

Before sleeping," said Mother Mary, "and while 'we are still awake and energized' – why not explore this issue further, namely: Why do so many incarnate Soul – once on Earth – chooses to forsake the best of their best intentions, deciding instead to indulge in an egotistic and self-centered way of life?"

"Born to an infinite God, nurtured in the most wondrous heaven, schooled by loving and insightful angels – and poof: a certain proportion of Souls – once they incarnate – deny or forsake their spiritual nature and ignore or neglect the contents of their heavenly contracts. Either suddenly or through cumulative neglect, they dilute, withdraw, pull back, reverse track. Amazing. Stunning. Sad."

"Yet despite My rather harsh commentary, I also want to acknowledge the difficulties all incarnates inherit once we're forced to face some of the harsh realities of the embodied state. The situation s complicated by the fact that many Souls bite off more than they can handle - loading their intentions, itineraries and goals with unrealistic and grandiose schemes. The new or the young incarnates can often be presumptuous. And those who by their account experienced difficulties during their earlier stints in the material sphere, may assume they can quickly recoup their so-called 'failures' or disappointments by then overreaching and trying to achieve too much, too soon - with the next one."

"Unfortunately, even experienced incarnates can become too ambitious in their subsequent reincarnations," said Gabriel. "Although their goals are spiritual in nature, some subsequently get overwhelmed by the earthly realities they - again - did not anticipate or learn to handle. Of all the physical environments, incarnating on Earth is known to be the roughest and most demanding. It has been the scene of a long list of miscues and casualties."

"Let's face it," said Gabriel. "The list of potential difficulties you incarnates face is a long one: losing a friend or loved one, going through a divorce, overcoming a long list of illnesses, losing a job, being treated harshly by authorities – on and on, all of it producing stresses and strains. Surviving no less attending to one's spiritual intentions in such a world is difficult - so unlike the relatively idyllic heaven from which you came. Cumulative difficulties can sap one's strength and forbearance, such that any given incarnate may begin to compromise if not jettison their best-laid plans. Quick fixes, a string of short-term compromises, anger and resentment over unexpected losses and tragedies plus a few serious miscues can overturn an intended way of life...the cumulative impact of which can undermine an incarnate's best and most loving intentions."

"And there are some who become so entranced with the delights of the physical realm that they periodically allow themselves to over-indulge – thinking they are strong enough to avoid getting entrenched in egotistic pleasures. But too often such Souls find themselves gradually succumbing to the worst of snares, all in a quest to attain whatever they consider success: so-called high and mighty positions of power, great financial wealth, whatever - as they make excuses for the corrupt means it may have taken to attain such silly indications of progress and success."

"Yet your Earth has also been the setting in which many incarnates have achieved marvelous spiritual breakthroughs and contributions. Look at the remarkable contributions made by millions of incarnates over the millennia. And consider the incredible advances made by the human psyche itself - as it has ceaselessly produced a series of ever-deepening cultural developments, as well as spiritual groups and leaders of ever-escalating renown. Is not the evolution and now full unfolding of Yeshua and Mother Mary prime examples of the progress that has and continues to be wrought on Earth - all thanks to the ever-perfecting power of the incarnational process?!"

Alas, Good Night

"These are the burning questions, all right," said I after a long silence, "but I think we have reached a point - with your permission, Mother Mary, and of course, Gabriel – where your combined energies are beginning to overcome the more limited resources available to we mere mortals."

Looking over at Magdalene, and getting her consent, I murmured: "Alas, I think our very human reserves are in need of rest and a good night's sleep. Please excuse us if we soon bid you 'goodnight.'"

"Besides, our fire is rapidly consuming our last sticks of wood. May its few remaining sparks serve to call our festivities – and most enlightening and fascinating conversation - to a close - as least for tonight."

"Yes, of course, I understand: well-taken," said Mother Mary. "But before taking the remaining issues to bed with us – let us thank Gabriel for joining us – and hope He will join us again soon."

"See what your presence has wrought – kind Sir - in just one evening! Perhaps you found us a bit bedraggled earlier tonight – but your presence has helped us to put things in perspective. No fear: we do labor on! Please know as well that we are ever receptive to both your sudden and planned appearances – and welcome whatever guidance You and the angelic realms are willing to spare us."

"And I thank you all," said Archangel Gabriel. "I greatly enjoy being in your company. So yes - I too will say 'goodnight' - for this has indeed been a very 'good night'. I – perhaps like each of you – am now feeling much more optimistic on your behalf. In fact, I am downright cheerful - about your individual and your combined abilities to not only survive but thrive as you live according to the 'Word of the Lord'. Thank you again. With blessings to you, each and all. For now, I bid you - adieu."

Assessing – All 'Round

The next night our conversation resumed, this time without the visible appearance of our wondrous Archangel. The twigs and leaves were just beginning to burn into the two logs of wood. We were each wrapped in a blanket. As I now recall, Magdalene was the first to speak.

"Picking up on last night's conversation, I pose the following issue: Assuming we personally are doing better today than yesterday, and presuming that many incarnates the world over – millions of us - are actually working effectively to achieve our best spiritual intentions, then how do we weigh, measure or account for whatever progress we may be making in helping to spiritualize the Earth?"

I noted that the number of incarnations - we each undoubtedly had gone through - have presumably helped a great deal as they also helped to make us more mature and effective in dealing with Earth's challenges. I also assumed – or rather guessed – that many, including the three of us, were each in the midst of incarnation number one thousand or perhaps twenty thousand. We have been here many times before - not in the same body and in the same circumstances - but surely our current incarnations are not our first (suggesting that Gabriel might clarify that for us – if He shows up again tonight).

Second, we three – like all beings – have presumably learned from our mistakes and been energized by our so-called successes or contributions, enabling us to be ever more effective with each successive reincarnation.

Third, I suggested we look at the nature of our trio: God's own Mother and a Master Soul, one of Its most recognized and blessed boosters par excellence, as well as Magdalene, one of Her most ardent followers, and me as one of It's devoted record keepers. Surely we must be doing something right by the very nature of the company we are keeping – which in turn may be strengthening the magnetic force that has and continues to bring us together as incarnates.

Picking up on a comment made earlier by Mother Mary, I also noted that it was indeed amazing that Magdalene and I, of the thousands if not millions of immortal Souls who were now incarnate on Earth and throughout the universe, are now actually companions to none other than Mother Mary Herself. We are also fortunate to be visited and encouraged periodically by Her Son, co-Master Soul and our Lord, Yeshua. And we have been assisted by Prime Source's esteemed messenger, Archangel Gabriel. Surely - I speculated, Raphael and Michael, plus Gabriel's many angelic assistants, are also ever waiting in the wings.

And last, it seemed that Mother Mary is, of course, our shining Light, and that Magdalene and I - despite our earned modesty - have contributed at least something to the creation of a loving and compassionate universe. Besides, the physical world may still be going through rough times – wars, plagues, bouts of egocentrism and even hatred - yet so many other parts and aspects are being responsive to the plight of the poor, actively seeking peace with their neighbors, and upholding the supportive role spirituality plays in millions of everyday lives.

Wonderful things have also happened, surely disasters have been avoided, and the basic goodness of many has been repeatedly revealed and celebrated. Therefore - despite our earlier doubts and misgivings - we have reason to be thankful for the progress we have made to date, confident that the new recruits will build upon it, and thankful for the progress - however incremental - that is clearly underway and leading in the direction charted by The Lord Itself.

Surprise, Surprise

"Well said, my dear friend," came the distinctive deep voice of Gabriel.

The three of us were suddenly wide-eyed.

"You're back!" said Magdalene.

"Fantastic," I exclaimed.

"Welcome, as always," said Mother Mary. "As you know too well, the first time you appeared to Me - lo those many years ago - it was both a surprise and of course an enormous blessing. Since then your appearances – although as sudden – including last night and now again today - are always wondrous and delightful."

"Sorry for the suddenness of My appearances. I am working on that. I just get so excited at the prospects of being with you again, that My actions seem to follow instantly from My wishes and intentions. I would prefer to warn you by flapping My alleged wings, but that is not possible since wings are not part of My or our equipment. I guess I hoped the extra heat you might feel as I approached you would serve as an alert. Hmm. In the future I promise to send you a gentle but definite warning signal of My imminent arrival – so My appearances do not startle you."

"At any rate," He said, pulling His earthly robes around Him, "I am delighted to be with this magnificent trio once again – a waking and inspired 'Trinity' if there ever was one."

"So," He continued. "I'll make this brief – just a few comments on all your self-assessments, if I may, and the impact of your respective incarnations are having on our beloved Earth. The heavenly realm salutes you – individually and as a trio. Please continue doing whatever now comes naturally to you. You are a joy to witness - since your contributions are continuous and very, very impactful."

"As to you, Mary of Magdala: please know your very presence enlightens everyone you meet. And John, the sensitivity of your actions – and your note-taking and writings – are so greatly appreciated by Our Lord that they are apt to be read and studied for generations to come. And Prime Source Itself sends love and dearest greetings to Mother Mary. Your presence, your aura, your dedication - continues to enlighten everyone and everything you meet and bless."

Ah - Tis Raphael

"And who am I to disagree," came another voice, one sparkling with joy and oozing with His characteristic good will. "It is Gabriel's sidekick, Raphael, the one who not only keeps Gabriel honest but who also seeks to amplify His ability to spread wisdom and joy."

"We know well of Mother Mary, of course," said Raphael, "as well as your blessed trio and the many contributions the three of you make every day - everywhere you go. I too feel blessed to see you all together - in person. Perhaps we have done something right – at least Gabriel continually harbors such ambitions," He teased with a giggle. "Either way, I am sure Gabriel agrees with Me: this is – for us - a fly-by supreme - enabling us to personally meet and greet those so blessed by Prime Source Itself. We especially thank your Souls and your inspired embodiments now serving on Earth. Blessings and love to you all - for everything you do."

Such august company was, of course, familiar to Mother Mary – although She smiled and bowed humbly in honor of the famed duo.

Magdalene and I, however, were again numbed into silence. We traded glances, of course, but frankly we were too awed to speak.

Magdalene Encounters Yeshua

Finally, Magdalene pursed her lips – which she often does before she is about to speak. "Wow - is this ever a surprise and absolutely incredible: Gabriel and Raphael – together. I never thought I would meet and interact with the two of you. But your appearance – together – in the fresh, so to speak – have given me the confidence to recall memories from some earlier incarnations."

"I now remember, for example, living in a community of Essenes during one of my earlier incarnations. We – at least our branch of the sect

- lived in Qumran, located on the northwestern shore of the Dead Sea, only a few miles north of Jerusalem."

"I was merely a child, one of very few," she continued, "since the group believed in celibacy. But my memories are clear - so distinctive and vivid was the Essene way of life."

"First, I remember the caves. We lived in one close to but beyond the base of the camp – that is until we came to live in a 'long' house - situated on flat land further down the road – one that accommodated many members of the community. There were also many other caves, much higher and further up the mountainside - seemingly impossible to reach. But word had it that such caves were used primarily to hide things – including scrolls inscribed with writings from the old days."

"We had a leader - known as 'The Righteous One' - a tall and saintly figure who led the group in daily talks and prayers, and who - together with a group of elders – supervised the spiritual customs of the group. They also organized our efforts to gather food, build cisterns to store our precious water, and raise defense if ever needed."

"Now here is the gist of my story. Years later, as a young woman no longer living in Qumran, I met someone at Jacob's Well in Samaria who also seemed to be a holy man. I thought He might be 'The Righteous One' of my childhood - so similar were the two in appearance and stature. Or I thought He might be a prophet of the Lord. He began by asking me for water, me a woman living in Samaria, supposedly or allegedly unclean – the kind of person with whom the traditional Jews had forbidden any communication."

"Yet this man – the one I met at the well - seemed holy at least other-worldly. He immediately mentioned my alleged sins – that is, my allegedly having taken a series of husbands – which I had - but serially over several incarnations."

"I was silent in the face of such comments for I did not know of His powers or authority. I sensed that He must have intuited an awareness of the number of honorable husbands I had loved over the course of many earlier incarnations. The one husband I had during that given incarnation had died many years ago - and I had taken up residence with an elderly friend of the family. We both lived in the same house but we were each solitary and celebrate."

"Our conversation did not last long, but before leaving me, this prophet, this heavenly figure – to my great surprise - revealed Himself to be 'the Messiah'. I had heard of such designations before - when much younger - but did not fully understand their implications - that is until I remembered listening as a child to an apparently holy person like Him speak at a large gathering of the Essenes. I wondered: could this man at the well be the same or at least the re-appearance of the 'Righteous One'?"

"So I asked Him about 'the Christ'. To my amazement, He simply said, 'I Am He'.

"At any rate, I met Him again years later, this time as part of a smaller group that had gathered in the home of my friend Martha. He spoke at length and answered questions - after which I was so taken by His words and countenance - and perhaps my memories - that I asked Him to accept me as His disciple."[39]

"In short, it is now clear to me that our Lord Yeshua was also 'The Righteous One' at the center of our life with the Essenes, the same holy one who spoke to me at Jacob's Well, and the same spiritual leader who accepted me as a disciple at the home of Martha."

"I wondered how many others had been so gradually drawn to Yeshua - and then like me - were finally inspired to acknowledge Him as 'the Christ'. So I am curious: what determined when and how such 'converts' as I came to serve Him and support His transformative mission? Was it the result of multiple contacts over several incarnations? Or was it a matter of meeting Him under varying circumstances – as was the case with me? And did anyone come to understand - who He was – immediately, during their first encounter?"

---

39 An expanded interpretation of the events outlined in John 4:16-24.

A Work in Progress

Magdalene rested for a moment then realized she had even more to say.

"Do you mind? I realize I'm taking up quite a bit of time today," She said, looking to Mother Mary and then me – and also getting an approving nod from us all.

"Go for it," I added, anxious for Magdalene to assert Herself, not waiting on anyone for approval. Having been raised within the Jewish tradition, however, She still tended to concede priority and dominance to any elder or adult male who was present.

We had talked often and earlier of her tendency to hesitate in asserting herself. So her so-called *coming-out* that day clearly signaled she had finally shed much of her earlier reluctance to claim equal status. She obviously was moving ever closer to being a living expression of her motto: 'Be a model unto to yourself - not hesitating to interact with others, contributing what you know to be is true.'"

She learned her lesson well - so well in fact - that for a while she went in the other extreme - as noted earlier - before finding a balance between humility in the presence of God yet confidently self-asserting with her incarnate affiliates.

Onward

And so Magdalene continued with her story. Moreover, she wanted us to know that she "simply loved being an Essene. There were only a few children – varying between six and nine at any one time - so the adults tended to indulge each of us. None of the parents were contemplatives or members of the leadership class, so we were given the run of the place – within limits of course."

"Like everyone else, we literally immersed ourselves every morning – walking through a small pool of water for spiritual cleansing – and praying daily after breakfast at a designated spot at the periphery of the adult gathering. We also studied every day with one of the elders, using varied writings from the books of the Jewish tradition and a series of so-called 'ancient texts'. And we were constantly urged – like all good Essenes - not to argue or get angry."

"Besides, we had to share – everything – for nothing was considered owned by any individual person. That was annoying, especially when I came to realize that my 'lucky' marble and the pottery I had slaved over was best gifted to someone who was ill or infirm. I even had nightmares at first – thinking my bedding could be taken from me in the middle of the night and given to another trainee."

"It now seems clear to me that more frequent my incarnations - and the longer each one lasted - the more I was offered the opportunity to interact with the man I came to honor as Our Lord. I came to realize my spiritual awakening was gradual but real. So I needed to trust the process - which of course unfolded first in listening to Yeshua at Qumran, then meeting Him at the well and then being accepted as His disciple while at the house of Martha."

The Underlying Unity

"As best I can now recall," Magdalene then observed: "You Mother Mary, and John, and I – as a three-some, have also been a work in process, parts of a larger unfolding that continues to this day. We came together – perhaps like all attractions and choices – not at once as a declarative and final announcement but by allowing it to evolve as our individual challenges emerged and brought us ever closer. Our development as individuals - and now as a group - has seemed to unfold serendipitously. Yet I also sense it resulted from the intentions we each set prior to incarnating, creating a mutual and cumulative field of energy that then attracted the approval and support and of Our Lord."

"I have come to realize - more fully with each transition in my own story - augmented greatly by this incarnation in particular - that my dialogue with the Lord has never been static. Rather it has always been ongoing and very dynamic. So too is the development of individual personality and our group cohesiveness. Both factors seemed to evolve in progressive stages - and surely never end or be complete - even though you and I, John, as pure incarnates will inevitably transit and emerge in new forms. That's another way of honoring Mother Mary as our sacred center and eternal point of continuity. Our continuous development – individually and as a Trinity - seems to be in sync with the never-ending dynamic of the universe."

"Like every other living organism, we as individuals and a group - seem to be are involved in a cosmic bio-spiritual unfolding: we each and all have - and will continue - to evolve as parts of a cosmic process – ever evolving from the simple and the singular to ever more inclusive - and extensive forms and expressions - of universal energy."

"And yes - I said and meant 'cosmic' – given the nature of our immortal Souls to create incarnations which live and serve within the flow of everyday earthly events. The combo of heavenly and the earthy, the infinite and the everyday – with all the transits that join, combine and blend the two realms - is so breathtaking a process that it can no longer be considered anything short of sacred and 'cosmic'!"

"That is our reality – a truism I now realize more fully every day," Magdalene declared. Then she stopped – her face a bit flushed. After taking a deep breath or two - she continued. "So my dear and esteemed friends: I now realize the essence of spirituality, what it is and how spiritual consciousness works and develops. I have never been so aware of how the everyday and the cosmic intertwine – and with such loving and I might say, 'exciting' implications for everyone in our universe."

Of the Essence

"I have never heard such wisdom articulated so elegantly," said Mother, "and, I must say, so succinctly. Such insights have been uttered - in traces and segments of sheer wisdom - throughout the ages but none have captured the essence of the process of *spiritual becoming* as well as you have, my dear Magdalene. Thanks be to God that you did not hold it to yourself any longer."

"And is it not fortunate that I have pen and pad in hand," said I. "I got it all – or at least almost all. We can fill in the missing words when we review it later. Congratulations! To think you hesitated – assuming Mother's divine status and authority, my 'alleged' superior male identity

- and in the presence of two Archangels. Surely your grand synthesis is the result of both your innate and acquired wisdom."

"Congratulations, indeed," I then added. "You may not realize it but I have already selected several of your insights for inclusion in a book I intend to publish one day, tentatively entitled, "The Essence of Spirituality". To borrow a phrase, that book is still unfolding - and thanks to you, it is getting closer and closer to completion."

"Oh my, oh my, oh my," was all Magdalene could say before being enclosed in a communal hug - outwardly offered by Her two traveling companions - and fervently supported by two smiling and delighted Archangels.

Me Too

And so it was that we soon resumed our lives – Magdalene and I walking hand and hand to the spot where our neighbor, Amos, his wife, Tamar and their family had gathered for dinner.

"Fish – delicious, succulent fish is the order of the day. Fresh from the lake, of course. Please raise your hand if you are interested?" said Amos, at which point he was pelted with bits of spent olive seeds.

"Okay, okay," he laughed, "as long as your verdict is unanimous".

It was primarily a family gathering that included a number of the couple's closest friends. We sat slightly to the side, with lingering memories of our earlier conversations leaving us more pensive than the festive atmosphere that surrounded us. In particular, I kept recalling Magdalene's comments about living in the Essene encampment in Qumran – to which I later confided, 'me too'. My father and I had also lived in Qumran during the time of Herod (72-4 BCE), his death occurring just around the time Mother Mary gave birth to the current incarnation of Yeshua.

At a young age I suffered from a very bad fall trying to reach one of the openings to a cave in a nearby mountain. I did not – unfortunately

- discover any pots filled with manuscripts nor uncover any sacred objects. That would be left to others much later on. [40]

I did, however, get what I considered wondrous opportunities to meet and then talk with the man called the 'Righteous One'. Everyone seemed to look to Him for advice and counsel - on matters both mundane and spiritual. The first time I met Him, all He said was: "Hello, John: how have you been?"

I said, "Rabbi – I do not recall ever having met you before."

Oh," He replied, "We have met many times during our frequent incarnations. For example, we met when you served as a scribe to several different prophets. And you will resume such duties soon - as you focus your pen on the activities of those known as Yeshua and Mother Mary."

Mother Mary leaned forward.

"That's it," She cried. "Besides sitting with me at the fireside chat with Gabriel so long ago, we worked together many times throughout history - as we incarnated together over the centuries in a broad range of roles – alternating with each incarnation as beggars, members of the royalty, tradesmen, scribes and even clergy."

"And I was there when you met Yeshua when He was the 'Righteous One' at Qumran. I served as the camp nurse, attended your wounds, and intent on befriending you for you seemed like 'a loner'. We did connect once but only briefly – that is until the 'Righteous One' told Me your Soul was needed elsewhere. Little did I realize at the time that the 'Righteous One' would later become my Blessed Son in a future incarnation. My-oh-my-oh-my. I can scarcely believe it: all these connections and continuities. Unbelievable."

---

40   Since known as *The Dead Sea Scrolls,* discovered in a cave in Qumran, Palestine by local citizens in 1947, and finally published as a text under the general editorship of James M. Robinson (San Francisco: Harper & Row, 1978).

"By the way," Mother Mary continued, "the Righteous One also told me - at that time - that I would soon be an integral part of a mixed three-some that would serve each other well into the future. We would each and all be reincarnated after the time of Herod – which of course turned out to be a most glorious time since it became the time when I gave birth to Yeshua as the Master Soul. Then much later, of course, you and Magdalene emerged as traveling companions, I was called by Prime Source to be the female aspect of the Master Soul during My Assumption back into Heaven, then choosing to return here only to have Yeshua ask you to be My guardian - at which time we left our dear Sanctuary and retraced our steps back to Palestine. Wow - and thanks be to Our Lord."

Shimmers of Love

Suddenly we were surrounded by a few additional voices – each clattering for recognition. Which voice belonged to who was not totally clear until the shimmer of animated outlines took definite form and we could clearly see the faces of several old friends.

"Such talk of our glorious work in Britannia and now your reunion in Palestine – had best include us in the circle of sharing," said one of the voices in a jaunty manner. "The others will speak in a moment but they agreed to allow me to join in your reveries first – bowing perhaps to my age and seniority and all that," said a deep voice crackling through the airwaves.

"Joseph, My Love," cried Mother Mary. "Be assured none of us – and certainly not I - would ever forget you or leave you out of either our remembrances or our thoughts of the future. How wonderful to hear your voice. When will you visit us – in person - and stay for a while?"

"Well," said Joseph, "I and many of us have been very busy at the Sanctuary. But in fact, we also have been discussing when and where we might connect with you again – perhaps joining the three of you there in Palestine and then bringing you-all back to Britannia."

"It has been too long. At any rate, we were alerted as soon as your recalls of so many wondrous events came through the airwaves. We dropped what we were doing to send you our kudos and thanks for celebrating so many of your - and our - adventures and connections."

"He also loves to talk," said Joseph of Arimathea. "He needs no excuse – and he is absolutely right when he tells You that any talk of any part of your combined missions automatically attracts his – and our - attention."

"Your sharing today certainly did spark our resolve to contact You and chat over the 'spiritual airwaves' - which also enables us to display our current and always charming faces," joked Nicodemus, "reminding you, please, to never forget us as we never forget and always appreciate you. The old days were tough in many ways, especially for you, Mother Mary and Lord Yeshua – yet they were also glorious days sparked with spiritual break-throughs galore, all of it elevating the role love and compassion continues to play in the interactions at the Sanctuary - and we sense, around the world."

"In short," Joseph said, "life is good - and progress here is unabated. We have extended the roof of the Sanctuary, opened a new 'soup' kitchen for itinerants, and added many newcomers to our community - including a few weddings and the birth of many babies."

"Yet we love you and just wanted to seize on the opportunity to tell each and all that we hold you in the highest and most loving regard."

"And We so appreciate your contacting us," Mother Mary answered as She kissed the outlined faces of Her husband and dear friends. "Be assured you are not forgotten or loved any the less than when we last show-ered our love on you in person. If anything, you have made us aware of how intensely we miss you. Yes, looking around me – I see and hear the others joining with Me with a chorus of 'yeses' - signaling our mutual desire to reunite with you in person very soon. Consider such a reunion to be on our calendar. Pick your best days or weeks and preferred meeting places and we will do the same. Our reunion – in person, so to speak, is going to happen!"

Cheers were then heard coming from both sides of the spiritual airwave.

Getting Closer

As we continued our journey - heading slowly toward Jerusalem - we made a series of mini stops at each of the villages we encountered, situated as they were along a fertile valley on or near the Jordan River. Everywhere we went we ate well and were treated with both interest and delight. Such small towns apparently did not get many visitors so they tended to appreciate a spark of newness in their midst. Yet most travelers - like us – tended not to stay long – ever anxious to make their way further south to the sacred city itself.

Ah, Jerusalem – the city of epoch events, the home of the Jewish Temple, the city Yeshua entered triumphantly so many years ago - then inaugurating what has come to be known as Palm Sunday.

It was the same Jerusalem in which I connected with My Lord in an additional way. I still recall the details of my choosing to form an extension of my incarnation and briefly became a soldier serving in the Roman Army. An epic event was about to unfold and I also wanted to experience it from an alternate point of view.

I watched Yeshua enter the Mount of Olives on a donkey, and then followed along His path into the city. I was dressed in the uniform of a Roman officer and only later changed back into the more modest clothing of an apostle - before then joining Yeshua, Mother Mary and Magdalene on the hill overlooking the subsequent display of lights and lasers.[41]

I also recall serving Yeshua much earlier and then throughout His mission in Palestine. For example, I initially responded to His call - along with my bother James - as well as Simon-Peter and his brother Andrew. It was the time when Yeshua urged us to also become 'fishers of men' as we fished along the shores of Galilee.[42]

---

41   See Chapter I, Yeshua Opens the Conference, especially the chapter labelled 'Setting the Record Straight'.

42   Mark 1: 16-20

I made notes of all these encounters immediately and later recorded them in full in my own gospel and subsequent letters. I was pleased to discover that some of them also found their way into the testimonies of Mark, Matthew and Luke.

Later, the famed painting of the so-called 'Last Supper' by Leonardo da Vinci would depict me embracing our Lord – just as I was becoming ever more aware of His majesty, a Master Soul and the incarnation of the loving masculine energies of Prime Source Itself. Until then, I – like the others – revered Him for His goodness, His insights and His healing powers. But to realize that we had been interacting personally with the now perpetual incarnation of the Divine Soul, still staggers me and often sends me into a state of deep, deep thanksgiving and reverence.

Of course, it is always worth remembering the rest of the story - especially the alleged passion, after which Yeshua, Mother Mary, Magdalene and I set out for the western coast of Palestine, gained access to the Mediterranean and thereupon completed our journey through Europa - finally encamping at Glastonbury, Britannia.

To realize – after so many years – that we were now within days or weeks of reentering the Jerusalem was almost overwhelming. Freed from the hassles of old, and apparently unbeknownst to the current Temple officials – we were about to come full circle and complete another phase of our individual and combined missions.

Sarah

Poignant events continued to unfold – seemingly everyday - as we continued our trek toward Jerusalem. One day, for example, while we were getting ready to leave Scythopolis, Amos's young daughter – the one who greeted us with so many questions and observations when we arrived – said she wanted to come with us.

Don't you think you ought to discuss such a decision with your Father and Mother, we advised.

"Oh, they know how I feel," she replied.

"Would you mind if we checked with them as well?"

"You really don't have to – but I think you will do so anyway," She said with an impish smile.

Amos and Naomi did know of their daughter's wish to travel with us. They reasoned it was in part determined by her fascination with the prospects of seeing Jerusalem, and in larger part with her fascination with Yeshua.

"You are good and caring parents," is what she said, "but sooner or later I must leave your side and seek my own fortune. What could be better than to travel now - to Jerusalem – and with Yeshua and Mother Mary?"

Obviously a word or two from Yeshua was needed – if Sarah's parents were not to be faced with a rebellious, defiant or sullen child.

"Word has it that you would like to travel with us," is all Yeshua said one day as He spotted Sarah.

"Oh yes!" she responded. "I am sorry I did not discuss it with you first but I guessed you might side with my parents and that would be that. Sorry."

"We are greatly honored," said Yeshua. "It is not very often a young woman so full of promise chooses to travel through the arid hills and deserts of Samaria, face the possibility of one hardship after another and leave their parents, friends and a good life behind – all to walk the great distance to Jerusalem."

"Sounds adventurous," is all Sarah would say.

"Well, I have what may sound like a better proposal, a combination of things you might prefer. And why would I do that? Remember, you are still young and have your schooling to complete. And if your Father and Mother are successful, you will soon have a real school established right here in your village. Besides, your parents would miss you terribly. You still have much to do here – responsibilities that could and will greatly help your parents, your community – and all your friends who are likely to be part of the new school."

"For example, who but you - is better able or motivated - to attract her friends to sign up for the school? And in the meantime, until it is finished, you can continue to help your Father and Mother with their business and thus learn a trade from such an innovative and well-known professionals. I have worked with both your parents and believe me, there is no better carpenter than your Father or wiser business person than your Mother. If I were your age again – your parents would be the ones I would yearn to be with and learn from."

"And - you may be taking their hugs and fine meals for granted. Just think of yourself as doing without such treasures – and on a daily basis; I assure you – in comparison - you would soon feel very lonely on the long road to Jerusalem, have little to eat and still have to use a great deal of energy to avoid illness and exhaustion."

"There is also something personal I need you to do for me," said Yeshua. That comment immediately got Sarah's full attention. "I need for you to provide leadership to the young people of the village: not only extolling the virtues of schooling but also in organizing all kinds of activities. Between you, your Mother and the other mothers of the village, you can teach the young girls how to sew and knit, make blankets and pillows, care for the animals and learn how to keep the books on the new business adventures you wish to start."

"As for the boys, they also need to learn new stills - including carpentry from you and your Father. Besides, I know for a fact that they would love to learn how to kick the ball into the net as forcefully and efficiently as you."

"Surely the others parents - mothers and fathers - will also need to be organized – and learn how to teach their own children - both the boys and the girls - what they know about sports, home care, working with animals and their own trades. I also know in your heart that you also wish to care for the orphans - as your Mother cares for you. In summary, you are of age and have the talent to become – especially in My absence - a leader of both the youth and the adults of this village. It is a most important assignment - and if you accept it, your parents will be greatly impressed - and Mother Mary and I would be eternally grateful."

"Besides, I will not be gone very long. In fact, I foresee our getting together again reasonably soon – if for no other reason than for you to give me a progress report on this very important assignment. Would you like that?"

"So I will see you again – and as you say - 'reasonably soon'?"

"Yes – and it will be fine quality time, one-to-one, one leader – namely you - telling another leader how much her new assignment is contributing to her own growth as well as the development of her entire community."

"Hmmm. I never thought of such possibilities. Can we shake on it – the way my Father does with his workers?"

"I will not only seal our agreement with a handshake. I also propose we also seal it - with a hug."

"Wow," said Sarah. "Wow."

Always Returning

Having completed one more negotiation, Yeshua excused Himself after telling Sarah - and all of us - that He needed to respond to an urgent call to assist someone in some other portion of the cosmos. It made us realize, ever more fully, of the untold number – perhaps millions - of aspects to His mission. We always assumed He would inevitably return to His beloved Palestine – and of course, Jerusalem – especially now that we were geographically so close to His sacred city.

And we sensed – actually assumed – that when He did return it would invariably be preceded by a long and deep humming sound, followed by a quickening of the air, then the inescapable feeling that time stood still. And suddenly we would know He was likely to reappear in the fresh, ebullient as ever, speaking as if finishing a thought in mid-sentence, wondering what was for dinner or breakfast. With each word He would advance upon us with wide open arms, first hugging His Mother, then each of us. Invariably, He would said: "It is so good to be alive - and be among those who are so outrageously blessed."

Inevitable

We traveled some ten miles today – first over a forested area, then down some very steep hills onto long stretches of what seemed like barren land. We stopped finally when we reentered a treed area near a small stream. The horse was tired and we were demonstrably weary. We pitched a tent and quickly found ourselves reaching for our blankets as temperatures dropped rapidly with the coming of nightfall.

I slept soundly for what seemed like hours - only to awaken suddenly to a bright sky illuminated by a full moon. I sat up – mesmerized by another of God's displays of natural beauty. Some stars could be seen that were closer to the horizons but overhead it was all moonlight in its full splendor.

The fire we built earlier was still glowing so I rustled out of my covers, grabbed some more firewood and stoked the fire to full blaze. Wrapped in a blanket I began to hum a song – one that sounded like remnants from a lullaby my Mother used to sing. I almost dozed off – until I heard Magdalene's voice.

"Hey: be careful or you will lose your balance and push me over."

Turning, I saw Magdalene sitting very close to me, wrapped in a blanket of her own.

"Oh, I'm sorry – I did not realize you were here."

"Actually your bumping felt good," she said with a smile and then a soft giggle.

"Yes," I shyly agreed. "In addition to bumping you I guess I could now lean into you – ever so gently, of course."

Linked at the shoulders, we gravitated toward each other. Gradually I noticed a half - then three-quarters of a face - coming into view, then definitely sensing the presence of increased warmth and a sweet aroma. Then - a definite fragrance ...and I found myself joining with the soft lips of my companion.

I placed my arm on her back - and with the slightest of shuffling – we were now face to face, kissing and hugging. I stroked her hair, gently placed one hand behind her neck, and was soon lost in an embrace I had once only dreamed of.

"Oh my," we both said in unison. Rubbing noses, we laughed...then traded a quick look – before easing into a series of longer and fuller embraces.

And so we snuggled in each other's arms - as I nibbled at her neck, blowing soft puffs of warm air around her ears, humming as I went, moaning gently as she returned the joy of being loved.

"Must be the full moon," I mused. Then surrendering to impulse, I sat up fully and facing Magdalene confessed that I had long imagined kissing her but never knew how to begin – trust my impulses – and risk rejection.

"Oh, you goose," said Maggie. "I too have been in knots - not knowing how to express how I felt, feeling the same hesitation and perhaps for the same reasons as you."

She then held my face, kissed me again. Blowing softly into my ear, she whispered: "Then let us always give thanks to the moon, the glow of the fire, and to the deep inner light that has brought us together."

Still Our Secret

"The two of you seem very chipper today," is all Mother Mary said the next morning. "Very chipper indeed."

"It is a fine day," said Magdalene.

"Very fine, indeed," I agreed.

Ever the taskmaster, Mother Mary urged us to feed and water the horse and get ready to face another day on the road.

"There are some hills ahead but nothing we can't handle," She said. "And thanks to something strange in the air – a very good 'strange something' mind you. I sense we have very good reason to step forward this morning with extra vigor."

Then She added: "Whenever emotions are shared, and good energy is released, it inevitably signals that good times - and loving times - are ahead."

Magdalene and I glanced at each other. Tilting then shaking our heads, we smiled. If Mother Mary could heal others, foresee events, dissolve with the wind and time-travel as well and return as if nothing happened, then it was no wonder She knew about everything that transpired around our campfire.

Sooner or later we were bound to go public. For now, however, it felt extra good to recall and fantasize, to daydream wondrous events, to act as if nobody in the whole world had ever felt the way we did. Mother Mary – and perhaps the entire angelic kingdom - knew. Yet by acting like it was our secret alone, a special something known only to the two of us, well - that made it feel extra special.

Ever the Twin Goals

And so it was that we made our way every closer to Jerusalem. We passed the town of Shechel, then Shiloh and finally entered Bethel. Still we had at least another day's journey in front of us. That evening, Mother Mary called a meeting – not just to talk but this time to plan.

"We have been edging closer and closer to Jerusalem – a destination that has not only returned us to the northern lands or Kingdoms of Zebulun and Galilee, but to the midlands and geographic areas of Manaseh and Samaria as well, and now down through the tribal areas of Ephaim and Benjamin and the lands of Judah."

"Frankly I never thought we would get this far so fast." She continued while looking over at me and smiling. "I hoped we would but so many unpredictable things have fascinated and thus diverted us en route that I slowly surrendered My earlier 'compulsion' to push on no matter what. In fact, I came to think we were meant to linger if not stay longer with some of the groups we met along the way."

"Still we always packed our things and headed to the road that led further south – as if some hidden map had also been burnished in our psyches and been etched into our feet and sandals. I don't recall ever discussing our route; we seemed always to take it for granted that each step would bring us closer to our destination."

"I - for one - always sensed that Yeshua - as usual - was also ever at our side – even returning personally several times along the way – approving and supporting what we were doing and where we were headed – nudging us onto to the next point of our rendezvous - enabling - even motivating - us to proceed as we realized our individual and combined destinies."

"Now we can almost hear the chants offered at the Temple, see the curved passageways of Jerusalem with all its shops and crowds of people, anticipating the many places where we once toiled and prayed, reaffirming our identities as devotees of our Lord God - Prime Source."

What We've Accomplished

Magdalene and I realized it was time to ask ourselves: What is it – precisely – do we wish to accomplish by returning to Jerusalem? What do we to hope to find? Who are we intended to meet and perhaps help? Is this where we will settle? Or are we intended to take the lessons of Jerusalem – past and those about to unfold – and continue to trek the land in the hope of fulfilling some other mission we outlined earlier in our respective pre-incarnation contracts?"

"I sense we may never stop posing and trying to answer such questions," I offered. "Often we are so tired by end of day and find ourselves without the energy needed to tackle and resolve such essential issues."

"At other times, we understandably got lost in the vivid interactions of the day or in any one of our millions of unforgettable experiences," Magdalene added. "Perhaps one of Yeshua's fly-bys - and all the involvements His presence generates – will help us to gain the clarity we seek. We have learned to take the future so for granted that we seemed to assume whatever we did on a given day was exactly what we were supposed to do, conceding that wherever we landed by day's end was exactly where we were intended to be."

"In other words," I continued, "if we wanted to make a contribution, or learn a particular lesson or experience something in depth, then we simply assured ourselves that we were in the midst of achieving what we needed to do. Actually reaching Jerusalem is still an illusion, a desire – still miles away in both geographic and psychological terms. But now we are on the cusp of achieving our supposed goal. There is no more time for simply 'assuming' or taking things for granted. We have reached the outskirts of our destination!"

"Let's face it," said Magdalene. "We have been and still are with Mother Mary, by golly, the Mother of the Blessed Yeshua and Herself a Master Soul. How could we possibly go astray? How could we – on any given day – especially today - be anyway else than where we were meant to be, doing anything other than what was intended?"

"God the Father has been on our side because Mother Mary has literally been at our side. You and I, John, have contributed our unique intentions and actions, which in turn hopefully supported and added to Mother Mary's spiritual presence. At a minimum – and fortunately - we learned how to allow our identities and commitments to be informed by - and flow with - Her divine energy."

"There is no resisting a divine magnet – which means we have been pushed and pulled by some irresistible force. In addition to the involvements of each day – yet seemingly supported by each of them - we have been inexorably drawn to achieving our goal, to the place and setting we could remember and identify, whose existence has always beckoned to us, urging us ever forward – drawing us ever closer to fulfilling our commitment to complete the journey – and attain both inner and outer peace."

Jerusalem and Our Souls

Mother Mary listened intently to our exchange and then offered the following: "You speak of the same kind of energy that attracted me to the Temple as a child, the same one that then sustained Me all those years until I came of age and met Joseph," She mused.

"Our betrothal also unfolded as if pre-planned - including the difficulties my poor Joseph experienced in trying to understand how and why God the Father had sent an Archangel – can you imagine – an Archangel who entered physical space to bring Me the news that I was – in a flash – pregnant with the Son of God, not just a male child but a male incarnation of the Lord Himself, a son by the name of Yeshua!"

"Talk about being 'drawn' into a situation that seemed as impossible as it did right and ordained. I experienced shock and trepidation but never any resistance. I dearly wanted what I was obviously preordained to create and deliver – all at the behest of God Itself. Goodness. I am still awed into both tears and thanksgiving by the seeming inevitability of it all."

"So," She continued. "I too know - all too well - what it is like to be drawn by the eternal, balancing it - en route - with the need to flow with the circumstances presented each and every day. Thus I have always said *yes* to the requests, the openings, the necessities and the impulses of the day, sometimes with hesitation and reluctance - but always 'yes'. Always I have agreed whole-heartedly to accept and work at whatever as it is presented, offered, gifted - even demanded. Once something unfolded, however, I was not sure if it developed because I wished and worked for it, and or was simply gifted; which happening was the result of my personal decision, which was ordained and which was the result of both forces. They seemed inseparable and interchangeable."

"As it often turned out that even so-called difficulties were often disguised as blessings, and vice versa. Our stories seem to evolve as a result of the constant interplay between personal decision-making and simply trusting or flowing with the energies presented. No matter what happens, there is ample reason to both affirm our belief in ourselves as well as our abiding trust in The Lord."

"Oh my – as Prime Source is My witness: I do so love My life and being granted the opportunity – and the wherewithal – to serve one more time, in one more place, in ever deepening sets of circumstances, with and for this world's continual flow of dedicated and soulful volunteers."

She sighed deeply – looked about Her - and then went on. "So it is that Jerusalem looms before us once again. Our full embrace of this goal still awaits us, as does the fulfillment of whatever tasks we may still need to complete once we enter the city. Giving daily assistance to others has been and still is our everlasting duty and aspiration, seemingly the Lord's way of insuring we've earned the right to reclaim our heritage in Jerusalem as we simultaneously realize the fullness of our intended agendas."

"Thank God we are together," said Magdalene. "Being part of such a wondrous trio – occasionally a glorious quartet, and recently a sextet – makes the immediate seem so much more poignant, the point that enables us to advance if not fulfill a major portion of our individual and group goals."

"Jerusalem does indeed beckon," said I. "I dare say we are ready. We certainly are willing. And surely the road before us is paved with God's good will and guidance - for us as well everyone who supports our quest."

Then a Miracle

As we approached ever closer, word reached us that a man – who lived nearby and was known as Lazarus - was extremely ill. His sisters, Martha and Mary, had spread word of his illness in hope that Yeshua would appear and somehow save their brother.

Unfortunately, Yeshua was away – but a man passing in a caravan shouted that he met Him on the trail and that He had a message for us: "We must go to Bethany first. Please meet Me there." And so we detoured - only slightly but still it once again delayed us from completing our intended rendezvous with Jerusalem.

A large crowd had gathered to mourn at the gravesite. Lazarus had apparently died while we were en route. Yeshua appeared suddenly soon after us. Martha, bereaved - rushed to Yeshua's side. Through her tears she reproached Him for being late – for she believed Yeshua had power to save her brother. "Had you been here," She said, "he would not have died."

Yeshua took Martha in his arms – and whispered: "Please hear and believe me: Lazarus, will arise again - here and now."

He asked: "Where have you laid him?"

Yeshua went to the cave where Lazarus had been placed - then ordered the stone that blocked entrance to be removed. Martha cried out, fearing the deterioration of the body. Yet Yeshua reminded Her, saying, "Did I not tell you that if you believed, you would see the glory of God?"

It was then the Yeshua called out to Lazarus.

"Come forth, dear Lazarus."

And the allegedly dead man, covered in strips of cloth, staggered to the outer entrance of the cave.

Yeshua said only: "Unbind him and let him go in peace." [43]

To witness the transformation of Lazarus was startling enough. For the average villager to attribute if not concede such powers to a stranger,

---

43   A modified version of the Gospel According to John 11: 1- 44.

however - no matter how great His alleged reputation - was to recognize what was both blasphemous and absolutely impossible.

The Long History of Miracles

In the meantime, Yeshua's words echoed throughout the square - and the taunts were silenced.

Then the roar: "Did you see that? Do my eyes deceive me? Look away children! Is this a sign of God or the devil? Never did I think I would witness such a thing. Thanks be to God and all the angels in heaven. Calling a man back from the dead! Is it possible? Knowing about Yeshua: we have learned not to doubt his capacities. But this - seeing it unfold before our eyes – is breath-taking."

Mother Mary merely smiled – then quickly said: "Oh, my Son – how proud I am of You...and.... how happy I am for Lazarus and his family."

I placed my arm around Mother Mary, as did Magdalene – and we walked slowly toward the home of Martha and Mary.

Miracles break the boundaries of nature; it is no wonder they seem so impossible. Even if you believe in the strength and will of the Almighty, miraculous events always seem impossible – and are impossible until a supreme force temporarily reorders things, breaks the boundaries of the predictable, splices in a bit of the improbable - and then transforms the ordinary with a bit of untrammeled spirituality.

The episode made me think of all the times we incarnates have been dazzled by such extraordinary events. What did the people think who were saved by the parting of the Red Sea as they escaped captivity in Egypt? What did Elijah say and do in order to revive the widow's dead son? How did the prophets of old bring about changes they wrought in the ordinary stream of events? Perhaps such workings were considered everyday happenings by the time Moses got to the Burning Bush, or when fresh water and manna arrived as if from heaven as many trudged through the Sinai desert.

What did the likes of Abraham and Jacob think when they were each confronted by the presence and direct vision of the Holy God? Surely Sarah was stunned by the sudden awakening of her fertility – as was Isaac who had been waiting all those years to incarnate as Her son.

And think of all the Israelites who had longed for entry into the Promised Land only to have their ancestors witness the Walls of Jericho come tumbling down. And how did the followers of the likes of Isaiah, Ezekiel and Daniel react when such prophets reported having a direct vision of God?

And was it later – or earlier – that Daniel and his compatriots were saved from the furnace, then starvation and then even the jaws of a lion. Who can forget the description in Kings 2 of Elisha's wild and wonderful set of healings and transformations – acts not only duplicated but expanded by Yeshua's frequent outpourings of love and forgiveness.

Recall as well the combined healings, exorcisms, transformations and feedings that Yeshua wrought during what the world considered the three most public years of His ministry. Among the most remarkable of Yeshua's interventions during those times - as later reported in the New Testament - included the feedings of the thousands with only a few loaves of bread; inaugurating the blessings and ritual of *The Last Supper* [44]; healing the man born blind; walking on and calming the waters during a storm on the Sea of Galilee; and creating a series of healings at the Plain of Gennesaret for any who managed to touch the hem of His cloak. [45]

I - a mere incarnated but immoral Soul - presented as I was in a mere mortal frame, initially denied what I had witnessed as flukes of nature or mere coincidences as I watched Yeshua transform people and events en route to and during His founding of the Sanctuary in Britannia. No one – not even Yeshua and Mother Mary could defy the laws of nature - or so I thought! Besides, so-called miraculous events could never occur in

---

44 Really the 'First or Next to Last Supper', given the fact that Yeshua had dinner with the Apostles once they were reassembled in Emmaus following the so-called 'Crucifixion'.

45 Mark 6:53–56

response to mere gentle commands and gestures, no matter how gifted and befriended by God.

Slowly, however, I absorbed the reality of the allegedly impossible and finally admitted the glory of the transformations wrought by Yeshua and Mary. Slowly but irrevocably I moved from denying and doubting their other-worldly powers, to gradually considering the possibility that something miraculous had happened - to finally, finally, *finally* affirming the reality of the obvious. Thereafter, although amazed if not stunned, I became unabashedly teary-eyed and ever so thankful as I witnessed one more display of their individual and combined powers to convert the everyday and the predictable into revelations of the miraculous energy of heaven.

Taking a Stand

Alas, we had come so close to the walls of Jerusalem that it was time to sell the horse and the caravan, and exchange it for a smaller but stout donkey. We no longer needed to traverse long distances but now anticipated negotiating the narrow and winding lanes and alleys of a large city. Luckily - soon thereafter - we were able to hitch a ride with a merchant's caravan for the last several miles, linking our new companion to one of the wagons by day and taking advantage of the communal feeding of both man and beast at night.

Such evening meals usually consisted of sharing whatever folks were willing to bring to the common table. The conversation stirred one night to religious and spiritual themes when someone shouted: 'The only way to gain God's favor and access to heaven is to abide faithfully to all the commandments, all the rituals, all the restrictions and all the advisory findings issued by the Rabbis'.

'Following the letter of the law was crucial,' said the man in the large hat and wraparound cloak, 'and that includes abiding by and fulfilling all the details. If you err, if you withhold even one hundredth of one percent, God will grumble, take offense and punish you – in essence saying to Himself: 'what kind of servant is this that does not serve his God faithfully and totally?'

'Well, many have tried to disobey God and look what has happened. You know it already: illness, starvation, disobedience by a wife or child, failure in business, a string of bad luck, loss of reputation. Who needs any of it? The ancients were right: the straight, the narrow, keeping you head down, being absolutely obedient – and even making sure you don't enjoy life too much. It is the only way.'

Some grumbled in agreement. There was one person in tattered clothes and a long beard who responded: 'What do you know? You are always playing mister smarty-pants. Ppp-leease, give it a break. You think you know everything. Humility is what is called for - since a new voice has arisen. *Bah* on your strict abeyance to silly laws and outmoded practices. Try getting some sleep already and maybe you will wake up feeling a bit more cheerful and optimistic. Either way, please stop telling us how to believe and behave – that is until your life is filled with joy and goodness. I continue to cry out for the true God who is kind and just - and whose sandals I am not worthy to wear.'

'That is an unfair and a rotten thing to say,' the man in the cloak said to the bearded one. 'If you go to hell, don't blame me.'

A few others chimed in – with equally loud and accusatory language. A chorus of voices was dominated by 'you this' and 'you that' - such that even the early sleepers were awakened and moved to sit up straight. Startled, they shook their heads, looked around, shook off their blankets and were seemingly ready to enter the flay. The theme of religion – as always - had an energizing effect on everyone within earshot.

"How about just doing your best to be a good person, a person who respects and even loves others, goes out of their way to help both friends, foes and neighbors alike, is cheerful in word and action, and as a result is beloved by all they encounter," said Magdalene suddenly, "the kind of person who is not swayed by the formalities of one's specific code or ritual but by the depth of their belief in and honoring of God, the kind of person who actively displays the kind of behavior that reflects God's love and compassion."

Well that really stirred things up. 'Believe in the code of your parents,' said one. 'Your actions and rituals ought to follow the laws set down by the priests whose beliefs and actions mirror their holy status at the Temple,' said another.

'Besides,' said a third, 'what does a beggar and a woman know? By my account - and that of my elders – both types know less than nothing!'

Aha!

"I am not only of this country," said a man in a turban and flowing robes, "but have also lived the world over. Where God the Almighty is concerned, I know nothing that justifies having only one set of laws and practices for all peoples. I hear of the ways of the Romans and their preference for many gods is still rampant – here and in many other countries. I also hear of an emerging offshoot to Judaism – followers of a man reportedly crucified because he threatened the religious and political authorities. I also know there is but one law that is prescribed and is dominant here – yet there are many other practices that are dominant elsewhere - as in the lands to the East, and the far West and the many territories where those from Palestine have yet to venture."

'You speak like a heretic. Be careful you don't end up like the Jewish heretic you refer to,' came the reply and the murmurs of many.

"Is not that the problem," said Mother Mary, walking over to Magdalene's side, and standing next to the man in the turban. "If a belief does not help to create love and compassion, then it could hardly come from God. If hatred and punishment for differing views is what a given belief system upholds, if it supports practices that honors or tolerates hatred, selfishness, greed and the dominance of whoever proves to be physically and militarily the strongest, then it can in no way be honored as coming from the true and loving God."

'You madam, your female friend, and the bearded one over there,' said one man in response, 'speak like the one who was justifiably crucified. Be careful, you are asking for trouble.'

Then the caravan leader added: 'Abiding to a creed of love will get you in trouble in this very troubled times. How did you come to join us anyway? Perhaps we should begin screening whoever we pick up on these roads. As the leader and owner of this group of wagons, I now ask each of you to leave us. We will have no blasphemers in this caravan.'

"We will claim our donkey in the morning," said I.

"No: you will claim it now," said the caravan leader.

Mother Mary and I signaled to the man reportedly from the East. He nodded. Then he and the other bearded one followed us out.

Not surprising, the supposed stranger with the turban and long robes turned out to be none other than Yeshua Himself.

And the strong voice coming from the man in tattered clothing proved to be John the Baptist – back for a fine-tuning with his beloved leader and extended family.

A New Day has Dawned

The scent of honey was in his hair – tangled, long, halfway down his back, the word 'repent' scrawled on his arm from repeated applications of grape juice. Yeshua hugged him – thanked him for coming – knowing his spirit could not long stay secluded in the mountain wilderness.

"Oh, my Lord, I hope I did not overstep my bounds. It is very difficult for me to stay quiet in the face of such nonsense. That big guy and the caravan leader: spewing all that old stuff extolling power, authority and 'the law' just as you, Mother and Mary Magdalene were offering the crowd your vision of love and compassion. Why can't most believe that the everyday person, freed from all formalistic and ritualistic restrictions, would be transformed if they simply practiced universal love and the inclusion of all – especially the ill, the downtrodden and the poor."

"Oh that we could wash their Souls of their embitterment and sense of entitlement," he added, "maybe even reawakening the counsel of your servant Isaiah who spoke of the wrath that these silly people unknowingly invite with their demeaning and superior attitude."

"My dear friend," said Yeshua, putting his arm around his old friend and compatriot. "Despite the physical death of your Soul's most recent incarnation you obviously continue to play such a wondrous role in getting people to refocus on the simple, the basic, the fundamental aspects of love and compassion – shorn of all the inequities of power, the confusions wrought by rusty theologians and the nit-picking of those whose attitudes are blatantly self-serving."

"And I thank you for continuing to be an advocate for the gospel of love. As you know, there were many times in the days of the old - as reflected in so many ancient testaments - where the hope of cleansing the world of over-wrought egos was paramount, where disregard for the counsel of God – even by the keepers of the Temple - was rightly chastised by the prophets."

"But a new day has indeed dawned," Yeshua continued, "when – as you note - the negative and protective focus of the old sectarians needs to be replaced by a new and positive *universal* – forged by a primary focus on love and compassion, one that is all-inclusive and instantly open to all."

"The old assumption," He continued, "that God would judge us has given way to a call for self-assessment - a self-monitoring of one's words and actions in terms of the eternal virtues of love and compassion. No longer do we assign the status and empowerments of the Soul to the priests and theologians. Rather - each person, each Soul - is asked to reclaim their direct link to Prime Source, thus proclaiming their personal responsibility to create love – unhampered by the rules and regulations imposed by any self-appointed and entitled class of would-be superiors."

Clarifications

"So," said Yeshua turning to the crowd that had gathered. "There have been a series of reaffirmations and upgrades to God's universal gospel. Prime Source is again requesting that we all uplift the quality of our intentions - and our actions – by applying the standards of love and compassion to everything we think, say and do. And Our Lord is again encouraging everyone to jettison the outmoded thoughts of a supposedly avenging God, the threat of hell and the fear of alleged damnation."

"The affirmations of *Love, Giving Thanks and Rejoicing* are now exalted – totally replacing any of the vestiges of the old negative emphases on *Fear, Worry and Repent.*"

"This is indeed a new era," said Yeshua, "one in which we extoll the sacred process of incarnation by which a beloved Soul chooses to become embodied in the physical realm and thereby work to enhance the spiritual evolution of the everyday material world."

"Each immortal Soul, by infusing itself into the difficulties and dilemmas of this physical domain, partakes in several opportunities: first, to love everyone and thereby accept and uplift all who have incarnated in the physical realm; second, to further the development its own potential as an incarnate Soul as they learn to love ever more fully and extensively; third, to so demonstrate their capacity to serve as a vital cell in the Living and Universal Organism of God; and last, through their actions, help this Earth and all the arenas of the physical domain become more like Heaven itself."

"Wow," gulped John the Baptist. "If I hear You correctly: all of us - upon the mortal demise of our latest incarnate forms, have the opportunity to re-incarnate again and again, thereby making a series of contributions to the integrity of our Souls while simultaneously enhancing the fate of the earthly domain. At the Soul level, I sense I already know that. But as an incarnate, I constantly tend to forget it as my spiritual reality."

"And, if I hear you correctly, in my next incarnation, I can again choose to be some variation on my old wild and wooly self, again crying out in the wilderness, helping people to be as authentic as You, My Lord. If so, I intend to continue helping others overcome their fascinations with religiosity, judgment, condemnations and the fear of hell – and simply learn to relax, and be the blessed Souls they already are - and become active ambassadors of love and trusting in The Lord."

"I can hardly wait for your next incarnation," said Yeshua with a hardy laugh. "I can hear the thunder now - you insisting – with your ever-stronger voice – that folks listen to their inner Souls, get moving and thus realize and become the fullness of their potential."

"Could be, my Lord, could be," said the Baptist - displaying his unique blend of hefty and back-slapping laughter.

"Just as long as I get to spend most of my time outdoors!" he added. "And surely it will make my work easier if I know I will again be entrusted to speak on Your behalf and thus continue to be a herald for the Lord."

From Religion to Spirituality

"While we are at it," said John the Baptist, ever open to learn more from Yeshua. "Earlier I argued against the corruption of many priests, their tendency to judge others by strict rules they never applied to themselves, and their very narrow interpretations of, for example, the Sabbath – where they often preferred the formalities of their own man-made prohibitions while ignoring others who simply delighted in placing primary emphasis on love and being compassionate – whatever the day, of the week or month."

"Was I wrong in doing so?" John the Baptist asked of Yeshua.

"Yes you were," shouted many from the crowd.

"No," said Yeshua immediately, "you were not wrong. When I refer to the continued evolution of spirituality I mean it must evolve away from the formalisms you decried - as adopted by many, many different cultural religions – to a more open and loving way of thinking and behaving, to where the essential standards of love and compassion are never compromised even if in conflict with man-made religious rulings and traditions."

"All formalities," He continued must be reinterpreted in terms of love and compassion. Any codes, rituals, ceremonies or proclamations that do not expressly acknowledge the sacred and eternal nature of these priorities must be changed or they will - in the long run - be deemed irrelevant."

"The evolution of religion has always grappled with this problem. In the beginning – when humankind was still jittery about its role and place in the universe - it tended understandably to opt for very definable ways: strict standards of right and wrong, preferring standardized rules versus trusting in the natural expression of one's joy, acceptance and inclusion."

"Those initial formalities often turned into strict systems. Once a separate and elevated priesthood was set in place, the formalities were understandably adopted as means of surviving in a seemingly hostile environment. But then they became the basis for sets of prescriptions and delineated do's and don'ts – each bearing both an alleged reward for following such edicts - or if disregarded - being potentially condemned to prolonged punishment in an alleged land of hell."

"Our goal, today, however, is twofold: one, to diminish the political power of the purveyors of outmoded formalities and black and white judgments. And, second, do everything we can to convince everyday citizens – tradesmen, parents, farmers, officials, politicians and clergy - to affirm and support actions that follow the natural rhythms of joy, love and compassion."

"As these kinds of breakthroughs multiple," Yeshua concluded, "the spirit of humankind will be able to express a more perfect expression of the divine - thereby ushering in an era that affirms everyone's right and ability to live according to the simple and direct norms of *Intrinsic Spirituality*."[46]

"Many people have yet to embrace the significance of these essential norms. But the momentum is on our side. So be prepared, my dear John, for the day when you and I will baptize primarily in the name of love, and the world at-large learns to adopt prayerful intentions that activate an era of universal love and joyful activity."

The Law of Love

'But the Law is the Law,' said a Sadducee who had joined the crowd and had been listening to Yeshua's comments. 'We are as we are – and how are you to change it? We are protectors of God's law and believe He decided on the truth long ago. It is incumbent on all of us to follow that Law."

'And yet - here we have a couple (pointing to Magdalene and I) deciding for themselves to enter into romance prior to the consent of their

---

46   The abbreviation of *Intrinsic Spirituality*, IS - is the third-person application of the verb, 'to be' - literally indicating a person's natural quality of being. The essence of the phrase can best be stated as: 'It Is What It IS' - or 'S/he Is what S/he Is'. Such an affirmation is, of course, an extension of the declaration that Prime Source shared with Moses when Moses was asked by God to identity Him/Her during their encounter with the Burning Bush. Prime Source's response, of course, was: "I Am What I Am", as recorded in Exodus 3:14.

families, who have not been formally betrothed and who apparently do not even intend to seek a blessing from a member of our clergy. Every aspect of their behavior violates our law and should be condemned by you, fair lady, and by you - there – the tall one with the beard leaning against the wall.'

"I certainly do beg to differ," came the voice from the shadows.

"In your definition and interpretation, the Law may only yield certain conclusions," said the tall figure as He approached the group of Sadducees.

"What you define as the Law seems designed to keep the average person from claiming his or her full rights as members of God's beloveds. Such interpretations may have been adopted to deal with the especially harsh conditions of old, when you were forced to move constantly and protect yourselves while traversing hostile lands. But such restrictions are not relevant to the situation at hand. The actions and intentions of this couple - who fell in love as they urgently served The Lord for years on end - was not the result of mere happenstance or the result of a whim but was clearly advanced in the sight of God by their genuine love for each other."

"Besides, we are the spiritual parents of this couple," said Yeshua. "We adopted them long ago – and now support their decision to profess their love for each other. By what interpretation of God and Its abiding love, can you possibly dispute this couple's assertion of their devotion to God and each other?"

Mother Mary then weighed in as Yeshua retreated once again to the shadows. "Your interpretation amounts to what you think is a violation of some code of behavior," She offered. "But that is not the view of a loving God – whose standing is greater and whose essence applies and takes precedence. The only law that applies here is the law of love."

"The views you present seem tainted by presumption, and dare I say, the politics of power and privilege. It seems you judge too quickly and loosely at a time when the application of love – the essence of God's teachings and behavior – clearly warrants deep respect for the devotions of this couple. It is indeed unfortunate that you cannot see and accept that reality."

Then Mother Mary added – pointing Her famous index finger: "If they wish to involve the clergy and have a formal ceremony including their families, so be it. But let is be their choice. Our wish for you is that you also learn to flow with the same wondrous energies of love exhibited by this couple. Look to them as your model. We pray that you find in your hearts to be like them: open, free, non-judgmental, in process, in love with life and each other. We wish you the likes of their great love, and pray that God's loving spirit pervades and inspires you - as it surely does for Magdalene and John."

The Gnostics Arrive

There was a shimmering in the background, setting off a rhythmic and enchanting pulsation. Then a white cloud of cumulative vapors emerged near the adjacent farm shacks and huts. Had the donkey broken loose? Was the commotion caused by a set of wandering gypsies having another cere-bration? Slowly the vapors dispersed - revealing a small group of men and women who were making definite strides to join the assembly of townsmen and the dazzled clerics.

One of the men, Basilides by name, bowed deeply to both Yeshua and Mother Mary: "We salute you My Lord and Blessed Mother Mary and Your compatriots, the Revered Magdalene and John the Apostle."

"We greet you from the other side, the one you know very well and helped to create - referred to here as the spiritual or heavenly sphere. My colleagues are named: Valentinus, Marcion, Ptolemy and Heracleon. We are figures from the constellation of forces that continually support you, my Lords - the cosmic arena where the events and figures of the past, present and future are stored and integrated."

"We are here," Basilides continued, "to confirm we are always avail-able to you wherever you happen to travel or reside – on This side or That. Prime Source suggested that we make ourselves visible to you today - since You are seemingly confronted by good but temporarily misinformed incar-nates who feel justified in obstructing your way back to Jerusalem."

"We have a special perspective," Basilides continued. "As noted, we come from the amalgamated totality of Life. Thus our views and experiences may be of special interest and assistance today. You and the other members of Your holy party may know us as *Gnostics*." [47]

'Love: On Earth as in Heaven'

"Greetings," said Mother Mary. "You are most welcome. We certainly are aware of how you labor in love against those who attempt to reduce spiritual teachings to mere institutions, restrictions and condemnations of alleged sins. You have been known for confronting any and all such denigrating views of the fate of incarnate Souls. We know your contributions include the ability to overcome a successive set of egocentric egos – particularly *male-egos* - who by self-proclamation and distortion, who have throughout history, sought to create a hierarchy of power-oriented political and religious rulers."

"We are also delighted to know you continue to support both individuals and groups as they express their diverse ways of applying the principles of love and compassion within their various cultures."

"It is also clear to us," said Yeshua, "that you are among those best able to advise the average incarnate during these trying times. As you know, we are about to re-enter Jerusalem and in so doing make a series of decisions which greatly impact on what We call, 'the ultimate love affair': *Prime Source's plans for this earth and beyond*. We seek, moreover, the

---

47 A collection of spiritual leaders who emerged as sects in both the Jewish and early Christian movements during the first and second centuries. Their systems varied greatly but converged around the conviction that the Christ figure was divine, and that each person had the ability to attain or intuit direct communication with God (gnosis). They also rejected the notion of sin and the need for alleged repentance.

Diverse groups espoused varied views on the origins and operations of the universe and differed in their respect or disdain for the material realm. See Elaine Pagels, *The Gnostic Gospels* (New York, Vintage Books, 1979); and *The Gnostic Paul* (Trinity Press International, 1975).

transformation of the material realm such that it no longer supports egotism, power politics and distain for others but rather yearns to mirror the spiritual intentions and actions of the heavenly domain."

"Our individual and combined missions of our incarnated lives may be summarized in a few words: 'Love: As Above, So Below', and 'Unconditional Love: On Earth as in Heaven.'"

Basilides conferred briefly with his colleagues. Finally, he turned to Yeshua and Mother Mary: "We love the essence of your summary headlines. We especially recommend the tone and tenor of the last one: "Unconditional Love: On Earth as in Heaven.'"

"So be it," said Mary. "That's our favorite too!"

Wonderful, Wonderful

Before proceeding, She looked over at Yeshua, who merely nodded and smiled. "You are on a roll, my dear Mother. Please continue. I too bow to your wisdom."

"Thank you my beloved Son," is all She said before turning again to the delegation of Gnostics.

"We realize that you are in the process of formulating views that sees the human body and mind as imprisoned by a so-called creator god or demiurge – distinct from and perhaps even overriding the presence and power of the transcendent God. As time unfolds, however, we hope you will help us affirm the fact that God or Prime Source is One, a most Creative Being who – as needs arise - adopts a series of transformations to assist It in creating, blessing and extending the cosmos. These actions include Prime Source's capacity to manifest as 'the Father' or the creating energy of the universe; 'the Mother' as the loving and nurturing agent; 'the Son' as the masculine and thus assertive forces of the universe; and/or 'the Daughter' or 'Holy Spirt' as Its equally feminine capacity to be loving, adaptive and supportive."

Mother Mary – then standing as tall as She could in Her material manifestation, concluded: "More on this – later as needed. In the meantime, we ask for your Gnostic and intuitive guidance as we reenter the complexities of Jerusalem. May your insights and practical assistance guide us as we enter the complicated arenas that await us - especially since your manifestations have lived in and contributed so much to the evolution of both Judaism and the newly emerging forms of Christianity."

And the Gnostics Speak

"We certainly wish you God-speed, dear Mother Mary, and offer You, Yeshua and your esteemed party - and offer you whatever practical advice we have as you - once again - interact with the political and religious pitfalls of the area," said Valentinus, another, and perhaps the most famous member of the visiting group of Gnostics.

"Thank you," said Mother Mary. "We are more than ready to listen to your counsel. But please forgive us if we seem a bit hurried; it has been a long journey and we are anxious – perhaps overly anxious to complete it."

"There will be those, chiefly from among the current set of clerics," said Valentinus, speaking a bit hurriedly, "who may attempt use you and your reappearance in Jerusalem to support themselves and their interests. Among the set of emerging authorities, soon to be called 'bishops and priests' in the new church - are those who adopt views and structures that justify their personal needs for worldly power and exert their 'spiritual' influence on both religious and civil affairs."

"As you undoubtedly already realize," said Basilides, chiming in to support his colleague: "the strict constructionists will arise again and have already formed tight bonds, determined to institutionalize their very conservative and frankly judgmental perspectives. Creeds, prescriptions, a multi-layered hierarchy, and a litany of alleged sins are apt to be at the core of such structures. We urge you to be very careful but resolute, encouraging everyday incarnates to believe in themselves and The Lord rather than the predetermined clerical formats that promise an automatic retirement in heaven and a sure way of avoiding the torments of an alleged hell."

"The emerging coalitions may also include many of your earlier followers and disciples, Peter and Andrew among them – good fellows but easily mislead by the advocates of an authoritative hierarchy and tightly defined belief system - based as it is on the silly superstition that redemption of the human race is needed because You and Yeshua - as Eve and Adam - stained the Souls of all subsequent incarnates with your supposed very obstinate and disobedient behavior in the Garden of Eden."

"If such conservative notions succeed, the result is predictable: a highly supervised structure will be slowly institutionalize and reach its height in the second and third centuries. So-called 'fathers' of the new Christian Church - like Tertullian, Hypolitus and Irenaeus - will be its purveyors. If they have their way they will institutionalize the church's growing power and pay only lip service to what we consider 'the essential spiritual norms' of love and compassion."

"Witness, for example, how the actions of a certain Bishop Athanasius of Alexandria and the future Emperor Constantine will converge to institutionalize the new hierarchy and thus wed the vast temporal power of the Roman Empire to the new church's increasingly regressive theology and authoritative tendencies." [48]

Fearful Warnings

"Forgive us, Mother Mary, for further delaying your departure for Jerusalem," said Marcion, the third member of the Gnostic delegation. "We think it only wise to warn you further of other pitfalls that may await you."

"The emerging coalition will be composed of some strange bed-fellows. Peter already sees himself as ordained to lead, and Andrew will support anything that determines immediate peace and clarity. Initially, such leaders will run the risk of completely misunderstanding Your – and our ideas - regarding the immediate and thus long-range need for everyone to behave with love and compassion. Admittedly, the general culture has not yet matured enough to prevent such imperatives from being considered

---

48   See Richard Rubenstein, *When Jesus Became God* (New York: Harcourt Brace & Company, 1999); Philip Jenkins, *Jesus Wars* (New York: HarperCollins, 2010); and Charles Freeman, *The Closing of the Western Mind* (New York: Alfred A. Knopf, 2003)

too mystical, too nebulous and thus not concrete enough to survive in the rough and tumble 'realities' of the world."

"That may be true at the moment when mere survival is deemed to be paramount. But both current and future developments argue for the diminishment of such structures and strictures. Once approved they will set the stage for tighter controls, expanding the sphere of proposed 'sins' and the solidifying the rule of a male hierarchy - all of which likely to intensify thereafter for many centuries."[49]

Flexibility And Commitment

"We readily admit our views sound nebulous to many," said Valentinus speaking directly this time to Yeshua - who had again rejoined the group - having completed another of His 'emergency assists' elsewhere on Earth. As usual, He seemed to reenter the earthly scene through some perennial 'side door'.

---

49   Of course, over the long haul, Christianity also produced many mystics, enlightened leaders and clerics, and those considered 'saints' by the Church - all of whom worked tirelessly to inculcate the civilizing norms of love and compassion.

But we get head of our story - focused as we are on this moment in history - a moment when such developments in Palestine and its immediate environs were still very much in their rudimentary stage of development. Even over the long haul, however, such forces had to struggle for recognition amidst the ceaseless expansion of the law and order perspective preferred by the Church's male-dominated hierarchy.

The teachings of Yeshua and Mary, however, were never explicitly excluded - and they were consistently hailed and practiced by the mystical wing of the established churches. But they have been systematically neglected and side-lined by official policy and practice, except during the hey-day of mystics like St. Francis, the advances made by many Anglican and other Protestant leaders and the coming of Pope Francis in 2013.

"Our views are no more new and strange than what You, Prime Source and most of the Jewish prophets have espoused for years," Valentinus continued. "You - Yeshua, and Mother Mary, as spokespersons for Prime Source Itself - have always espoused the overriding need for love and compassion – which is why, we Your followers, espouse the views we do."

"Acting through the various spiritual leadership roles you have assumed over the generations - we realize You have enabled the various cultures of the Earth to optimize the degree of love and compassion then possible in their societies - given the at times slow and consistent progress made during the evolution of human consciousness."

"Given everything we have said, we now rest our case, urging You, Mother Mary and your sacred party to persist championing love and compassion - even as you reenter Jerusalem's highly charged political and religious turmoil. In all humility, we - Your servants - urge each of you to realize that dealing with the forces of Jerusalem will take special handling, suggesting the need for even greater degrees of determination - and flexibility."

"Forgive us for coaching You, our divine leaders - but you are incarnates as well - and it is to that portion of Your identity that we speak - and thus encourage - and wish 'Godspeed'."

Yeshua and Mother Mary smiled and then hugged each of their Gnostic disciples. "We thank you for remembering - and so aptly applying - the essence of the message that We and our colleagues Magdalene and John, continue to emphasize to all incarnates." said Yeshua. "With our Father's help, We will inevitably succeed – and soon: not by overcoming the so-called opposition but by enticing them - slowly but surely - to join the greatest revolutionary movement of all, the one dedicated to instilling a universal commitment to the sacred norms of loving one's neighbors as much as oneself."

Destiny

It rained hard the next day, and the next. The populace was jubilant given the long season of drought. But anyone on the road was in for a rough slog.

First the donkey would not move. Can you imagine: we were about to have a major encounter with destiny and the otherwise pleasant and forbearing donkey would not move.

Magdalene stroked its chin, ran Her fingers through the hair that curled along the back of his neck, sighed and finally sat back down to serenade it with songs of energy and motivation. "Have we not given you enough attention and rest?" she asked him.

"Is this forced delay - 'the donkey-delay' (as it soon became known) - a sign? – an invitation for us to slow us down? – to not advance too quickly or enter prematurely into a new and potentially dangerous situation?"

"Who knows?" was our group's initial response, and then "well, maybe", which was followed by "perhaps there's more to it", leading to the final acceptance: "whatever it is, we might as well relax and flow with it."

And so we laughed, pet the donkey, gave him an extra portion of fruit, and together intoned, 'mea culpa, mea culpa, mea culpa" just in case we had driven him too hard. Then, suddenly, he slowly raised himself on all fours, shook himself from head to toe, stomped a bit, grunted and displayed his famous toothy grin.

"Seems like everyone is now happy or at least happier," said Mother Mary as we laughed in recognition of our donkey's changed mood. That left us to the recognition that getting to Jerusalem today really was really not imperative. Neither was tomorrow. We decided to rethink our initial premise - deciding that we leave only after we prayed for guidance and insight – just in case, giving our donkey one more stroking and an additional portion of oats.

As it turned out, it was indeed fortunate 'Simhah' - the donkey's Hebrew name meaning 'happiness' - proved to be so stubborn. Once delayed, we did the work we were avoiding all along. Better late than never, we realized that we needed to clarify what we individually, and collectively, wanted to achieve in Jerusalem - and how we intended to attain it.

When the sun set that evening day - we knew we were fully prepared to meet our fate. We were now within several miles of the city's gates, well fed and feeling rested. We even set out our best or our least-tattered clothing. We were breathing fully and freely, increasingly assured in the justice of our mission and desired outcomes. Moreover, we were convinced that we were indeed walking figuratively and literally with God - oh-so very thankful for the opportunity to continue serving Our Lord as we set about the joy of finally fulfilling our destiny.

Chapter VIII

Jerusalem

Resolved

YESHUA WAS THE FIRST TO AWAKEN THE NEXT MORNING. "My gear is packed and on my back. My sandals have been laced. I have washed and I even combed my hair and beard; good thing – I found a few burrs," He laughed.

"The breakfast of bread and fruit was perfect. Even the sun is shining – and our water jugs are filled to the brim. We best not delay any longer. What say, everyone: shall we complete the last loop of the journey we started so long ago?"

"There appear to be but a few more towns to traverse, and then it will be 'Jerusalem redux' - restored, yes – but also rendered anew, this time with special focus and vigor."

"I," Yeshua continued, "am in an expansive and ebullient mood this morning. So please indulge Me – for I have much to share."

"First, I sense from the sentiments we exchanged last night - that this final leg of *this journey* (for surely there will be others) represents more than an assertion of *our right of return*: it has also been hailed by our dear friends, the Gnostics; actively supported by our followers; cheered on by the many God-inspired people we met en route; waved off by those continually overwhelmed by their own personal interests; and trashed and condemned by representatives of the fearful, the privileged and the power-seekers."

"Yet this next phase includes a harking back to the past - for it is more than a revisit: this next – and final phase of what we can earnestly experience as a *renewal* - represents the opportunity to generate a revolution in how people view life and how they wish to live it."

"So as we embark on the completion of our special quest, one most solemn as well as joyous. If I may so proclaim, the venture that lays before us is most sacred. It is one of deep spiritual significance – for each of us individually, for all of us united in spirit, and for all the generations who will henceforth heed our message."

"Surely, our Father, the Creator, the cosmic being we rightfully refer to as *Prime Source* - is ever mindful of our hopes and dreams, and is - as ever - totally supportive. So We are hereby invoking the essence of Prime Source, requesting that It's divine integrity be continually infused into our bountiful Earth. In so doing, we embrace, love and spiritualize the totality of everything we have come upon, encountered and experienced."

"May this increased convergence of Earth and Spirit continue to guide those who will follow us – doing what they can to enlighten this realm with their special applications of the sacred auras of heaven. May that be Our common bond: We have each and all been created by Prime Source - to serve as Its representatives, and entrusted to bless and love Life as It has blessed and loved us."

"Jerusalem – with all its alleys and dialects, all its foods and customs and cultures, all its strange and familiar faces, all of its ingrained love and all its suspicions and oppositions – has been and henceforth will be so ever more: the crucible, the oven, the vessel within which we rededicate our Souls and help to fortify and render its essence anew."

"So We start again - here on cusp of our journey. Prime Source is our agent and inspiration. 'Now' is our opportunity, and 'Jerusalem' is indeed the focus of our celebration."

There's Luv and There's Love

Ah, but first - dear reader - is the latest report on another very important development. It concerns, of course, relations between Magdalene and I. Interested?

AHA: thought so.

Well - I, John the scribe and apostle - must admit that communications between my beloved Magdalene and I have intensified slowly but surely with each passing week. Increasingly we eyed each other through one single lens – the one generated by being absolutely besotted with the other.

For example, I admittedly am emoting more than ever – down one minute and ebullient the next. Magdalene, in particular, has commented on how easily I could be sad then at the next moment giggle at the slightest provocation. And where I once watched Magdalene faithfully attend to the needs of others, I increasingly perceived her as angelic, 'the lovely one' able to quiet ruffians as easily as she comforted the afflicted.

Mother Mary has also been quick to notice how much we now teased one another and how innovative we were in inventing endearments for different occasions. Mother's keen intuition and ever-watchful eye made Her abundantly aware of all She needed to know. And Her reaction? Apparent delight, sheer delight. Yet She confessed to being a bit wary as to how we would work things out.

"People fall in love all the time," said Mother Mary: "what better and more glorious match could there be. But I hope your love for each other will not diminish your capacity to notice, understand and respond to the needs of others. Will you – in the toughest of times – allow your personal attraction for each other override and even miss the immediate needs of another or the fuller context of a given situation?"

Privately, She told us later, She hoped the recent flare in our relationship was not just a passing infatuation – just a luv affair, if you will, one that did not subsequently develop into enduring love. Tough issues, for sure, She reasoned: best wait - and see - and adjust – if and when the need arose.

Meanwhile, we were also concerned. We would not only embrace and cuddle until the last of the logs turned to cinders. We also shared our concerns about what to do next: continue to nourish our separate but related identities? Just wait and see what happens? Or was it time to commit, deepen our relationship - and even go public with a public betrothal?

Did we owe Mother a fuller explanation – or at least a confirmation of our plans – whatever they turned out to be? We were after all Her closest earthly compatriots and companions – and I in particular - at the explicit behest of Yeshua - was Her earthly guide and protector.

What to do – if anything?

Finally, we both agreed: we must talk with Mother – bring Her up to date (which was what?), outline our plans (as if we knew!) and anticipate and resolve any difficulties (the greatest mystery of all!). Whatever it is, we vowed, we'll handle it, do what was best for all. Besides, we reasoned, if there was anyone who could help us figure things out, it would be Mother Mary.

Love Magnified

She spotted us walking toward Her – hand in hand. Once we rounded the bend we let our hands drop to our sides – separated our bodies a bit and deliberately created an amount of space that we deemed appropriate for two friends walking along the road.

Yet we kept glancing over at each other.

"Nervous?" we each asked, almost in unison.

"Oooo – yes," we uttered, again almost simultaneously.

"Remember to breathe," I counseled.

"And remember: we trust Mother Mary – and – each other."

Mother Mary had been sitting on a bench and rose quickly to greet Her two protégés.

"Lovely morning," She said as She reached out to kiss us both, first on one cheek then the other.

"First, let me say we are embarrassed to be seeking your advice at this juncture," said Magdalene, her head bowed slightly, "when it is obvious that everyone is now aware of our love and our growing relationship."

"We hear the titters and the whispers – as must you. Apparently our connection is known to everyone including the disciples that follow us daily - as well as those whose numbers triple in numbers whenever Yeshua is visibly at our side."

"I guess what we want to say is this: we are sorry if this has put you in an awkward situation – one, of not being informed directly or formally, and two, leaving You with the issue of having to defend us against any barbs and gossip."

"And why should I not defend you – for I am delighted for you both," said a wide-eyed Mother Mary. "You have both served Yeshua, Me and The Lord's cause with great diligence and effectiveness. It should come as no surprise to anyone that you might be attracted to each other. Consider how much you share in awareness and common experience. And look at all the time you spend together, how well you work together, and how lovely and handsome you look - and are together."

"If there was anything that might generate gossip about you two, then it might be news that you were arguing and not really in love."

"Men and women fall in love - thank goodness! Why should it not affect the two of you? Besides, it is our Lord's plan and secret weapon for promulgating the species and giving us more options and opportunities to incarnate," She said with endearing laughter.

"If there is so-called talk – so be it. Here I am a married woman traveling while Her mortal husband is off on some related mission in another country. I am also a woman who earlier left Her homeland to serve Her Son, the Mother whose only child is now gallivanting about the cosmos – the same one who years ago was accused of treason against both the Temple and the Romans. And given the nature of His and our work, all of us are periodically accused of not following the law of our fathers and participating in dubious healings and miracles."

"Perhaps the only thing about us that may be viewed as 'normal' and 'within the law'," said Mother Mary laughing, "is the fact that *the 'young couple' traveling with that older woman* - are apparently very much in love."

"Oh, Mother, leave it to you to see the humanity - and the humor - in all this - and put it all in perspective," signed Magdalene. "The way you put things obviously makes us laugh too. It is true that almost every aspect of everything we do and stand for - as a trio, and when Yeshua is with us, as a foursome – is a challenge to most people's sense of normalcy – living as we do - champions of the authenticity of everyday people. From that wider, spiritual and more inclusive perspective, all John and I are doing is adding a bit more love to the equation – and expressing it in a most natural way."

Perspectives Vary

We all started laughing again - realizing that our trio - and occasional quartet - must be quite the sight to everyone raised from a different perspective, in a different culture, and with a different set of standards.

"Even when things started to settle down," said I, "when we returned from Britannia and lived the semblance of so-called predictability, who do we delight in seeing and following? - the Person who seems to be number one on both the purists and the hedonists' lists of 'most reviled and feared.'"

"And who might join us an honored guests," said Magdalene, "but the most notorious leaders of the Gnostic sect, and then a perceived savage dressed like a mountain hermit. To the average citizen it would be quite normal to harbor suspicions about such characters - and even judge them for their oh-so different beliefs and strange behaviors!"

"And we need to remind ourselves that the negative 'whispering' did not start with hints of your romance," said Mother Mary, gesturing with open arms. "We have been under surveillance, in the glare of public opinion and deep concern - if not condemnation - since day one. Remember the Romans in concert with some of the leaders of the Temple tried to kill our beloved Yeshua. That involved a lot more than an occasional whisper."

"As to your formally telling Me of your romance: there was 'no right time'. My sense is that it was not until very recently that even you realized – no less admitted - that your affections for each other had been building for some time. Then some lovely moment occurred that allowed your love to be affirmed and shared. Now – that is simply marvelous."

"You did not tell me sooner because you yourselves did not fully realize it any sooner than a fortnight – if not several days - ago. I am sure you have spent most of the last few months sorting out your confusion and doubts before you could actually admit and then affirm the depth of your feelings for each other."

"So thank you now - for telling me – formally – about this marvelous development – one that I frankly anticipated for some time. Yeshua, of course, already knows. And We both celebrate the two of you and offer you Our full support and blessings."

"As to what you and we do next, and how we continue to go about our work: well, I think nothing has changed – except perhaps the assurance that the amount of love emanating within - and from - our foursome is growing at a very fast rate indeed."

Rebecca

And so it was that we proceeded further south - with each step moving ever closer to the heart of Jerusalem. But the sun was at full strength today and so by mid-morning we paused and relaxed a bit, even stopping at a field house situated near an extensive grove of olive trees.

Our fine mood was reinforced when a young woman walked into our campsite. Her name, we soon discovered, was Rebecca. She emerged first as a blur and then gradually as a whole person. She bowed and asked to speak with Mother Mary.

When the two women met, they each hesitated and then expressed a sense of familiarity and attraction – soon embracing each other with cries of joy and familiarity.

Rebecca was woman of middle height, perhaps a bit taller than Mother Mary. Her long robe hid a view of her feet which - we noticed - never seemed to touch the earth but rather seemed to glide along or slightly above it.

Mother Mary looked up – felt a shivering along Her spine – then called out to our unexpectedly guest. "Rebecca: can it be you?" She asked. Rebecca answered immediately: "Yes...my dear Mother Mary - it is I."

"What brings you here, My dear ?" She inquired.

"T'was Gabriel who sent me."

"We are delighted – but to what end do you appear before us?"

"To bring you good news and happy tidings. The heavens are bestirred with news of your imminent reentry into Jerusalem and we all wish to herald your arrival with song."

"Did you say, 'song'?" asked Mother Mary.

"I did indeed, my Lady – just a chorus or two – and, if you wish, as offered to You with the aid of a children's choir."

"Do we wish? – I should think so, my dear girl. We just stopped for a break before entering the walled city - so now is the perfect time to receive your greetings."

"With your permission, my lady," said Rebecca, "Gabriel has arranged for the musical greeting to emerge in a few stages – with perhaps just an inkling for much more this evening – and even more as you enter the city proper, if that all seems agreeable to you."

"Wonderful: please let the music begin," said Mother Mary. "Oh, Yeshua: isn't this grand! And John, please: please arrange for water for Rebecca and the children. And Magdalene would you mild fetching a bit of bread, cheese and perhaps some fruit. Rebecca: please sit with us."

Then Mother Mary cried out: "Gabriel – you most caring of Archangels – please choose an embodiment and join us. And please, of course, bring the mischievous Raphael with you – as if you would ever leave Him behind! Oh my, oh my, oh my. It does indeed seem like the perfect way to begin celebrating."

Heaven on Earth

Once we were settled - there was a long period of silence. And so we waited – for what we were not sure – but given past experience, I anticipated some sort of heavenly music.

"Perfect," Yeshua whispered. "The silence is inviting and so pregnant with creation."

It was then that a horn sounded: a long and harmonious blast from a shofar or ram's horn echoing through the canyon.

Again silence.

Suddenly - the clash of the tziltzal or copper cymbals: once, twice, three times - their vibrations slowly giving way to a long and escalating hum

– a distinct shimmer that was mesmerizing but had not yet proceeded to full volume.

Then we heard voices – first as if on high and then gradually descending – followed by an encirclement of children, rows of them - intertwining, forming various symmetrical patterns – apparently choreographed – creating the form of flower petals: cascades of singing children formed in circles, one to our right, another to the left, then others above and below us as a fifth one appeared in the center. There we were in the middle of circles of harmonious voices.

The soft tones of the nevel or harp then evoked the auras of the heaven – which in turn gradually gave way to the multiple vibrations of what seemed like a full orchestra.

We listened intently – what else would one wish to do at such a moment – and were even attempted to sing – or at least – hum along.

Through it all emerged the voice of a cantor singing in deep baritone – offering one, two – then a series of lyrical verses - each one prompting a melodious response from the dozens of children.

Who was directing such a display? Who and what generated such a spontaneous evocation of celebration and thanksgiving? How was it that such a musical display was coordinated: the sacred instruments, the orchestra, the resonant voice of the cantor, the exuberant children, the multiple choruses - this honoring, this remarkable outpouring of love – emerging so spontaneously, so quickly, here of all paces - surrounded by clusters of olive trees, at the juncture of our formal return to Jerusalem?

"Oh – we are delighted that you love what we have arranged on the spur of the moment," said Gabriel. "It just seemed right – a divinely inspired moment - no more than a light-year in the making," He laughed, "something we do when inspired by a special moment in the life of someone like Mother Mary."

Dressed now as a Bedouin from the desert, He bowed as He waved His colorful scarf. "Remember we have known you, Mother Mary, for some time – through many lifetimes and through your giving birth to Yeshua at His epoch making Annunciation. And who can forget your Assumption into Heaven, your coronation as Queen of Heaven and joining Your Son as a Master Soul now serving the physical realm in perpetuity."

"Let this – then – be a show of appreciation," said Raphael as He too suddenly appeared in the form of a shepherd. Putting an arm around the shoulder of Gabriel, standing some seven feet tall and arrayed in radiant garments, He addressed Mary directly - yet seemingly was speaking to the entire assemblage as well: "This indeed is but a glimpse of what is to come – a set of rolling salutes to Mother Mary and tributes to Her ever-cascading series of contributions."

Leaning forward, He added: "And you really haven't seen anything yet. Just wait. We've also have some other, really big ideas - planned for the future. Ah - the mystery. Ah - the joy – on *Earth as it is in Heaven.* T'is indeed a time to *rejoice.*"

The Lines of Time

The chorus of children soon gathered around Mother Mary. A few of them were almost as tall as She - well, not quite - but in reaching up they could touch Her face - and that is what one little girl insisted on doing.

"What is it you want, child," Mother asked.

"Your face tells a story," the girl responded.

"A story?"

"Yes – this line here: it is beautiful – it curves and is so deep. Look: there is a similar one on the other side. They are especially noticeable when I look directly at you. Did you have them when you were a little girl?"

Mother Mary laughed and hugged the child.

"Perhaps I had the beginnings of them when I was a little girl," She said, "but the years have surely added to them. I think they are called *life lines.*"

"I am especially happy today - because of your beautiful songs and elegant dancing. Yet as you may learn one day, life is not all happiness and celebration. There are – inevitably – difficult times as well - faced by all who serve the Lord by incarnating. I assure you those challenges have contributed greatly to the making of these very deep lines."

"Can you tell us a story about those times."

"Oh, child – you nick My wounds with your innocence."

"Please – just one. Were you anything like us?"

"Well childhood begins with parents - and My parents were very old when I was born. Their names were Anna and Joachim. They never thought they would have children. And then – suddenly - I came along. I had no brothers and sisters so quickly learned to rely on Myself, to look deep within and trust in the visions that soon arrived."

"I was a good student - like you, helped My mother and father and loved playing with friends. Yet I also prayed a lot. I especially loved to chat with God and the Angels who visited Me. That was My way of life for many years until I entered the Temple as a ward of the priests. I stayed there until I was betrothed to My husband Joseph and had a son of My own. Thereafter, I..."

Suddenly She stopped. Reaching up to stroke the left side of Her face, She deliberately retraced the groves of that one particular line.

"You may not understand what I am about to say, yet you are the one I wish to credit for helping Me to recognize - once again - that learning leaves its mark on our faces and on our hearts. So does love and anxiety and the search for peace and quietude. I would not trade the grooves on My face for anything – yet as I think back, I do wish some had not cut so sharply - and so deeply."

"I didn't mean to make you cry," said the little girl.

"Oh, you did not make me cry, my child...but life has...and I sense always will. The celebration this morning made Me cry, and as you see, the recalling of My childhood and My life story - also made Me cry. Sometimes life is too vivid, too overflowing with intensity – overwhelming us with memories of loss as well as all the opportunities we had to experience great love and joy."

"It seems that our hearts, our sensitivity - our insights are predisposed to attract - and automatically open to the presence of joy and life's opportunities to celebrate. With such heights of emotion, however, also come the downturns and the bouts of worry and loss. Ah, the lines of life: they serve as signs that we have loved deeply, and appreciated everything that has left its mark on us."

"I am sorry, My child, that I have become so – what we adults call 'pensive' and 'philosophic'. It is part of the risks of growing older."

"Oh, no, my Lady. Please don't apologize. Perhaps we understand more than you think. We love your tears as much as we love your smiles. We simply love you – whatever your mood, whatever you are experiencing at the moment, whatever you wish to say and do."

"We also talked among ourselves - and together composed a poem - that we now wish to share with you." She signaled to the others and so they sang in unison.

> 'Mother Mary,
> May we too grow strong
> Attain your strength and wisdom
> Become privileged
> To grow life lines like yours
> Learning from everything
> Framing our faces
> To resemble ...
> Your lines of love,
> Acceptance and joy.'

Ever Vigilant

The thrashing of sticks could be heard in the distance...accompanied by loud shouting and what sounded like angry threats.

Over the hill came a band of Sadducees.

"Blasphemy. Revolution. Death to the infidels," came the repeated cries. "Go away. Stay away. You are not wanted here."

Into the circle of children they marched, not knowing who to confront first or who or what was responsible for what they called a 'disturbance'.

Mother Mary stepped forth.

"Who is it you seek," She asked.

"The trouble makers."

Turning around, surveying the crowd of children and musicians, Mother Mary opened and extended both hands: "What do you mean and who do you accuse? We are in the midst of a festive gathering, singing and dancing. And it is not the Sabbath. What could be wrong?"

"We hear of trouble-makers – foreigners who crossed the borders into Judea several days ago – apparently headed for Jerusalem – naysayers who deny – nay, challenge – the laws and customs of our land."

"And what are their names?"

"We have no specific names – only the testimony of those who live just north of here in the small villages. They tell us a band of thieves and malcontents have entered our land and are heading to Jerusalem."

"We are indeed heading to the sacred lands of Jerusalem – but have met no blasphemers or malcontents. We gather here with children, sing the songs of Judaism and the universe, praise God for His mercy and kindness. Surely these musicians, these singers, these dancers, these children, the kantor - are guilty of nothing but love and goodwill."

"Well – should you meet any unbelievers and blasphemers, sinners spreading false lies and stirring up the people, please report them to the authorities."

"By the way, who are those two lurking in the background," asked one of the Sadducees, pointing in the direction of the shadowy figures standing to the side of the musicians?"

"They are with the musicians – stout fellows, ready and able to help any and everyone, especially children, travelers and those carrying heavy burdens. They seem to come and go as need be."

Mary Magdalene then stepped forth.

"One is my uncle and the other two are like grandfathers. They are indespensible to our operations - central to its core and our essence. Their aged hands and wise voices handle any and every difficulty we have or might yet encounter. In fact, they both protect and guide us. They be good, hardy, dependable – in fact, essential - folk: Gabriel and Raphael are their names accompanied by a very revered shepherd from the very high north."

"Oh, by the way, this is Mother Mary, this is John, and I am Magdalene. We are pleased to meet you and appreciate your watching over us during what are apparently difficult times – what with alleged marauders wandering about. We salute and thank you for protecting our welfare."

The stoutest of the Sadducees bowed.

"We love to be appreciated," came the response, "and now wish you well on your journey farther south."

As they departed, Magdalene noticed that the shadows had moved quietly to the side of the musicians - then vanished. She heard a distinct sound, a sort of 'frumm' – like the sudden departure of the wind. The threesome, apparently sensing all was well, had chosen to recede – cloaking themselves in a veil of invisibility - at least for now.

Yet another energy continued to pervade the scene: a vibrant, pulsating cosmic presence – a reflection of the All that embraced *the everything*. It too hovered – silent - yet ever vigilant.

Recalling History

The closer we advanced upon the inner city of Jerusalem, the greater the number of people who travelled with us – sensing, even expecting that something special was about to unfold. We detected the continual buildup in energy and nodded to each other, signaling that all was well. We did not envision anything immediate or out of the ordinary - although we were indeed headed into the heart of our destination.

On the itinerary were brief visits to some of the sites of old - recalling and celebrating earlier breakthroughs as well as healings they reflected: a revisit to Bethlehem and Mother's delivery of the latest incarnation of Yeshua; then a bit west to Qumran to honor the days when we all were Essenes; to Emmaus where the Apostles had reunited with Yeshua; and finally to the Mount of Olives and the winding passage to the walls of the Old City; the Damascus gate that led to its markets and complex alleyways; the site of the crumbled walls of the Temple destroyed by the Romans in retribution for the recent Jewish revolt; and, of course, the hillside overlooking the site of the staged passion and crucifixion.

We also anticipated reliving the deep sense of relief we felt lo those many years ago - when finally we left behind us the negative taunts of the Temple and military officials, moved first west and turned north once we sighted the sea – whence we sailed west along the Mediterranean, traversed Europa and eventually settled on the shores of Britannia.

Wisdom

We realized that wherever we had stopped for food, to wash or simply obtain a respite from the heat and the dusty roads, we were immediately surrounded by crowds – knots of people curious to learn about these alleged famous or perhaps infamous people moving through their land. The happened again last evening.

"May we ask you questions?" said one man - for example - holding the hands of two youngsters. "My children urged me to come – but I do not understand why. Are you prophets?"

"No," Mother Mary answered. "But we do seek to live according to the norms of the loving prophets and God."

"Are what are those norms?"

"There are several. Chief among them is *to love your neighbor as yourself.*"

"The way to God then is through loving our neighbors?"

"You put it well."

"But what of the Temple elders, the ancient traditions and now the rulings being issued by the leaders of this new Christian church?" shouted another man to the rear of the crowd.

"We are free to follow the particulars of the various sects as we see fit – but only as those practices flow from, lead to and follow the overriding imperative of love. If, however, the codes and specifications of any group lead you to judge others, defame or condemn them, then those codes and specifications – we feel - must be set aside in favor of accepting the common humanity of us all – each of us serving and being guided by the love of the one loving God."

"You make it sound so simple," we recalled one child saying.

"It is indeed very simple," we answered. "The theories of many religious bodies and their spokesman make the spiritual process seem very complicated – seemingly placing all sorts of structures, rituals and codes between us and God. But the process of communicating with God is simple.

Words - and actions - of love and compassion come before anything else - and in fact - are all that is needed to attain a direct contact with God."

"Our perennial advice: 'We encourage you to speak personally with God – one to One – not through intermediaries who purport to interpret our experiences and God's response. We need no such interpreters. God is kind, caring and forgiving. The essence of God is empathy. As both our Mother and our Father, God is ready and willing to listen to us and guide us. God is always available and is able to offer us whatever advice we seek: how to overcome a difficulty, how to be gentle with oneself, and how to give – as God has given - love, healing and comfort to others.'"

Political Structures

"I am a member of one of the new Christian communities that has emerged since the death of one called, 'Yeshua,'" then said a woman walking with a cane . "The leaders are supporting a new strain of authorities – a set of bishops and priests and deacons. What do you make of this development?"

Mother Mary walked up to Her, held Her hands and answered: "Those who have gained power within the Christian movement are themselves loving Souls. Unfortunately, however, they have become so anxious that they have overreacted and opted for success through centralization over what we admit are the relative vagaries of an uncoordinated and thus individual approach to love and compassion. Unfortunately, good people are understandably frightened and thus tend to overreach in their attempt to safeguard their beliefs. So they adopt strict codifications of alleged sin, opt for a ruling clerical hierarchy that claims the right to do all the thinking for their followers, and adopt what is to Us an overly solemn theology based on the false allegation that their leader died on a cross."

"It will take more than a few words and perhaps several minutes to tell you the whole story. Are you really interested, have the patience to listen to the details?" Mother Mary asked.

By then a large crowd had gathered. This is how I recall what happened next.

Several people cried 'tell us more."

That's all Mother Mary had to hear. So She resumed Her explanation.

"First, Our Lord Yeshua did not undergo a crucifixion and is not dead. He is very much alive. He has and continues to make appearances in many parts of the world and universe - including Britannia and here in Palestine and Jerusalem. He has, in fact, travelled with us recently and will soon return to assist us in re-entering Jerusalem."

"The alleged passion was merely a show – displayed through God's mastery of nature – this time simply using beams of laser light and creating the appearance of Yeshua's passion and death. God the Father would not agree to the supposed death of His Son! Thus the show - arranged to neutralize the hatred and incessant pursuit of the Temple and Roman officials and allow Yeshua to pursue His healing mission without further interference. And the mirage transpired as Yeshua Himself and our Holy Family watched, unharmed, from a nearby hill - after which We left Jerusalem to fulfill a next facet of our mission in far-away Britannia."

"Unfortunately, the laser show itself sparked a recall of an ancient prophecy of Isaiah, namely the one referring to a 'suffering servant'. The formers of the new church quickly used the reference it to their advantage: having an innocent martyr as one's founder became an effective way of attracting new followers."

"Thus the image of a crucifixion was falsely adopted as the central symbol of the new Christian movement. The reality of Yeshua's continuing and abiding love for humanity, our Palestine and our entire Earth was ignored, pushed aside. Pity!"

"Such misinterpretations, however, did not, change our reality: the mission of the ever-living Master Soul was not extinguished nor did the 'light show' (as we refer to it) that created the mirage of a crucifixion affect the mission of Yeshua in any way."

Empathy

"How are you doing?" Mother Mary asked the crowd - as Magdalene distributed the water and fruit that had appeared from some unknown source.

Apparently we were meant to stay with this crowd and answer all their questions.

"It is complicated but significant stuff," said one man. "Things we seem not to hear otherwise - at least not from the Temple, the Roman Army or the new Christian groups. But what you say makes sense. I especially like the emphasis on loving and doing what you need to do, surviving, even thriving despite the opposition. *Brava* for you and your colleagues - especially Yeshua!"

The crowds tended to approve - overwhelmingly - which is why many of them continued to follow us.

"One can empathize with the leaders who emerged dominant in the early Christian church," said Magdalene, allowing Mother Mary to rest for a moment. "These continue to be difficult and confusing times. Since Yeshua was born as a Jew it was natural for some of His followers to either continue worshipping as Jews or later join a branch of the early Christian movements that wished to meld some of the new ways with some of the old. That was risky since the group that emerged as dominant increasingly organized itself around a very defined agenda, governed by a hierarchical structure of bishops, priests and deacons."

"But Prime Source did not and has never needed any intermediaries although It has encouraged the assistance of the Archangels and Angels and the various prophets of every time and culture, including - of course - all the earlier incarnations or appearances of Yeshua and Mother Mary. Any attempts to install human intermediaries as go-betweens with Prime Source are unnecessary and really silly - for they deny and undercut our direct link to God and Its ordained embassies."

Prompted by Insecurity

Magdalene then turned to me: "John, would you like to take it from here?"

"Ahh," said I. "I would be glad to make this a team contribution. But I urge you or Mother Mary to intervene should my understanding need your support."

"Well," I said, "such authoritative structures understandably appealed to those who needed tangible intermediaries to attain a sense of firm and defined mooring – especially during the chaotic years following the destruction of the Jewish Temple by the Romans in 70 A.D. But the price they paid for obtaining such a sense of false security was profound. Supposed intermediaries and a growing set of alleged aids to living religiously - such as a growing list of ornate rituals, strict codes, defined hierarchies and lists of do's and don'ts to which the adherents were bound - were not of God's making. They were invented by well-meaning but insecure clerics – usually all male - who allowed their imaginations – and their human egos – to overreach, and thus erect unnecessary structures and adopt overly defined paths of devotion - which increased clerical power as they destroyed everyone's direct link to their God."

Mother Mary rose, and with a nod - I passed the baton. Her emphasis was clear.

"It is more than sufficient, however, to simply love and thank God for the gifts of being alive, and to support the desire of one's neighbors to do the same. *Simple, direct* and *love* are the key words describing the central activities involved in honoring God, others and oneself. Interpreters, theologians, authors of catechisms, the proponents of rank, authority and complex structures – are all both manifestations of and supports for a false religiosity dependent on layers of human power and authority."

"Such constructs are superfluous, unnecessary and counterproductive since they play to the most base of human infatuations with one more predetermined and thus misleading way of connecting to God. They prove to be but silly add-ons - for they denigrate personal responsibility and ensnare the innocent into believing in a God posing as a series of human stand-ins."

"We are sorry to be so harsh - but reality is reality and it needs to be stated directly and honestly," said Mother Mary, who by now was out of breadth and reaching out for an arm or a chair. "Being loving does not mean being so tolerant that one forfeits the right – and the need - to set the record straight."

How Far Away

As the crowd dispersed, we gathered our few things and got ready to get back on the road – for our destination was now so very, very close - when a small child tugged at the hem of Mother Mary's cloak. That stopped everything, of course.

"Lady, where is God? I look for Him but don't always find Him."

"Well, let's help you to figure this out. I take it from what you say, that sometimes you are able to find God when you are looking for Him and sometimes you don't. Is that true?"

"Oh, yes, He appears to me, then quickly disappears – even if I am not finished saying my prayers and asking my questions. I just enjoy being with Him, and then suddenly 'puff' - He's gone."

"Do you remember where you are and what you are doing when He does appear and answers at least some of your questions?"

"Oh, yeah – I am usually alone, walking my dog or just out walking along a stream or among lots of trees. It is then that He usually appears and talks with me. Sometimes I get the feeling He is standing in front of me - especially when I'm feeling lonely. Then there are times when I can hear Him whispering to me – but that's usually when I least expect it."

There was silence, until the little girl looked up - and after taking a big breadth - resumed her chat with Mother Mary.

"So He does visit me every once in a while - but He never stays. Where does He go? And when He does leave, how far away does He go... like, does He have a home or tent like the rest of us?"

"I have several reactions and a few pieces of advice," said Mother Mary smiling. "Let's sit over here - and ask Magdalene and John to join us. They are good people and I trust their advice. Would that be all right?"

"Yeah – four of us: like a quartet. The three of you – a trinity – and with me, a quartet. I like that."

"First, it sounds like God visits you – which is wonderful news indeed - since there are so many children – and adults – who want some time with Him. He does not stay with any one person very long, it seems, because He wants to spend at least some time with as many children and adults as possible. Does that make sense?"

"Yeah, I guess it is not right for me to think He only has me to cheer up."

After hesitating - and seemingly talking to herself - the little girl said in a strong voice: "Okay, then - its official: I hereby announce my willingness to share! In fact, I realize that's a good idea since I would hate to be the one who's left out."

Then a quick follow-up: "Does He have a home?"

Mary Magdalene looked up. "God never goes to any one 'home' because He is at home everywhere. There once was a famous spiritual leader by the name of Hermes Trismegistus from Egypt who summed up God's wanderings - something like this: 'God is a loving energy - whose home is nowhere in particular - but who is capable of being present everywhere'. The means God travels a lot because there are so many people to see and love and talk with. So He is at home everywhere He goes."

"In other words, the spirit of God is so big and expansive that God does not live in just one place but feels at home everywhere He visits - because children and adults like you make Him feel so much at home when He does arrive. So God's family includes everyone and all families - including yours and mine."

"Is this making any sense?" I asked.

"Yeah – kind of," she said - slightly scrunching Her face.

"That's a lot to absorb for any of us. So please allow me to put it in even another way," said Magdalene. "God is both so loving and so gigantic that He can be - and thus is - 'at home' any and every where He goes. So as soon as He finishes talking with other boys and girls - and as you know, there are a lot of them - He is then able to chat personally with you - which I am sure He loves to do - because you are kind enough to greet him, love Him, wish Him well and - I am sure - always remember to ask how He is doing as well."

"Wow," nodded the little girl. "That's a lot to think about. It also makes me feel lucky that God visits me as frequently as He - or She – does, given all the kids and adults who love Him all over Palestine and the world, and – who knows – even those who live high up among the stars."

One More Question

"Okay, I think I got that," said the child. "But I have one more question. That is if you are sure 'you're not tired yet' – something my Mother says all the time."

"No, no: we are fine. Thank you for asking," for I so loved getting involved in a child's very incisive way of raising the great issues of our or any time. Besides, this little girl's questions revealed a wisdom well beyond her years – greater than what accrues in one lifetime - suggesting she was indeed a very old and loving Soul - one who had experienced and learned a great deal over many if not generations of re-incarnation.

"So - is God a child, or an adult like my Mother and Father, or is God a prophet, priest or a wise man or woman? How big and how old is God anyway?"

At that juncture I started to feel as if I had volunteered too quickly. I looked over at Mother Mary and then to Magdalene – and all they did is look back. Finally, Mother Mary said with a broad grin: "You're still up, John. Time to let us know how much your Soul has absorbed over all your many incarnations!"

"Thank you, Mother, for what I hope is a vote of confidence," said I with a bow and a chuckle. I then turned to what I now perceived as an ancient prophetess - clothed in the garb of a young Palestinian girl.

"You pose several questions, one greater in scope than another," I observed. "Let's take them in order."

One By One

"It seems that God is capable of doing a very wide variety of things - depending on the needs of the person God happens to be talking to. He or She - we will get back to the issue of male or female in a minute - can assume the role of a child and speak as a child when with children - yet easily speak the language of an adult when sharing with people the age of your Mother or

Father. God can communicate with both men and woman of any age given Its totally unlimited love, insight and wisdom."

"Got that?"

"Yeah - that I understand. Thanks."

"Now, in terms of gender, God is neither a man or a woman but rather is a creative combo of both. So God can be as assertive as most men seem to be most of the time, and equally receptive – that is, willing to listen very attentively to others - as most woman do – well, most all the time," said I, snickering to myself.

I snuck a peak at both Mother Mary and Magdalene for any reaction. Receiving only smiles, raised eyebrows and Magdalene's comment, "we'll talk"...I continued.

"Since most people – men and woman, boys and girls – are capable of both kinds of skills, that is - able to get things done, which most men think they are good at, as well as being very good at listening and helping others - which most woman really are very good at! God is perfectly able to do both – just like you. Although you have the patience of a girl you certainly also have the ability to be as assertive as a boy – like your Mother, capable of listening and absorbing new ideas, and also like your Father, able to choose and achieve what you want or need to do next."

I checked in: "All right?" I asked. "Is this making sense?"

"Yeah - I think I got it. Please go on."

"Now the second question: So what is the appropriate pronoun to use when referring to God? A fully capitalized 'It' would be fine as would be She or He – again because God contains the natural skills of both girls and boys, women and men – and thus is the perfect blend of both nurturing and listening to others which seems instinctive to girls, and then choosing and doing thing, which seems to be the way most boys like to operate."

One More Time - Once

I thought by now that I had clarified the young girl's questions, but was quickly reminded that I still did not say what 'we're supposed to call 'God."

I took a deep breathe and found myself uttering the following: "Once we establish a deep and loving relationship with God - and you know in your heart when that happens - God is perfectly all right with our addressing Him or Her with any one of a variety of names."

I forged ahead quickly - without waiting for the girl's comment or additional questions - hopefully concluding the conversation with the following:

"Some prefer to use such endearments as "Dear God, or 'Dear Lord' while others might prefer something as familiar as 'Dear Father' or 'Dear Mother'. It seems to me a child or young person, might even use something as personal as 'Hi God' refer to 'My Special Friend."

"There are certain biblical terms that might do as well - such as of *Yahweh* and *Adona*i, terms used within the Judaic religion yet are also closely associated with those who become warlords - bad people who think they deserve to be treated as *gods* but who clearly are not since they rely on intimation and violence. So we advise you to stay away from those phases for now – that is until you are of age and then make a choice that feels right to you."

Again, I looked over at Mother Mary and Magdalene and sighed, realizing that these allegedly simple questions were harder to answer than I assumed. But I labored on.

"The most accurate term, however," said I, "literally translates as *Prime Source* – meaning the first and only source of Life, creator of the universe and guide to all who love Him or Her."

I looked up at the sky – unsure of the source of my alleged insights - hopeful that I did not use words that an adult - no less a child - might have difficulty understanding. I also wondered if I had just participated in what is known as 'automatic uttering' – speaking from sheer instinct and hopefully a bit of inspiration - a verbal form of *automatic writing* that has apparently prompted much of what I have been writing recently.

Had I just learned something profound – at least realized it with greater clarity? By simply trusting my inners, I responded with assurance - and spontaneously - to the mini-giant who stood before me, saying things I did not realize I knew - replicating the process I increasingly used each evening as I recorded the day's insights in my journal.

Mother Mary came over to hug me – saying, "dearest John: you have become our teacher. There is a multicolored halo around your head – a sign that you are indeed being blessed with deep spiritual knowledge."

Magdalene simply grabbed my hand, and whispered: "How proud I am of you."

The young girl was wide-eyed, her mouth slightly crooked and ajar. Her face seemed to mirror shock and wonder - yet she also seemed to glow with a rich inner awareness.

She took a deep breath, then let her shoulders drop. She looked around - then directly at us, and finally sighed: "Talking with the three of you is like talking with God – excuse me, 'Prime Source' - directly – that is, to both Himself and Herself – the One who apparently roams from heaven to here - and everywhere in-between."

"I like it," she added. "No - I love it! I truly hope we meet - and talk again - soon."

We each realized it was now best to be quiet - and simply bow to the angelic figure before us.

Various Opinions

A couple then stepped forward.

I quickly noted: "It is getting late so we had best make this our last question for now. We are bound to make our way to Jerusalem later today" - or in looking over as my colleagues, was moved to say, "tonight or first thing in the morning?"

"I understand," said a woman who had worked her way to the head of the crowd. "I will try to make this brief."

"We take to heart the teachings you have shared with our daughter. But so many different groups offer different answers. For example, those who have become increasingly vocal are the ones that prescribe beliefs, mandate precise ways of devotion and advocate submission to a growing number of those they call 'priests' and their superiors known as 'bishops.'"

"The same people also promise us salvation but only if we follow their prescriptions. We are practicing but questioning Jews. Why should we become so-called Christians if we have to surrender our right to question their mandatory views? Do they possess a superior insight into the ways of God?"

The man standing next to her added: "The views you express seem more tolerant of freedom and personal experience - even dissent, at least more willing to listen to and heed those of us who are still groping and feeling our way. Is the way to God really as specified as those who urge us to join their church, a church that apparently consists of a series of set meeting times, a definable gospel and an established hierarchy bent on prescribing sacraments, creeds and behaviors. No one apparently has checked with those of us who long to update our practices as Jews but are not ready to embrace what the Christian's present as 'Judaism's heir apparent.'"

"I agree," said a third person. "I am a gnostic, one who believes Judaism like all 'isms' can evolve - in this case, not toward rigidity and a new authoritarian structure but hopefully give way to a new philosophy, one willing to accept individual variations in what we believe and how we behave. The Jewish Testament speaks often of a 'god' who urges our leaders to kill one set of people or another, forcing others into servitude and admonishing still others if they do not follow their prescribed codes."

"Many of our revered Judaic prophets, however, have spoken of integrity and personal responsibility – even encouraging us to love our neighbors. But such pleas too often are either ignored or negated by many of the authorities - who in sharing the stories of their people - seemingly brag about their capacity for vengeance, retaliation, even war and wholesale punishment."

"From what I hear," said the Mother of the little girl, "the proponents of some new church say it is founded on the words and behaviors of a man named *Yeshua* who also spoke of personal responsibility and loving one's neighbors. Yet the new church set up in His name seems bent on adopting strict codes and proposing hierarchies that tell us what to believe, how to behave and whose dictates we must obey. If true, they apparently advocate the formation of a new class of self-appointed clerics, overseers and author-ities – whose edicts must be obeyed or we will be assigned to hell when we die."

"It is also reported that Yeshua had a series of apostles that He chose personally," came another voice from the crowd. "Why should those twelve men now have the right to choose their successors – and establish what Yeshua never did, namely a physical church complete with a hierarchy, formal credos and prescribed activities ruled by a special class of designated successors. And – and worst of all – the masses of people now find their God-given right to speak directly to God either dismissed or scorned."

The Gnostic Perspective

"There are other issues as well," said a woman stepping out from the shadows. "There are also those of us who call ourselves Gnostics, folks who speak not of buildings and hierarchies, creeds and judgments, or one prescription after another – but who champion the simple right to love God and one another. We Gnostics think it is best – and our right - to trust in our nature, and through our experience learn to adopt the words and behaviors that display love of self, others and our community."

"We," she continued, "perhaps like you - don't offer a church with defined physical and psychological boundaries but rather speak of a community of free and like-minded seekers who glory in and seek God in both the narrow cracks and larger dimensions of life."

"What a lovely way to put it," was all I could mutter to myself.

"What lovely alternatives you offer," said Magdalene speaking directly to the woman. "Can you say more."

"We offer spiritual directness as well as individuality" said the woman offered, looking over at me and getting my cheerful salute. "As you have already testified, Judaism currently seems lost as it stumbles between the words of certain 'gods' and leaders and their talk of war and vengeance on the one hand, and the more insightful and loving words of their prophets on the other. This new Christian group, however, seems too anxious to erase the past and Judaism's dilemmas by in turn being overly assertive: it's in a hurry, advocating immediate obedience to its still unproven hierarchy, and relying heavily on their interpretation of a mythical couple who allegedly betrayed God and thus brought about cycles of deprivation and hardship for all their ancestors – including us."

"Who are the truly sacred people in this tangle of old and new?" the woman asked.

"Apparently it is those of us who are beginning to cluster around this third perspective – the Gnostic one. It avoids the errors and unfulfilled promises offered by Judaism yet perpetuates its love of God and life. Yet it avoids the rush to audacity with the unquestionable authority proposed by the new Christians. A new rigid discipline, monitored by a self-appointed hierarchy is hardly the best way to continue the best of the spirit and practice of Judaism and link it with your renewed emphasis on unconditional love. Finding the best in all approaches to God is surely the best way to create a community of loving individuals who truly yearn to trust in God and themselves."

We looked at each other – clearly overwhelmed by the raw energy and the wisdom being expressed by this set of everyday people, people ready and able to express their frustration with what they experience as the dominant views and practices of the day.

It was late, growing ever dark - much later than we anticipated. So we finally begged to be excused - for we had yet to complete our journey, recalling once gain that we were destined to get to Jerusalem but would in the process, never pass on the opportunity to work with others as the need and the opportunity arose.

So we decided to leave these concerned citizens with a repeat of our best advice:

"We hear you and love you - and urge you to continue espousing your experience and your love of God. Follow your instincts, trust your experience, and join no group that demands that you follow the dictates of their authority. Love your neighbor, and persist - above all: continue to talk to God directly and with love and thanksgiving. That is more than enough for God to admire you, value you and love you in return."

Onward

Onward we traveled – affirming that Jerusalem was the draw... packed as it was with history, our history, Yeshua's history, the site of Mother Mary's greatest vision and triumph.

To reenter this sacred city – to bend with its disjointed corridors and undulating walkways, to negotiate its streets of broken pavements and swirls of sand – was to enter into and reclaim our past as well as proclaim our new reality. Here we were – ready to recompose and reorder our lives. In coming full circle we knew instinctively that we were about the business of achieving our long-awaited vision.

On the trail, we traded insights – and our hopes and visions - as we negotiated the roadways leading to the city. We anticipated our delight in again celebrating Yeshua's declaration of freedom from the static and negative experiences of old: those insulting taunts of the agents of privilege and hierarchy; the continual denigration of woman in both civic and religious matters; the intermittent confrontations between the Romans and the religious and political leaders of Judaism; the cries of the money lenders who pervaded the grounds of the Temple; the continual smell of burned animal flesh; the distortions created by convoluted theologies and the antics of power-oriented clerics; and the concrete walls, the high towers and the endless physical, mental and emotional partitions of the city and its Temple.

In short, it dawned on us that our seemingly endless trek, our slow, at times arduous but constant advance on Jerusalem, mirrored the course of our internal struggle to determine what to do when we got there: what specific outcomes should we expect, and how should we best honor the loving messages of Yeshua once we are again engulfed in the raucous give-and-take of Jerusalem's tumultuous political environment.

The endless roadways, the villages visited and bypassed, and now the walls, corridors, hills and walkways of our sacred city – all seemed like metaphors for what both obstructed our path as well as that which would help us clarify and declare our identity - and the next stage of our ever-emerging mission.

Both clear memories and vague anticipations were now woven into one entangled yet unraveling story, one we hoped – would, after all, fulfill our immediate spiritual aspirations as well as serve the longer range needs of our earthly and cosmic community.

The Crucified One

It seems the team of Sadducees was not finished. They waited for us again the next morning – just as we were entering the formal district of Jerusalem - fortified this time by a contingent of the Roman army.

"Let us assume – as least for now – that you are and will continue to obey the law and abide by Judaic practices and traditions as you enter our Holy City. We will be watching you carefully – especially now that you are so close to the regions of our Temple. We remember that the last time you were here you were led by that famous rabble-rouser – Yeshua? was that His name? – yes, Yeshua."

"As we recall," said one of the Temple leaders, "this Yeshua and His party caused a great deal of commotion, even threatened the overthrow not only of the Temple authorities but a revolution against the Roman command – such that the army had to haul Him away and put Him to death."

"We notice, of course, that not even an apparition of the dead Yeshua is in your company today and apparently - or obviously - is no longer your leader," said the leader of this band of Sadducees. "Pity," he added, sniggering as he turned to acknowledge the laughter of his compatriots.

"Let us assume His total absence removes the possibility of your repeating any of your earlier threats to undermine the peace and safety of our people. But please be aware that we are still watching you very closely. You now appear to be a much smaller band of potential troublemakers but perhaps you are still pernicious. What have you to say for yourselves?"

I stepped forward.

"It seems you will be very much surprised to learn that Yeshua is very much alive and well – still as vivid a human presence as you can ever meet. He is away at the moment – but remains, as ever – a very powerful force for love. We assure you: He is not to be trifled with – having the capacity to best the finest of your clerics in debate, able to tongue-tie the allegedly brightest of you and unseat the proudest of even your military's most experienced horsemen."

"What is this? Do you challenge us?" a guardsman asked as several soldiers rattled their swords.

"No, but I do," came a voice to the side.

Everyone turned to see a tall, bearded man walk deliberately to Mother Mary's side and thus flank Magdalene and I.

"And who are you, might we ask?" inquired the captain of the troops that accompanied the Sadducees. "A thief? A madman, perhaps? A total stranger to the political and military realities of this area? Identify yourself and mind you be supplicant – that is if you care for your life."

"You should know Me well, for we have met before," Yeshua answered. "In fact, you spoke of Me just moments ago – when you besmirched My reputation and existence, and accused My brethren of malicious intentions."

"You - the one we crucified along with two other thieves several years ago? That rebel died on the cross! Now – are you - an imposter - looking to undergo the same fate? I think you are not only mad but brazen and insulting - standing here and challenging the established representatives of the Temple and the Roman authority. Do you want us to arrest you, torture you, crucify you as well - as we did the revolutionary you now claim to be?"

"Know now that you are surrounded by those who would arrest you on the spot. If you wish – we'll even throw this three-some into the lot: wipe you away – all at once - while we have the chance. The audacity of you, the insanity of your challenge."

Turning to his men, he scratched his head and wondered: "Have you ever?"

At that moment a haze - a thick dark haze - began to encase both the delegations from the Temple and the Roman Army. Few were spared - as Yeshua, Mother Mary, Magdalene and I walked to the side, heard what sounded like the flapping of wings, and saw the outlines of several angels.

The eyes of all others - including their horses - were instantly blurred. Memories were erased. Heads drooped, sticks and swords dropped to the ground and nothing could be heard except the prolonged coughing and slow retreat of the Temple and Roman officials. Above it came with the swooping sounds of the blessed ones - who promptly lifted - and transported - us to saver grounds.

Affirmations

Word of our presence in Jerusalem continued to spread quickly. Expectations of our continued confrontations with both the army and the clergy grew crowds wherever we went. They dogged our every step. Thus so did the questions as to why we attracted the attention of the officials, and what we represented.

"There are so many ideas and theories circulating that we are often at a loss as to what to believe," a shop owner reached out to ask Mother Mary as we paused before a small crowd in a square just before the Mount of Olives that overlooked the old city. "Can you please clarify your perspective, perhaps spelling out the particulars - thus revealing why you are so controversial."

"My beliefs, our beliefs," said Mother Mary, "stem from the words and work of Prime Source. They have also been voiced – repeatedly - by My Son, Yeshua. We call such truths 'Affirmations' or 'Convictions'. In most cases they are simple and reflect generations of spiritual insight and experience. Our beliefs and proposed actions are not, and should not be presented as catechism for children, giveaways for the uninitiated, fill-ins for those unsure or those willing to recite anything as the price for being accepted by any established authority."

Turning to Magdalene and I – Mother Mary asked us "to please chime in as wished or needed." Receiving only smiles and nods from us, She continued.

"There are a set of Affirmations, however, that we do offer as guidance to any who would join us and support our cause. They are not mandatory. They are presented only to communicate the tone and tenor - the quality and reach - of that which forms the fabric of our lives - and which affirms Life - and all lives."

"So please hear us:

"We affirm the eternal presence of 'Prime Source' - the divine creator of the universe."

"We affirm that God - also known as Prime Source – created each and all of us as immortal Souls."

"As immortal Souls we are part and parcel of our cosmic God, serving the supreme being as cells within Its universal body."

"All of us – all now residing in Palestine and everywhere on the Earth - have incarnated, that is, our immoral Souls in Heaven have agreed to embody themselves in the mortal or incarnated beings we have become."

"Thus we all serve in a dual role: first and foremost as immortal Souls who reside in Heaven, then, as well as the very people you see before you, all of you who inhabit Palestine and those now incarnated throughout the world."

"When our bodies have completed our work on Earth, when we incarnates have fulfilled the terms of the contract or mission, we - as immortal Souls - will return to Heaven - where we review our achievements on behalf for love and compassion while we were here on Earth, and then choose what good will we intend to create if and when we again re-incarnate and return to Earth."

"All of us incarnate for three major related reasons: one, to speak and act with love and compassion for all we meet; two, in so doing become more like our loving and cosmic God; and three, give thanks to the Lord for the opportunity to serve Him."

"Those are the basics. Any questions?"

The crowd stood in silence. As did we.

No one said a word.

Questions

Finally, a man with a weathered face, asked: "Now that we hear what you profess, I am a bit sorry anyone asked. I do not doubt you, my lady – but what you believe may sound so very simple to you. But it still is so very, very complex to us – and frankly is beyond our comprehension."

Another chimed in – pointing to the older man: "I want to agree with you, kind sir - for I too am stunned and amazed. The stories of what we now call the Hebrew or Holy Testament have their complicated parts – but nothing like the seeming impossibility of the story you tell."

Then a woman standing with three children called out: "I believe in you, Mother Mary, and know you would not lie or mislead us. But I am stuck with choosing between you as a loving and true person - and the seemingly impossible ideas you just shared. I also fear there is more – and that worries me. It is all more than I can absorb – as least for now and in one hearing."

"What you shared is about honoring God and learning to love," said another. "It is bit different from what we hear from the Temple folks – and on that basis alone it is worth considering. In fact, most of what the lady said makes sense to me."

"Me too," said another, and then another.

"Nonsense," yelled one member of the crowd: "It was all nonsense." Others followed with shouts of "blasphemy," "the devil's doing," "may God strike you dead," and "you are surely bound for hell."

Small knots of people continued to argue as the sun faded and the crowd slowly dispersed. Mutterings continued to be heard in the hamlets surrounding Jerusalem - including its many alleys - as people returned to their homes and shared their reactions with their families and friends.

Assessing Reality

"Well, at least they did not attack us physically," I said with a laugh.

"I can appreciate the resistance," Magdalene whispered, as we spread our now very late lunch - or early supper - out on a blanket at a leveled spot just short of the entry point of the old city, realizing it was too late for us to be admitted into the city proper at that hour.

Like everyone else we continued to process our most recent set of interactions. "I am proud of those who at least tried to reconcile their current beliefs with the reality of cosmic love," said I.

"It was another *beginning* - although our going public again and again continues to feel like we are always at the beginning," said Mother Mary with a sigh. "It felt right to share what motivates us – and to do so publicly - yet I am concerned that I may have over or misstated our beliefs or make them seem so very complex to the average person."

"It takes a lot for folks to absorb what are to them totally new realities," said Magdalene: "Yeshua - the Son of God; our coming into this world through the process of incarnation; our Souls each taking on a physical body in order to do the work of the Lord here on Earth; and thus viewing things from both a cosmic and local dimension. That's a lot. And it all involves an enormous leap of faith – understandably straining the flexibility of the average person – especially since it is - to most people - so new and, we must admit, so comparatively revolutionary."

"And if you have always thought of religion in terms of only concrete rituals and religious activities, then our spirituality - explained mostly through the use of metaphors and references to inner conversions of the spirit, can seem unreal and far-fetched - indicating the divide between us and the general public is still very wide and deep."

"Frankly, at times – our simple truths initially felt far-fetched for me as well," said I, "except that I – like you, Magdalene - have spent years living with Yeshua and you, Mother Mary – seeing Your actions and absorbing Your gospel directly. And Your testimonies have been repeatedly reinforced by a whole set of tangible reinforcers - such as recently receiving the wise counsel of Gabriel and Raphael, the appearance of a band of Gnostics and then the real support of Angels – all of which have continued to fortify and greatly strengthen the intuitive prompting of our Souls."

"The same living and tangible referral system is not available to everyone. Most are not blessed with direct access to Yeshua and you Mother Mary, and are not yet aware of their capacity to gain the insights they want by simply asking to access Our Lord directly."

"It is wise, then," said Mother Mary, "to include the issue of people's understandable resistance to that which we have experienced and know so well. Our beliefs, based on our experiences, are so familiar to us. But that awareness will take time for the general public to accept. In our current time of turmoil, our affirmations - for the average person - understandably involves enormous leaps of faith."

The Price We Pay

"Yet many people seemed genuinely interested," I mused. "but they were so fearful that they tended to fall back on the old ways of thinking. Our message involves changing one's attitude and approach to life – and thus entails a great deal of work. The simple act of loving - unconditionally - seems so utterly new to so many. And it is very hard to do in the face of repeated provocations!"

"So it is easier for most to adopt a specific ritual or a creed than learning how to trust in themselves, their direct link to Prime Source, and just being in love with the world – especially when their daily experience suggests the best way to survive is to be distrustful, obey authority and participate as best one can in the mandated ways often presented to them."

"Yes – but it's inevitable that the word of the Lord breaks through here and there - and inevitably everywhere. Our work is helping to bend the curve – at least among those who continue to ask questions. Yet the opposition is strong and set in its ways," said Magdalene, ever the teacher and anticipator of history. "Unfortunately it will continue to include those who are about to emerge as arch-conservative clerics in the new church."

"There's Irenaeus, for example, the future Bishop of Lyon and author of the infamous 'Against Heresies'; the fierce Tertullian, the early apologist for the new church and severe critic of Gnosticism; and Ignatius, the eventual Bishop of Antioch – who along with the future Augustine, the famed Bishop of Hippo in North Africa - will doggedly espouse such debilitating doctrines as 'original sin'. Then there will also be such philosophers as Hippolytus and Polykarp who will strongly oppose any deviations from the norms established by what turns out to be the victorious orthodox clergy and their supposed very christian church."

"Among those to be condemned will include the future exponents of Yeshua's perspective - such as the highly spiritual and free-thinking Gnostic leaders Basilides, Valentinus, Marcus and Marcion [50] - whose spirits

---

50   See Stephan A. Hoeller, *Gnosticism: New Light on the Ancient Tradition*

we met recently. These men will adopt many of practices sponsored by the emerging Catholic majority - sacraments like baptism, matrimony, and the Eucharist. But they will avoid and reject any dependence on bishops and their string of assistants and intermediaries, instead insisting on their own natural sense of Gnosis and direct access to The Lord."[51]

"Some Gnostic theorists, however, have added a lot of explanatory theory to their work – much of it now seeming to be very silly. It alleged divisions and power plays among what they deemed the original divine energies of the universe. In truth, of course, Prime Source is and always will be One - although It invokes such Master Souls as Yeshua and our Mother Mary, the Archangels and a host of Angels and Ascended Masters [52] to deliver its messages and implement Its visions throughout the created realm."

---

of Inner Knowing (Wheaton, ILL: Quest Books, 2002).

51   For an excellent summary of the Gnostic perspective see Elaine Pagels, The Gnostic Gospels (New York: Vintage 1979). For the diverse sets of materials developed by the various Gnostic authors, see Marvin Meyer (ed.), The Nag Hammadi Scriptures: The Revised and Updated Translation of Sacred Gnostic Texts (New York: Harper One, 2008).

52   An Ascended Master is an immoral Soul who has attained great spiritual depth and experience through multiple incarnations and has thus volunteered to forgo returning fully to Spirit, choosing instead to serve other incarnates as they struggle to complete the terms of their contracts. Having experienced life as incarnates and attained the great spiritual depth desired, Ascended Masters are able to empathize with the spiritual dilemmas faced by the Souls embodied in the physical realm. Among the most frequently invoked Ascended Masters are St. Germain, Maitreya, Lord Lanto, Lady Nada, Lord Metatron and Kuthumi. Ascended Masters are likened to the Bodhisattvas of Buddhism who have earned nirvana but have chosen to postpone it in order to remain incarnate and assist others.

So Many Options

We approached the city initially from then north, followed the road as it bent south until it gently turned east and led us to the high grounds of the Mount of Olives. The outer walls were now in front of us – as they had been for Yershua when He entered the city on what became known as 'Palm Sunday'.

We could now see the full array of the city's eastern walls and could sight the upper reaches of the Temple. Before us lay lines of green olive trees - and to our left - the hundreds of tombstones that had been breached white by the arid sun.

Some portions of the outer walls of the city had deteriorated but all were still thirty feet high - each portion connected, thus enclosing and presumably protect ing its residents - just as they had when Yeshua entered the city years ago on Palm Sunday.

We stopped or paused frequently – as if to catch our breadth and to take in the realization that we had actually arrived at our destination. The Eternal City with its the seven square miles of homes and stores and religious expressions - containing a mixture of Jews, Arabs and an untold number of armed Roman soldiers - was as last before us.

Taking these last or culminating steps turned out to be a daunting task. We had arrived at our destination yet were still unsure as to what we wanted to do next. Make claim to what? Proclaim our arrival - yes. But on behalf of what particular memory or credo? Celebrate our return? Share our assessments of what we had learned since leaving so many years ago? Think of setting up a school – once we were settled? Form a community, build a Sanctuary - as we had in Britain? All worthy projects, each involving a great deal of work. And which would come first?

Or perhaps - we increasingly sensed - it would be enough to simply pause and acknowledge the essence of our accomplishment. Later - once inside the city - we could then share with whomever was within earshot, summarizing as briefly as we could - our experience of traveling first on land, then on a series of boats, sailing the length of the great sea, and then completing the journey by traversing the several landscapes of Europa. Or should we finally let all our reveries go and live purely of the moment – concentrate on the realization that we had achieved our goal – and then, and only then - go about the formal business of establishing a presence. Was it not enough to simply bask in our innocence, joy and wonder.

We wondered if we might again be confronted by a set of Sadducees and Roman troops, and asked once again to refute our beliefs in return for safe passage. Perhaps – no matter what – even at the price of being turned away – we knew we were there to assert what we had come to know as essential: if in any way provoked, we would speak softly, lovingly but with enthusiasm for the wondrous perspectives of our divine Lord and God!

So much, so much.

Finally, Mother Mary suggested a way to resolve our quandary. "Let's just stay in the moment: We made it! So let's enjoy this magnificent view of the city, relax, unwind here on this lovely hill just above the city gates, and, of course – give thanks"

"I love it," said Magdalene.

"Let's make it unanimous," said I.

Individuality in Unity

Mother Mary noted that She also wished to excuse Herself - and run what She called and 'essential errand'. "I shan't be long," She said.

"I would also appreciate a few moments to mediate upon a special intention I have carried with me since we departed our Sanctuary in Britannia" said Magdalene.

"Fine with me," said I. "No hurry. Let's take as much time as we need to get as centered as we can. Our very next step is indeed highly symbolic. One great adventures is about to be completed while another surely awaits us. Besides, I want to finish making notes on the last few days. I could use a few moments to bring it up to date and celebrate this momentous occasion."

"Let us make that unanimous," smiled Yeshua – who arrived and departed so often of late that we were never sure where He was at any particular moment. "I just ran a special errand. Why shouldn't you?" - He said with a broad grin. "It took us a long time to get here - so you would think we would be disposed to rush ahead. Fully embracing the future, however, is not an easy task. Best we each be settled in mind and spirit before pushing on the Damascus gate and finding our way through the city's maze of streets. Surely much is the same but much has also changed."

"The central reality is that We have indeed made it. We are here at the walls of our sacred city, peering down it in all its glory. I agree with Mother Mary: Let's enjoy and celebrate the moment. So - everyone: take your time, and do whatever you need to do before We cross the final border and embrace the next phase of our journey."

Gifts Galore

Mother Mary was the first to return to our spot atop the Mount of Olives - returning an hour later with an assorted bouquet of flowers. In it were cultivated blossoms purchased at a shop outside the walls to the Temple. The assortment also contained many sprigs of olive leaf. And placed within the bouquet were a sprinkling of wild flowers – the colorful kind that grow along the roadside.

"I wanted to dedicate these flowers to us: to all the love we have shared and created since our parting."

"I too arrive with a gift," said I. "In this bag is an assortment of rocks – small ones, of course – that I have collected at many of the various points to which we traveled when we last saw and departed from Jerusalem: Joppa, Crete, Malta, Gaul, Britain, our Sanctuary at Glastonbury, the Sea of Galilee, and since then, remembrances of the many towns we visited since making our way through Israel and Judea. Each pebble or rock serves as a reminder of our progress and determination. Together they commemorate both our initial journey and our fateful return."

"Well, it looks like it is my turn," said Magdalene cheerfully, nodding in my direction. "I have been writing as well - as you may know – focusing on writing short phrases and poems. I wrote my latest just last night. It speaks of the paths we have taken and the many internal walkways we have learned to investigate and affirm. I note their existence now - in commemoration of our reaching our sacred City."

"As for Me," murmured Yeshua. "I too have been planning and plotting to offer you-all a commemorative gift. I would love to share more with you now – but prefer to do so a bit later after I have counseled with our guardian Archangels - Gabriel, Raphael and Michael.."

A New Beginning

Down the winding path along the Olive Trees we went, following its slanting and downward slope all the way to the eastern wall of the citadel. The old city was rectangular in shape so We followed along that eastern wall until it turned sharply north at the corner. Within fifty paces we found ourselves at the steps to the ancient Damascus gate.

It was there that we paused, realizing that we were finally ready and able to reenter into the sacred grounds of the inner city of Jerusalem.

But Yeshua - our magnificent, unpredictable and ever playful leader - was not with us - causing Mother Mary to recall – once again – the similar incident that happened many years ago when the young Yeshua stayed behind to interact with the Rabbis following His bar mitzvah.

We looked in every direction but he was nowhere in sight.

"He always has His reasons - always something to do with counseling with The Lord. Let's be patient. He will join us as soon as He can."

Depth Spirituality

His momentary absence once again created a temporary gap in our foursome - leading us to be ever so aware of His pivotal role - not just in completing the physical journey from Jerusalem and back - but in providing the motivational energy for both.

Yeshua's initial decision to enter Jerusalem so many years ago was an epic moment in the history of religion - for it laid the foundation for the most loving version of spirituality the world had ever seen. His incarnation - following His nine month incubation within the womb of Mother Mary - was the culmination of all His earlier appearances as a sage, adept and spiritual leader throughout the world's varied cultures and historical timeframes. It also marked the inauguration of a new chapter in the history of the world, one in which the long history of religions – those past and about to emerge - gave way to the advocate and purveyor of Pure Spirituality. He had finally fulfilled His intended role as the anointed one who was to serve as Prime Source's perpetual representative in the manifest universe of creation.

Yeshua's assertion that each person has the capacity to create and mold his or her own individual spiritual practice - superseded all the earlier efforts to harness people to one institutional religion or another. Devotions to the Lord henceforth were to be based – not on adherence to cultural practice or institutional mandate – but on an individual's commitment to lead a life of love and compassion. Such dedicated individuals – bonded as they would be to a universal community – were henceforth encouraged to affirm their identity as integral cells of the cosmic body of the All, Prime Source.

Suddenly

Suddenly there He was there - singing a song that went like this:

> "I am as ever - with you,
> "Long have we been united,
> "Portending what will always be.
> "I too celebrate our journey
> "Both to and fro.
> "So may I walk with you
> "As ever
> "As we complete the cycle
> "As One."

"Yeshua," cried Mary. "I knew it, I knew it, I knew it – and I have prayed for it – and now here You are in your rightful place - as you always are and ought to be."

"How could I not be part of this final step in our Our return," said Yeshua, "I have been waiting for you. I even thought of reentering the city earlier – thinking I would use the time to obtain a sort of sneak preview and make any special arrangement needed. But neither My spirit or this body of mine could be forced to go beyond the portal to this main gate - without you."

"Besides, this mission has always been a joint project – one in which we intended to use our earlier experiences throughout Palestine as spring-boards for expanding our mission - inviting everyone we met to join in our crusade of love."

"We have entered through many a gate before...and always together. This should be no different - especially since none of our earlier crossings have been as meaningful as the one that lies before us today."

He was greeted with such responses as 'indeed', 'yes, My Lord', 'thanks be to God' - and shouts of 'onward', 'inspired' and 'blessed.'

And So We Danced

Yeshua then motioned for us to loosen our packs and find a spot on the large slabs that served as the steps to the fabled point of entry.

"Now for My special gift - My offering in thanks to all of you for making our return possible. We left this wondrous city many years ago – and did so under trying circumstances. We did not want to leave, of course, but a series of negative forces were aligned conclusively against us – signaling that we needed to pursue a new, adventurous – and yes, we should realize – an inspired way of expanding our message. And we knew we needed to deliver that message beyond any one geographic or political border – instead inviting the entire world to hear and heed our call to live with love and compassion."

"And so we have travelled - and will continue to do, together, alone and with others – having loved the distant lands and all its people - yet anticipating, even longing - for the day when we would mark a return to Spirit's greatest celebration. Today is that day. And this gate marks the point of our return, the closing of the circle, the completion of one entire turn on the spiritual spiral."

"I am sorry to have surprised you – but I needed to seek advice from our famed trio of Archangels on the staging and wording of a short but very special chant and ceremony. I scampered back here as soon as I could, however - hurrying so that I was actually early," He said with laughter.

"So let us celebrate – giving thanks that we are indeed together at this special moment. Surely we have reason to celebrate - in fact - to sing - and to dance."

Up we jumped, retreated a step or two to flat ground, formed into a circle, and began to clap and shout to a beat of our own making.

"Let us form and be as whole as a circle," said Yeshua.

And the rest of us repeated the refrain.

"And let us give thanks," cried Mother Mary.

And the others repeated the refrain.

"And may we ever seek spiritual adventure," said Magdalene.

And the refrain was repeated by all.

"And may we always love God, ourselves and each other," said I.

And the others – naturally - repeated the refrain.

There We Were

Our reentry into Jerusalem obviously was no ordinary event. Epic, revolutionary, awe-inspiring, cosmic in impact – these are the words we later used to describe the emotional fullness of our return.

It was no surprise that Yeshua and Mother Mary led the way. Together they sighed deeply, reached up, touched the gate, pushed it open - and re-entered the City.

We peered at the shops, purchased some fruit and water, looked up at the buildings and were surprised by the heat emanating from the paving stones. We heard birds singing – from both cages and roof tops – and listened to those advertising their foods, bowls, scandals and freshly woven garments.

Down the alleys we went, inhaling the scents and sounds, pointing to various portions of the city as they appeared in view, moving through the curving alleys and negotiating the undulations in the terrain, even smiling at the consistent bleating of sheep - rounding one bend - then another - until we finally gazed upon the hilltop from which we once witnessed that horrific yet stunning light show.

The Eternal Presence

We agreed: it was indeed very wise and significant that we revisit the scene that had so shaped our lives and led to the clarification our missions. For Magdalene and I, our return made us realize all the more that our journey to Britannia and founding the Sanctuary fulfilled the promises each of us made when we transited as incarnates from the spiritual to the material realm.

For Yeshua and Mother Mary, however, it marked not only the completion of the Jerusalem-to-Britannia circuit and back. It clearly and once again honored their joint status as the Master Souls - as well as their capacity - as incarnates - to come full circle from their initial earthly appearances as the mythic Adam and Eve.

Prime Source created the world – and humankind – and as noted in the Hebrew testament, declared each incremental step as "good." But – as we know – physical creation was only a précis to achieving the deeper and longer-range task of then sending two eternal guides to the incarnate world to help us learn how to live with love and the joy of making a contribution to the lives of others.

Standing on the heights as we did so many years ago, we gave thanks for the many embodied luminaries who - through the centuries - encouraged everyone to contribute to the Earth's spiritual evolution and thereby help to transform the incarnate realm.

In fact, we surely owe double thanks to Adam and Eve - who in bringing the process of incarnation to Earth - set off generations of 'begots', not just of human incarnates as noted in the Hebrew Testament [53] but staged manifestations of divinity Itself, culminating in the evolution of our Master Souls, Yeshua and Mother Mary.

As noted earlier, masculine forms of Yeshua highlighted in biblical writings included Adam, Seth, Enoch, Moses, David, Joseph, Joshua and Melchizedek. The biblical references to the incarnate forms of Mother

---

53   Numbers 26.

Mary include Deborah, Esther, Hagar, Jezebel, Lilith, Miriam, Rebekah, Sarah and Tamar. [54]

Besides the references included in the Bible of the Middle East, each major culture also had its own representatives of the Master Souls of Yeshua and Mary. That listing for Yeshua includes the Asian Buddha and several Bodhisattvas, the Hindu incarnates of Atman-Brahman, the early Middle Eastern mystics, such revered messengers as Mohammed, the various leaders of such Indian tribes as the Shoshoni and the Hopi, and the tens of other spiritual adepts and cultural leaders who emerged throughout the world's cultures. It was our own Yeshua and His Mother Mary who continually embodied the essence of the Divine Soul, opening one door after another for Prime Source to manifest Its presence throughout the physical reality.

Last and Least

And so Magdalene and I assessed the significance of our part in and hopeful contribution - in particular - to our Lady's and our Lord's journeys and their perpetual presence as guides and healer to all the Souls who enter the incarnate world of embodiment.

We did our best to fulfill our assignments – giving witness, for example, to Yeshua's decision to honor Isaiah while disclaiming the fate of the 'suffering servant'. Then we assisted the journey of the 'sacred family' through Europe. We helped them get settled in Britain as they established a community to serve the public, founded a Sanctuary and inaugurated a revolving liturgical service that honored The Lord in each of Its hallowed directions and aspects. We then served as companions to and protectors of Mother Mary as we traveled back to Palestine. And most recently, we helped Mother Mary and Yeshua complete their triumphant returns to Jerusalem.

---

54   See earlier references to: 'Realities', Chapter 1. Yeshua Opens the Conference, especially footnotes 15-18.

Each step Magdalene and I have taken en route has had a special meaning. Each experience has strengthened our resolve to serve, tested our capacity to be flexible and find the wit to handle each emerging problem with a set of skills we never knew we had. We served Yeshua and Mother Mary best by allowing ourselves to be guided by their words and actions, expressing our love of God with each new adventure – and adding our intentional love and our compassion as we were able.

It has been a long, fulfilling and at times bewildering journey. We have talked about it often - and we both agree we have reason to feel blessed, enabled in our dialogues to be devoted friends to each other. Given the millions of Souls who choose to place their embodiments on Earth around the same time as our Souls' most recent incarnation, it is astounding to us that we chose and were chosen to serve the Master and His Mother so directly.

We realize, as well, that we have been ever so fortunate to not only meet and talk with Yeshua and Mother Mary but then given the opportunity to interact with them - very day - for weeks, months and now years - and even live with them under the same roof - so to speak. Through a series of adventures, chats, hugs and both tearful and cheerful encounters, we learned to love them as real persons as well as revere them for their divine presence, radiance and power.

By following their counsel, by walking with them and learning from their example, we learned - above all - to love ourselves and value the people and angelic figures we encountered en route. Not bad for two walk-ins, two mere mortals privileged to have Souls who chose to place their incarnates in such blessed and glorious situations. How miraculous is that? And - indeed – how very fortunate are we!

Whole Cloth

Yeshua took off His cloak and spread it on the ground.

"Every part of this garment is important. Each part plays a role in keeping Me warm. Yet I do not attend to one part only – washing and mending only a pocket, or the hood, the sash, the hem, or just the inner versus the outer layers. It is one garment and all of its many aspects are valued and appreciated as integral parts of the whole."

"So it is with our incarnate world - Jerusalem, Britain, Europa, India, China, the North and South Americas and the great seas - all countries, parts and aspects that border, support and lay adjacent to each other. In short, it is about time that we launched another foray into the land of 'universality' - a spiritual perspective that invites everyone to honor all parts of our universe, love all peoples and all of our brethren who now or will soon inhabit this globe as integral facets of the cosmos."

"May individual variations and cultural diversities always exist – for they are essential ways of honoring the diverse aspects of the Lord and Its wondrous variety of appearances. The basis for such variations, however, is the oneness of its unity, the centrality of all who are destined to love and affirm each other despite outer appearances. The variations in birth place, language, race and culture are simply God's way of displaying Itself through our diversity. Every variation is thus a play on the theme of Oneness, each a slice of Our Lord's ubiquitous presence contributing to the unity of the whole - each reflecting an aspect of Its eternal presence in each and every nook and cranny of the universe."

Full Circle

"Thus the circle, our circle, the universal circle," cried Mother Mary, "is about the business of becoming complete. The rational and sequential findings of the West will soon be wedded to the intuitive processes and affirmations of the East, the masculine essence with that of the feminine. Experiential contact with the cosmic Creator through the prayers and actions of the West is finding its complement in the Eastern emphasis on direct communication with The Lord through in-depth meditation and contemplation."

"The West's cultural empowerments to heal, bless and affirm are balanced by the Eastern emphasis on enabling through patience and receptivity. And the fears of the West – such as the alleged need for redemption from the so-called sins of Adam and Eve, the goal of being 'saved' from a supposed hell, and the tendency to depend on the mandates proclaimed by a hierarchy of ordained clergy – is being tempered by the Eastern love of relaxing, accepting and appreciating the insights and resonance of the moment. Thus does *willing* partner with *allowing.*"

"This revolutionary unity of perspectives, approaches and behaviors," Yeshua continued, "was on display when We walked through the Damascus Gate and reentered the Old City. We wanted to make the journey and then allowed it to unfold. The spiritual pathways of humankind of each complemented one another, thus creating a holistic and unified approach to The Lord. The old and the new have alternated for centuries and are now meshed together. Even the clergy who present their respective churches as the exclusive home sites for Prime Source are gradually allowing themselves to let go of such silliness and accept the reality that every creed and theology, every city and glen, every walkway and tent presents a natural dwelling place for the Lord."

A New Epoch

"Soon everyone will realize," cried Mother Mary, "that everything – including every object and aspect, all flowers of all shades, the faces of every culture, all the diverse forms of art and music – although valued in themselves are best appreciated when experienced as vital parts of the overall fabric of Life, as distinct contributors to the essential resonance of the *Essence.*"

"The future is both now and incessantly becoming. What is fading is any reliance on all-powerful hierarchies. Yearnings to rule over an obedient and disemboweled laity are set to disappear. Any emphasis on *sin,* and the need to be *saved* from a destination that never existed will also evaporate. The need to obtain the imprimatur of a state or religious official in order to voice one's beliefs or manifest ones's soulfulness will also wither away."

"The repeated emphasis on fear, the concern for crossing the line of what those in power deem correct, the risk of being judged an apostate by any self-proclaimed advocate of superiority – will each be replaced by the sounds of freedom rendered in song and dance. Simple conversation will demonstrate the glory of being a joyful and creative aspect of the cosmic reality. Sharing with one's neighbors will reveal an abiding belief in the unity of life – willed and supported by an ever-creating God who is always learning, always adapting, always loving, and always growing as it continually expands and deepens Its capacity to love."

"Recognizing God's ceaseless development and expansion – and our individual roles in making Its presence manifest - will lead to the celebration of continuous re-creation and extension of the universe. Such is the cycle of organic growth and development - each phase of the creative process supporting the next cycle of the the double spirals of the Loving God - one going ever deeper and inward as the other expands ever outward. An all-pervasive aura of peace and harmony will bubble forth and shine through - on a New Earth that affirms the glory of the Universal ALL."

Old and New Memories

Mother Mary smiled at last - relieved to once again be on the hillside that overlooked the epic events of yesteryear. She knew now that Her Son was very much alive – in body and spirit - so alive that She hugged Him in earnest - again and again. Still there were mixed blessing: She had years to love and adore Yeshua as a child and youngster. Yet the later years forced Her to experience a million and one fears and a series of mini-deaths as they struggled to avoid the taunts and treats of Temple and Roman officials. Through it all, She learned how to exert unconditional love in any and all circumstances, appreciative of all the blessings She received while bearing the burdens of being the Mother of a person who was loved and adored by thousands but who also had to undergo continual pursuit and condemnation.

Despite the memories and lingering concerns, She was now assured that Her Son was well, whole, protected – there beside Her – even as She remembered with horror the beams of lights emanating from the heavenly lasers and depicting the hateful intentions of some very angry and very frightened Roman and Temple officials.

Admittedly, the bond Prime Source had anticipated Yeshua making with the Jewish people had proven difficult to implement. Still Mother Mary paid tribute to the many prophets who honored the Lord during the worst of times; She recalled, for example, the stirring and encouraging words of the many prophets who for the sake of justice admonished the self-proclaimed warlords of their generation. And She anticipated the continuous contributions the Jewish people would make - century after century - to family, tradition and the abiding love of the Lord.

The practical wisdom acquired by all the earlier incarnates of His Soul enabled It to acquire the behavioral skills needed for Yeshua to become the Master Soul and navigate His way through the politics of Palestine. His indebtedness and continuous linkage to His Jewish roots and upbringing would always to be honored, as would His connection to the stamina, goodwill and devotions of the Jewish people He met during His mission to Palestine.

Through it all, His ultimate status - and all the empowerments and responsibilities that went with it - increased exponentially as He completed His destiny and became a Master Soul. He was no longer in training, accumulating the insights of the work He completed in one culture after another. He had – at last - arrived at His appointed place - both in Heaven and in the earthly domain.

Good portions of His upgraded mandate obviously transferred to Mother Mary in the form of empowerments, blessings and increased responsibilities. Yet none of those infusions came easy for Mother Mary: learning to acquire the depth of Soul needed to live in solitude in the Jewish temple; later being bequeathed to an older man; confronted by an angel with a most incredible message and commission; giving birth to the Master Soul while traveling on the road and doing so within an animal shelter; delivering Yeshua to a world that wavered between loving devotion, benign neglect and outright resistance and violence; living the life of a devoted wife and guide to Yeshua and the sons of Joseph; weathering the blows of Her Son's uncertain and at times tumultuous commissions; standing with Him on the fearful days of the staged passion; energizing our long and arduous jaunt to Britannia; bringing to life to and then sustaining the Sanctuary at Glastonbury; then being Assumed into Heaven and honored as a Master Soul before deciding to return to the physical realm in order to continue serving all who needed Her love and guidance.

Fortunately, She – and He – weathered each storm and transition and did so together, overcoming the initial concerns of being ordinary incarnates, intent on inspiring everyone They met and healed all who needed Their blessings, and in the process laying the foundations for the likes of you and me to both serve and thrive as each new era of the universe unfolds.

Birth, life, love, purpose and transformation - had triumphed. The loving destiny Mother and Son had worked so hard to imprint on the incarnational world had succeeded. Their work and dedication created a glorious agenda, their combined energies manifest a fierce determination and vibrancy, and their messages and actions created a spiritual revolution that continues to unfold as we speak. And their combined and continuous missions have not only been appreciated and ordained - in Heaven and on Earth. They are also venerated for having fostered an endless supply of love and compassion for, within and throughout the universe.

Mirror Images

Through it all I have come to realize the glory and profundity of that which we oft tend to take for granted. How remarkable, how incredible, how awesome and yet how mysterious is the creative process of life.

My experiences of Mother Mary and Yeshua have left their indelible marks, helping me to understand the depth of some incredible truths. Those truths may sound too simple to some. But they have had - and are still having a transformative impact on me: on who I am, what I value, and how I wish to lead my life. Witness the following utterly horrendous realizations:

- Incarnation - whereby an immortal Soul chooses to serve in the physical domain - is the remarkable process by which we immoral Souls become human.

- The joining of male and female energies is the creative force that leads to the physical birth of nothing less than an incarnated Soul and the creation of a fully empowered human being.

- Women beget children – which is a miraculous process in itself – but is superseded by their capacity to simultaneously give birth to the incarnation of an immortal Soul.

- Sacred seeds are shared by males who through the miraculous impact of their love ignite the formation of a fetus that in only nine months is transformed into the embodiment of an immortal Soul.

- Before, during and after the birth of an incarnate, the process of incarnation thrives on love as it produces a human capable of contributing to the welfare of both the spiritual and physical realms of life.

- Incarnation is an avenue of exaltation – one that leads to and celebrates everyone's ability to sponsor a series of divine-like activities in the everyday world.

- Divinity in Itself involves the intention and capacity to transmit Its energy into concrete forms – manifest through the empowerment of Its immoral Souls to incarnate in the material realm and thereby extend and deepen the presence of divine energy throughout the cosmos.

- Mother Mary, Yeshua and Prime Source are together a sacred Trinity that perfectly manifests the unity of the One as our supreme benefactor.

And so it has been and will assuredly always will be. The story of Mother Mary and Yeshua's journey from Jerusalem and back again has also become a mirror of our own development, coming full circle, heaven to earth and back again, carrying the creative power of the Lord into a form that enables us to contribute to the continuous development of the universe.

Oh-my, oh-my, oh my…

Chapter IX

Prologue

Unfinished

THE CONFERENCE HAD RECONVENED.

Yeshua stood tall, folding His hands as He looked at the heavens. Finally He looked up and smiles. His hands are open and His arms extended as He bows to the large gathering assembled to honor Mother Mary.

"You may remember we convened this conference in order to celebrate the one and only: My Mother - Mother Mary. Having revisited the most significant and telling portions of Her incredible story, We wish now to conclude by dedicating this finale as a special honoring of Her."

He paused - then resumed.

"I will first summarize the essence of Her story and its string of incredible events – and will do so s-low-ly - in order to remind everyone of its heavenly and earth-shattering significance," He continued.

"Once back here on Earth, Mother, as you now know, She heeded the wishes of Prime Source, My and Our Father, and – following the annunciations of Gabriel – conceived a Son to whom She gave birth – a miraculous feat unto itself – all so that I too might incarnate and complete My chosen Mission. She so loved Me, and everyone She engaged throughout Her many incarnations, that God the Father choose - as you know - to

honor Her again by first assuming Her back into Heaven and then desig-
nating Her as a Master Soul."

"But," said Yeshua, "Mother Mary - always looking for another challenge and another opportunity to give of Herself - chose to leave the heavenly sphere and re-incarnate, return to Earth still again – for no other
reason than, in Her words, She 'had another incarnate life to live, and more
contributions to make to My beloved friends in the physical realm.'"

"Thank God for Mother Mary," someone called out, and the crowd
applauded vigorously.

"Enough of concluding remarks - at least for now," laughed Yeshua,
and the crowd roared, Yeshua quickly adding: "In this regard, I follow the
lead of my earthly father - our beloved, Father Joseph - who is so adept at
ending a presentation - and then immediately including just another thousand words or two. We will hear from Father Joseph again, I am sure, before
this special gathering is convened" - to which the crowd of guests roared
its approval.

The Story to Date

"Let me be clear," Yeshua added, "Mother Mary will, of course, continue to
live among us – as will I - and do so in perpetuity. You should know, as well,
that Our combined purviews have expanded to encompass all those who
have incarnated - not just on Earth - but everywhere in this planetary system
- including those who will soon incarnate on and/or relocate to Earth II. [55]

---

55   The Earth and its inhabitants will experience a series of very difficult
changes - beginning around 2010 and continuing for some 20 years. Those
changes will include a series of catastrophes such as a series of viral pandemic
infections, volcanic eruptions, meteor showers, and severe climate changes
that will provoke a slow but substantial rise in temperatures, severe melting
of the ice caps and massive flooding.
Such changes are the result of the continual expansion of the ozone zone in
the Earth's atmosphere, and the failure to switch from fossil fuels to the

Our individual and combined areas of responsibility, so to speak, are well on their way to including the entire cosmos and all the Souls and Beings who choose to serve in the far-flung domains of our ever-expanding universe."

Instantly, there were shouts of approval: "Go Mother Mary. Go Yeshua. Go Prime Source!" "May You never stop sharing Your wisdom with us," "You are our eternal guides."

"Let's not too excited," said Yeshua. "Then everyone will want to say a word or two – including you know who – and we will never be able to return to our intended focus on the beliefs and impacts of Mother Mary."

A spirited group in the rear then started a rhythmic chanting of: "FA-ther JO-seph, FA-ther JO-seph, FA-ther...."

"See what I mean," said Yeshua as He waved to His earthly Father seated just off to His left, who in response waved, laughed and then shouted, "I'll be patient, I'll be patient: my time will come!"

"Now – back on topic," said Yeshua as the crowd slowly quieted down.

---

cleaner and thus healthy reliance on wind and solar energy. These problems have exacerbated the historic need for Gaia to cleanse the many areas on Her Earth that were and continue to be devastated by war and degraded by the cumulative effects of human avarice, greed and neglect.

The formation of *Earth II* will literally involve the migration of two types of incarnates to the new planet: many of the Souls now anticipating incarnation, and many now on Earth who are dedicated to fostering ecological and spiritual health of their new home.

The appearance of *Earth II* may not become noticeable - physically and spiritually - for several more years, but certainly emerging some time between 2026 and 2032. Those who chose to ignore and/or support the continuing neglect and devastation of the original Earth will - by inference and choice - remain on it and thereby inherit the deteriorating conditions they directly or indirectly helped to create.

"For starters, I realize many Souls were misled by the false interpretations of Mother Mary's life and thus My current incarnation - propagated by some overly assertive and presumptuous clerics who let their imaginations build on some very distorted misinformation. For some - there is still the silly issue, for example, of My alleged death by crucifixion and thus Mother's unending grief and sorrow."

"The evidence - and thus the emphasis today is on our obvious good health and well-being, and in particular on Mother Mary's continuing capacity to guide, serve and inspire everyone She encounters."

"So be forewarned. Mother Mary's life of dedication means you either have been or soon will be affected by Her grace and radiance. Given all the testimonies we have shared to date regarding the life choices made by Mother Mary, we urge you to emulate Her graceful style, Her sensitivities, Her devotion, Her ability to achieve what She intended, Her ability to heed God's counsel and not only work for but with others. Model your life on Hers; it offers a prime example for what you - and everyone - can achieve when motivated by unconditional love and compassion."

"With your prayers and affirmations, Her presence will continue to evoke a spiritual revolution in this world and throughout the cosmos. As we salute and join in Her mission, we do our part to create - in Her name - a world filled with untrammeled love, joy and peace."

Increasing Spirituality

"So allow Me to expand upon what We once referred to as *religion* but which - given Mother Mary's impact and your many contributions - has become a gospel of love, which over the centuries has expanded and deepened into the affirmation of and growing call for – *"Universal Spirituality"* *('US')*."

Each of the many cultures in which we incarnated throughout history, for example, has made a contribution to honoring an important facet of spirituality. Despite their shortcoming, the many religions of humankind have continually expressed their human instinct to honor the supernatural or what we now know as 'Prime Source'. And in each of Our many appearances, We have tried our best to at least advance some aspect of the spiritual essence without totality overturning the sponsoring culture or doing more than a given historic epoch would allow. Thus progress was evolutionary - each advance We affirmed setting the stage for the next and the next spiritual contribution - until We recently and finally embraced the fullness of Our destinies." [56]

"Take for example, the earlier advances made by the Upanishads and the proponents of the Daoism; then exhibited in the life and work of Confucius and the Buddha; followed by the aspects of religion embraced progressively by selected leaders of the Sumerian, Akkadian, Assyrian, Semite and the Egyptian civilizations. Such contributors often overlapped the contributions made by the various leaders of the many religious sects of India, Japan, and China; followed by those displayed by the prophets of Judaism, Christianity and Islam; subsequently expressed by our appearances as spiritual spokesmen for many MesoAmerican, South American and Native North American Indian tribes. Later We even incarnated as advocates of a few of the spiritual-psychological approaches that emerged in the modern era; and now continue to sponsor many of the ecumenical movements helping to establish greater unity among the various religious and spiritual perspectives."

"The continual and progressive nature of all things religious and spiritual is as old as the universe itself. The inclusive nature of generic *spirituality - with its* emphases on love and compassion - is now being adopted on a global scale as the heavily defined, bounded and denominational forms of religion fade and expire."

"The urge for 'Universal Spirituality' began with the first incarnation of the Soul we now honor as Mother Mary, and underwent a series of unique manifestations and upgrades as it progressively appeared in culture after culture though the eons of time. Despite many attempts to extinguish

---

56   For a list of Our earlier incarnations, see the sections 'Realities', 'Evolutionary Progress,' and 'Continuous Unfolding' in *Chapter 1: Yeshua Opens the Conference,* including footnotes 16-20.

Her varied expressions, the divine feminine has always re-emerged with ever greater vibrancy. The tenets of love and compassion have proven to be - not only the underlying thread of most religions and spiritual philosophies throughout the centuries but are now being increasingly affirmed as *the essence of spiritual living.*"

"Thus the need to remind - all of us - that eternity is also much larger, longer, more complex and varied than mere earthly time can even imagine. The one and only constant referent is *eternal time* – a bit of an oxymoron but one that puts our earthly or incarnate times in perspective. The current expressions of *Soulfulness* - as significant as they are - are only a small part of the much deeper, extensive and ever-evolving reality known as the 'Spiritual Universe'."

"Be assured that many of the current articulations of religion - and even spirituality – will continue to exist because they have been created by and thus tailored to the needs of particular cultures and traditions. Having made their contributions to the continual emergence of the spiritual needs embedded in humankind, the many distinct denominations will continue to fade in popularity and gradually disappear or implode under the pressure of their own exclusivity and resistance to the more inclusive calls for generic love and compassion."

"Each generation of incarnates increasingly wish to become a tribe of one or simply ally informally with those have a similar perspective, those spontaneous congregations of kindred Souls who neither want or need structural support or hierarchical distinctions. Moreover such individual and informal groupings will be disposed to honor and be guided by those among them who display the greatest insight and devotion to the guidelines of love and compassion - a natural style of leadership that circulates the individuals and issues and determine."

"As we world-citizens increasingly follow the transcendental themes of natural inclusion and spiritual camaraderie, the benefits of our actions will not be confined to this Earth alone. Rather our work will become a model for 'taking it on the road' - so to speak - championing the universal gospel of love and compassion in every arena in the cosmos."

Unity

"Soooo," Yeshua concluded. "Mother Mary's contributions will continue to invigorate the evolution of the entire material domain. If any philosophies and religions of the Earth define Prime Source as a denominational preserve, they will inevitably be ignored and become irrelevant and obsolete. If they choose to interpret their cultural interpretation of religion to be anything more than a contribution to spiritual consciousness, they too will be swept aside by the continued unfolding of spiritual reality."

"But if...

- they believe in, support and honor Prime Source – the Creative Being who continues to expand and deepen Its cosmic expressions throughout the physical realm.

- honor the primacy of love and compassion,

- respect and defend those who choose to display their spirituality through customs, rituals and elemental rules that are different from their own,

- then, they surely will continue to contribute to the flow of an all-inclusive and Universal Spirituality and live in the spirit of Our Mother Mary."

"Got it?" asked Yeshua.

"Got it!" roared the gathering of representatives from the entire range of physical and psychic activity. Cries of support could also be heard from the millions of want-a-be incarnates still in-training - anticipating the contributions they too intended to make to the continued evolution of the Earth.

"In conclusion," said an increasingly earnest Yeshua. "There are three sets of affirmations to which the life of our dear Mother has been dedicated: 'universal inclusion', 'unity through diversity', and 'love and compassion'."

"Alas, will we all be 'on the same page' - so to speak - working in our various ways, in our particular arenas to achieve the universality of love for all beings. Everything, everywhere, all the time: that is the goal. And that is Mother Mary's call to action."

The Evolving Future

"So when it comes of Christianity - in particular - and its silly and false references to My alleged passion, crucifixion and resurrection - although well-intended - only continue to confuse things and serve as obstacles to the truth. Please - gently remove all the crosses, all the paintings of Me and My Mother in alleged agony, all the expressions of alleged passion – all that erroneous, misleading and negative stuff. Twenty centuries of portraying something that never happened, namely My allegedly hideous death and Mother Mary's resultant agony – has historically done its best to try Our divine patience - not really - but you know what I mean!"

"Now the purveyors of Christianity have attempted to balance all that false negativity with a positive event, namely the *Resurrection* – something that should indeed to be celebrated - not as a one time event - but as a perpetual reality. Mother Mary and I have been assigned by Prime Source to be here - fully resurrected for eternity - and that is a fact!"

"The world, the consciousness of humankind, the old but weathered practices are finally giving way to a simple and direct gospel that espouses the global standard of love, the pre-eminence of tolerance and compassion, and the affirmation of Prime Source's continuous creation, development and expansion. Like the rest of life, the esense of *Universal Spirituality* continues to evolve in depth and influence – ceaselessly learning how to reconfigure the past, inspire the present and advance a future that unites *Logos* and *Mythos* into ever greater expression of *Spiritos.*"

Look to the Feminine

"So what lies ahead?"

"Here's a hint: look to the feminine to take the lead, inviting the masculine to join with it in remaking both the immediate environment of the Earth and long range development of the universe. Look to the feminine priority on love and compassion – the overt manifestations of the feminine archetype of Mother Mary - to affirm and expand the role that intentional unity and wholeness play in the continued evolution of the entire physical realm as it learns how to emulate the dynamics of the heavenly sphere."

"As to the immediate future of our planet, Earth: please do everything you can to encourage and support the role of the feminine wisdom in medicine, in business, in sports - and especially in politics where every aspect of the current and cruel imbalance exists. It is time such historical injustices are corrected – not just for the sake of the individuals involved but for all of society. Our world badly needs the infusion of feminine energies and perspectives if it is to minimize and then eliminate both the systemic damage caused by the past and still ongoing dominance of an overly-assertive and self-centered male ego."

"The natural inheritance of all living creatures combines what are considered masculinity's finest psychological contributions (goal setting, assertion, differentiation, consciousness and clarity), with the best of the feminine empowerments (empathy, compassion, love, inclusion and intuitive insight and understanding)."

"So everyone has the capacity to be a fine blend of both. But males, of course, more readily access their masculine psychological inclinations, while women more naturally express their feminine affinities for love and nurturance. The genitalia of the sexes is demonstrative: males display their creative potential with organs that are on the exterior of the body. The female creative genius is basically internal - with the capacity to conceive, birth and nurture a new being."

"Unfortunately, the greater muscular physical bulk of most males relative to most females, plus their innately assertive propensities - have, one, tended to suppress their own innate feminine capacities while, two, literally pushing the physically smaller and instinctively more accommodating females aside, thereby fulfilling their self-fulfilling prophecy to 'be in charge and in control.'"

"The question now is: has the male drive to dominate the positions of power and influence - served the human race well? The appropriate and wise female reaction is: you have caused enough wars with your over-assertive and inflated egos, neglected the need to create cooperative relationships and allowed many aspects of our planet to deteriorate and face devastation.

It is time for you to move over, stop trying to play 'top dog', share the agenda and incorporate if not embrace your capacity to be both caring and decisive. Only then will both sexes reach more nurturing, win-win solutions to the world's problems."

"I know Mother Mary agrees: it is time for the natural female energies within both sexes combine to overcome centuries of male dominated decision-making. Men and woman can and should work together to enact policies - that benefit not just the already rich and powerful - but as many people as possible - especially the needy, the youth, children and all those who tend to be neglected when pure male energies dominate the scene."

Affirm the Mixed Combos

"I do indeed agree," said Mother Mary, jumping from Her seat. "This brings us to the need to overtly affirm the rights and abilities of people of all races, skin colorings and cultural backgrounds. Long has the 'white race' attempted to assert superiority and denigrated the black, brown, tan, yellow and red skinned coloring of other humans. All skin colorings and bodily postures are reflections of divinity and thus are of equal essence and ingrained talent. Please realize: each is a product of the divinely-inspired desire to vary skin color and bodily characteristics to the various geographies, cultures and living conditions of the world."

"The long history of the so-called 'white race' considering the other more tinted-races to be inferior - thus relegating them to second class citizenship, discrimination and enforced subservience – must, and will, come to an end in a truly spiritual society."

"In fact, the colors ascribed to the variations in skin tone are – in themselves – both silly and inaccurate since the supposedly 'white skinned' people are *colored* as well since their skin shading is decidedly not white - but actually 'tan-pink'. Everyone has a *skin coloring* - not of any primary or even secondary color - but various shading and combinations of tan-pink-black-red-and-yellow. A *rainbow* of those muted colors is probably the best way to describe the coloring of the lot of them - actually, the variety of our incarnate colorings."

"Only through mutual and universal acceptance of our various combos will humanity become increasingly aware of who and what it really is: a composite of male and female characteristics and a rich variety of sin color combinations - composed of old Soul incarnates and those recently arrived. Each combo has the capacity to adapt its cultural perspective to history's changing circumstances, each having inherited the empowerments needed to deal with the challenges they face and attract."

"The central factor now facing all incarnates is the fact that everything throughout the entire cosmos is in the midst of change. The pace is getting faster and the repercussions of any action or inaction are growing more significant. Each successive turn in the ever-evolving spiral of Spirit, in the cosmos and in our individual lives - reveals a destiny that portends we be ever more flexible in meeting the transformations that lay ahead. Such realities will also necessitate that we become ever more aware, ever more affirming of the divine and ever more loving of everyone and thing we encounter."

Continuous Communication

"To this end, both Yeshua and I return periodically to the purely spiritual side - for direct conversations and counsel with Prime Source and Its heavenly advisors - on everything including the next phase of Its continuous creation and development. The resultant visions set by Prime Source in turn determine the parameters of Our respective goals and how We can best fulfill Our service - as the ground under Us literally continues to evolve."

"Theologians and philosophers – meaning well and intending to help us understand the context of our choices - have frequently referred to My Assumption and Yeshua's Ascension as epic, archetypal and stand-alone events. Be assured, however, that We have had many, many – in fact - millions of such mini assumptions and ascensions over the millennia – interactions that might be more accurately described as in depth and 'personal meetings' with Prime Source."

"Both of Us contribute greatly to those interactions and decisions though ongoing conversations. Thus We occasionally 'disappear' or temporarily put our bodily appearances on hold as we consult and communicate directly with Our Lord. Obviously, We also serve in and through our embodiments - using prayer, meditation and contemplation to communicate directly with Our Lord."

"For example," said Yeshua, "My purpose in first meeting with Magdalene following My alleged passion, and then meeting with her and then all the disciples in Emmaus, was to demonstrate that I had returned from another of My 'ascended' meetings with Our Lord in the heavenly or archetypal realm, [57] the arena some psychologists will thereafter come to describe as the super-conscious."

"I basically did the same thing," said Mother Mary. "In addition to the one return to the Purely Spiritual realm that was mentioned in the Bible - advertised as My Dormition or alleged My earthly death - actually My Assumption [58] - I too have hand and continue to have repeated consultations with Prime Source. Like Yeshua, I - like My Son - communicate directly with Our Lord and Its heavenly hosts on a daily basis. I make such 'round trips to and from the heavenly realm through a series of psychological or mindful 'assumptions' and 'returns' - using the best media I know of, namely prayer, meditation and acts of contemplation."

"The direct meetings and interactions with Prime Source 'on the Other Side', are invaluable for they gave Me – and Us - ample opportunity to both give and receive advice and counsel - before resuming Our missions to and in the incarnate world."

---

57   See Matthew 28:1-10

58   There is no direct or specific description of the Assumption in the biblical narratives, although the Catholic Church interprets Chapter 12 of the Book of Revelation as referring to Mother Mary's 'Assumption'. Pope Pius XII, however, would eventually define the Assumption as dogma in 1950 in his Apostolic Constitution Munificentissimus.

The Team

"Now," said Yeshua, "I think it best to focus for a moment on the role our beloved disciples, the Beloved Mary Magdalene and the Apostle John, have and will continue to play in uplifting the spiritual impulse of Earth and elsewhere in the cosmos."

"As you know, John has been watching over and interacting with Mother Mary on a daily basis - ever since he and Magdalene traveled with Me and Mother Mary from Jerusalem to Britannia. He then worked with Mother Mary at the Sanctuary, and – at my specific request – not only traveled with Her back to Palestine but subsequently lived with and cared for Her for the last several years. As his latest narration of those events reveals, his devotion has been and continues to be both loving and protective, and his notes on Our travels to Britannia and Our Return have been remarkably perceptive and ever so enlightening."

"Now - our Beloved Magdalene has also set an example of loving insight and action, ever the one to spot a need, fill it and then move on without fanfare or explanation. She has been both a joyous and helpful companion to Me and Mother Mary - always available with an arm, a calm voice and wise counsel. Perhaps it will be Magdalene who will write - or inspire - the next book about this and future developments."

"And needless to say, My - or really Our, Mother Mary - being in the best of times none too shy, continues - as you see –to be in full voice, totally accessible, always helpful for anyone in need of moral, mental or physical assistance – at least, that is, when She is not in deep mediation and contemplation."

"Of course, She will continue to guide others, complete umpteen more acts of love and compassion, and handle whatever difficult situations arise with utmost care – all in the process presenting both a loving and insightful solution to whatever issue or problem arises."

"T'is quite a team Prime Source has assembled. So I am delighted to continue having them at My side since Our work is hardly complete: My dear Mother, and our two most remarkable 'disciples' – each well informed and resolute - with surely continue to speak, write and act for and in the ways of the Lord. "

"Fortunately many others also continue to support our mission – folks like each member of this assembly, the intrepid Souls still serving in Britannia, all the wondrous incarnates we met and continue to meet on the road – and you the individual reader - obviously intrigued enough to follow us this far, and now hopefully committed to affirming and even joining our cause."

"Each - and all - have been and continue to be the source of inspiration. You serve as our best examples of everything we love and admire. Your many diverse yet related ways of applying the best of heaven to the physical arenas in which you serve - continue to create models of informed action, sure to inspire all the incarnates who are sure to follow your wise counsel. To each and all, We offer our heartfelt blessings and deepest appreciation!"

Wait, Wait – 'Just a Minute

"Opps," said Yeshua. "Did I forget any one or any thing?"

A figure of some repute then made his way to the microphone. He walked slowly but with a joyous yet fierce determination, seeming to glide on air as if to complement his flailing arms. He bowed to Yeshua, rushed to hug his wife, send a series of a two-handed waves to everyone on the dais, shook a triumphant fist or two in the air, reached up to adjust the microphone, pull it down to his height, and stand as tall as his puffy profile would allow.

"I am here," he bellowed, "to never say 'goodbye.'"

The auditorium erupted, and Father Joseph received a standing ovation - which he acknowledged with several bows, and a series of waves to old friends and neighbors.

"Thank you – my brethren from several lands and states of consciousness," was his opening comment.

"And," noting parenthetically: "I do seem to love the word 'and'...for it so fits my personality."

"At any rate," he continued, "as you well know, ours has been and continues to be a journey of service – establishing fellowship with and expressing love and empathy for all."

"I especially want to thank all those willing to read - and heed - one more of my reputedly infamous commentaries...copies of which – I am assured – you already have tucked in your pockets, ready for immediate reference as well as constant review."

Father Joseph bowed once again, and then and again – as a chorus of 'bravos', 'you tell em, Fadder' and 'God loves ya' - swept through the arena.

"We have all helped to build this ever-escalating affirmation of Spirit – evident throughout both our past - and our ongoing dramas. Through it all, it has always been Our Lord who has provided the direction - [many then crying out: 'thanks be to God]' - while my son, Yeshua, has given so abundantly of His devotion and energy; and my bride, Mother Mary, has supplied and offered Her velvet hand, Her fierce determination and devotion, and the love of Her continuously open heart."

"Then there is John – the ever-present scribe who has again produced a written record of our comings and goings - and in the process – found a way to both praise and explain our finest hopes - and dreams - and occasional accomplishments."

"Ah: who can forget Magdalene, ever the radiant and emerging one – the damsel who has never failed to resolve each difficulty faced by this fearsome foursome as they traveled the known world - and who has continued to do so with the charm, delicacy and strength of fine spun lace".

"And so - as this joyous celebration is living testimony – I hereby, again and forever, register my heart-felt thanks to Our Lord for including me in this set of epic encounters – enabling me to contribute what I could - all of it energized and supported by all of you."

"Truly, our individual and combined energies will inspire the generations of incarnates who follow us - as they too make their contributions to spirituality, world peace and cosmic enlightenment. On behalf of myself, my most inspiring and beloved Wife, our most remarkable Son, and the esteemed members of this panel, I offer you all an abundant and continuous blessings of love and godspeed. Thank you!"

Tumultuous applaud erupted, followed by undulating waves of outstretched arms – all chanting 'thank you, Fa-ther-Joe' and cadenced cries of "Jo-seph, Jo-seph, Jo-seph " – all climaxing in a series of cheers and cries of "for-ever... and ever... and ever."

To Serve

Both husband and Son - serving as an honor guard – then escorted Mother Mary to center stage - so She might bask in the spotlight of soft pinks, golds and vibrant blues.

"I have little to add – but frankly did so wish to appear once again," said Mother Mary, "both to offer you My love and - in turn - bath in the love your lives have created. I am, as ever, Mother Mary, an incarnate like us all, and who, given your support, will continue – ad infinitum – to do Her best - as we together joyfully enact the intentions of Our Lord."

"I am here – like you - to serve: that is it - and that is all."

As She prepared to leave the stage, She suddenly turned back.

"*And* - one more thing, if I may," She said with a full smile and then laughter - "a phase and habit I picked up from My husband."

"Please know as well that I have always been guided by your insights, your tenacity, and your loving example. And I assure you I always will be inspired - and enlightened - by your creativity and dedication. As ever, I am deeply nurtured by your presence and will forever be energized by your love. So thank, thank you, thank you."

All As One

You would think anything could top that. Well – you would be wrong. Mother Mary beckoned to Her Son and Her husband. Then all three bowed – and bowed again – to one and all – not just to acknowledge the outpouring of love but in tribute to all the Souls and incarnates who gave and continue to honor Spirit with their love and devotion.

"The loving and the forgiving - are to each other - loving and forgiving," Mother Mary said softly to Herself - yet it was seemingly heard by all as if voiced by a heavenly choir.

With hands over hearts, the now silent crowd bowed in reverence to Mother Mary – followed by a long silence.

Finally and suddenly the crowd erupted - cheering – turning to hug one another. Affirmations galore and gentle backslapping became the order of the day...which soon gave way to singing and dancing and many a glass of wine.

Hours passed yet everyone continued to mill about – retelling stories, recalling the details of one glorious event after another, not wanting to say 'so long' - never 'good-bye' - or even 'good night'.

Those on the slightly elevated and makeshift stage joined with the rest of their colleagues – symbolizing the merging of divinity on and with the earth. Everyone, but everyone - the esteemed, the experienced, the recent and wide-eyed, the glorious, the everyday, the angelic and ever-loving incarnate - melded in body and spirit – there and then - knowing they will inevitably meet again - on earth as in heaven – yet expressing the total glory of the moment - a distinctive, unique and loving collage of Souls - naturally connected - joyfully behaving as One.

About the Author

William Francis Sturner, Ph.D., is the author of fourteen books, father of two children, playmate of six grandchildren, lover of art and music, psychotherapist and a very spirited and joyful presenter and facilitator.

Raised as a Roman Catholic, he gradually investigated other religious perspectives before devoting himself to the study and practice of mystical traditions and universal spirituality.

His work combines the perspective of growing up in the Bronx with the disciples and experiences Jungian, Gestalt and spiritual psychology. His university appointments have included professorships at four American universities (Oakland, SUNY College-Buffalo, Massachusetts and Maine) and vice presidencies at two (Oakland and Buffalo State). He has also been awarded visiting appointments at the universities of Limerick, Ireland; Istanbul Technical, Turkey; Santiago de Compostela, Spain; and Moscow State, Russia.

His degrees include a B.S.S. from Fordham University (1957), a Masters in Communications from the University of Wisconsin (1960), a Ph.D. in Political and Organizational Studies at Fordham University (1965), and a Post Doctoral Certificate in Gestalt Psychology from the Gestalt Institute of Cleveland (1973).

Sturner's training includes forty years of studies in Jungian Depth Psychology with such centers as the Jungian Center in Kusnacht,

Switzerland; the New York Institute in Jungian Studies; and International Studies in Jungian Psychology (NH and VT).

Sturner founded his 'Open Heart Sanctuary' in 2002 in East Aurora, NY, and has since moved it to the Sarasota-Nokomis area of Florida (2021). He now devotes his energies to communing with nature, offering workshops on creative and spiritual development, investigating various mystical traditions, and writing books that express the love and compassion of *Universal Spirituality (US)*.

His earliest books on leadership, organizational development and creativity have given way gave to volumes on mythic tales, a Jungian interpretation of creation, and the spiritual traditions of reincarnation. His most recent books have also focused on the various themes of spirituality and the continuing contributions of the Master Souls - Yeshua and Mother Mary.